DE VALERA'S IRELANDS

DE VALERA'S IRELANDS

Edited by

GABRIEL DOHERTY & DERMOT KEOGH

MERCIER PRESS

MERCIER PRESS
Douglas Village, Cork
www.mercierpress.ie

Trade enquiries to CMD DISTRIBUTION,
55a Spruce Avenue, Stillorgan Industrial Park, Blackrock, Dublin

ISBN 185635 414 8

10 9 8 7 6 5 4 3 2 1

Printed in Ireland by Colour Books Ltd

CONTENTS

FOR MY MOTHER, HELENA DOHERTY

INTRODUCTION

This collection of essays has been commissioned as part of the UCC Department of History's Higher Education Authority research programme 'Culture Contact – Nation and State'. The volume has its origins in a particular historiographical context: there has been a dramatic increase over the last decade of the twentieth century of popular interest in, and associated scholarly re-interpretations of, the history of post-independence Ireland. This has resulted in part from the long-overdue opening of Irish state files together with general access to ecclesiastical, business, private and other archives. The National Archives Act of 1986 and the 1997 Freedom of Information Act are the product of, and have contributed widely to, a greater spirit of openness in Irish society in the latter part of the twentieth century. (It is for this reason that both editors regret the current proposals to limit the scope of the Freedom of Information Act.) The overall effect has been to stimulate a most-welcome debate on all aspects of contemporary Irish history.

The years that saw the apogee of the influence of Eamon de Valera are central (both chronologically and thematically) to this climate of revision and reappraisal. His actions and role, both as a leading actor in the making of modern Ireland and as a metaphor for its defining narrative, have been the focus of more extensive scrutiny than most of his Fianna Fáil contemporaries and his rivals in other parties. Despite the high volume of fine scholarship now available in monograph, the contributions in this book will demonstrate that many interesting lines of enquiry remain to be pursued. An auspicious beginning has been made to the study of de Valera's Irelands. But, as the contributors to this book argue, historians are really only in the foothills. There remains the major challenge of scholarly investigation combining a study of personal, official and international sources.

Some explanation is required regarding the title of the volume, *De Valera's Irelands*. This has been chosen consciously and deliberately to emphasise the principal theme of the volume: that the role that de Valera played personally in the development of independent Ireland, and the social experience of that period which is indelibly associated with his name, was a more sophisticated, differentiated and evolutionary one than many authors (particularly modern social commentators) have been willing to concede.

The different members of the generations who lived through what might be termed the de Valera era had radically different experiences of growing up, education, work, marriage, emigration or entry into religious orders. Much depended upon economic and social status. Thus the experiences of a farm labourer were distinct to those who employed them on larger farms; children raised in industrial schools had different experiences to, for example, boarders in a diocesan college; the Churches had differentiated influences on their members; being an orthodox Irish Jew was distinct to the experience of a co-religionist of a liberal or secular tradition; all Irish people did not have a uniform experience of the impact of censorship. There has been a trend towards reductionism in some of the scholarship relating to de Valera and to the society that he helped form. He is made to shoulder personal responsibility for many of the defects of that society. He is held accountable for the strong conservatism and resistance to radical change in post-independence Ireland.

The essays in this volume take a different scholarly tack. Whether this be through Owen Dudley Edwards' illuminating study of the American aspects of 'Dev's' persona; Ged Martin's delicate examination of the manifold (and at times contradictory) perceptions of him over time; or Seán Farragher's subtle delineation of his adolescent formation in Blackrock, the picture is clear: de Valera, as a political creature, defied easy categorisation – and continues to do so. Likewise in the social sphere: Caitriona Clear's challenging re-examination of the position of women during the era; Gearóid Ó Crualaoich's forensic analysis of the modern, urban 'hidden Ireland' of these decades; the calculated reappraisals of cultural policy by Gearóid Ó Tuathaigh and of arts policy by Brian Kennedy; and Brian Walker's investigation of identity as revealed by public commemoration, all point to a similar conclusion – that the experience of these years is a more nuanced one than is usually entertained. A similar line emerges in the political sphere, in, for example, Tom Garvin's synoptic essay on the legacy of the Civil War, which points to the complex impact of that event on the 'entire fabric and quality of public life'. The point must not be pushed too far of course: John McGahern's personal recollections of childhood during these years indicate an enduring antipathy to 'an insecure sectarian state … guided by a philistine church' – and that perspective, too, is part of the narrative. Thus, the conclusion reached by Garret FitzGerald, in the final piece of the volume, could equally apply to the work as a whole: 'Even today judgements on him are bound to be no more than provisional, both because we are too close to the man himself – barely two decades after his death – and because much research remains to be undertaken, and many veils remain to be removed, before the achievements and failures of this remarkable Irishman can be evaluated in a definitive way.'

We have, therefore, sought to produce a volume that seeks to address this challenge, one that both encapsulates existing knowledge and lays down challenges for future investigation; it is for the reader to decide how far we have succeeded in either or both of these tasks.

ACKNOWLEDGEMENTS

This volume is part of a series of works currently being undertaken by the Department of History, University College Cork under the aegis of the Higher Education Authority research project 'Culture Contact – Nation and State'. As such thanks are due to the HEA for its assistance in supporting the project in general, and this volume in particular, in its initial stages.

Thanks are obviously due to the various contributors to this work. Many were participants in a conference of the same name held within University College Cork at the outset of the research programme. Others were invited to contribute papers on specific topics. Our thanks to them all for their patient co-operation in the enterprise.

We would like to thank Professor Michael Mortell (former President of UCC), Mr Gerry Reynolds of Radio Telefis Éireann, *The Sunday Tribune* and the UCC History Department for their generous sponsorship of the initial conference. Thanks also to Professor Gerard Wrixon, current President of the College, for his support of this project in particular and of the Department in general within UCC during his term of office.

We are grateful to Charlotte Holland, Norma Buckley, Margaret Clayton, Veronica Fraser, Geraldine McAllister, Deirdre O'Sullivan and Mary Ring, secretaries in the Department of History, University College Cork, for their unceasing assistance to the manifold tasks of a modern university Department.

We thank all the postgraduate students of the Department of History, who assisted in the organisation of the conference and who helped it to run so smoothly. Thanks are due to all the staff of the Printing Office in UCC for their help in producing material for the conference, and likewise we would also like to thank Orla O'Callaghan, Ruth McDonnell and Marie McSweeney for her help in pre-publicity. We are grateful to Donnchadha Ó hAodha, Denis Bannon and the other staff of Áras na Mac Léinn for their help in staging the proceedings.

Our thanks, as ever, to the staff of the Boole Library within University College Cork, particularly those members working in the 'Special Collections' section: Ms Helen Davis, Mr Peadar Cranitch, Ms Anne Cronin, Ms Teresina Flynn, Ms Catherine Horgan and Ms Mary Lombard.

We would particularly like to acknowledge the assistance of the *Irish Examiner* in providing the several photographs used in this volume, most notably Suzanne Crosbie, and Anne Kearney, Lilian Caverley and the other members of the paper's photographic library.

We would finally wish to thank Mary Feehan, Eimear O'Herlihy, Aisling Lyons and all the staff of Mercier Press for their assistance in producing this handsome volume.

Gabriel Doherty, Professor Dermot Keogh,
Department of History,
University College Cork,
September 2003.

The American identity of de Valera

Owen Dudley Edwards

'But, Doctor,' said Caspian, 'why do you say my race? After all, I suppose you're a Telmarine too.'

'Am I?' said the Doctor.

'Well, you're a man anyway,' said Caspian.

'Am I?' repeated the Doctor in a deeper voice ...

'So you've guessed it in the end,' said Doctor Cornelius. 'Or guessed it nearly right. I'm not a pure Dwarf. I have human blood in me too. Many Dwarfs escaped in the great battles and lived on; shaving their beards, and wearing high-heeled shoes and pretending to be men ... But never in all these years have we forgotten our own people and all the other happy creatures of Narnia, and the long-lost days of freedom.'

'I'm – I'm sorry, Doctor,' said Caspian. 'It wasn't my fault, you know.'

Aslan said nothing.

'You mean,' said Lucy rather faintly, 'that it would have turned out all right – somehow? But how? Please, Aslan! Am I not to know?'

'To know what would have happened, child?' said Aslan. 'No. Nobody is ever told that.'[1]

'I am deeply honoured,' said President John Fitzgerald Kennedy to the Teachtaí Dála and (Irish) Senators in Leinster House on 28 June 1963, 'to be your guest in the free parliament of a free Ireland. If this nation had achieved its present political and economic stature a century or so ago, my great-grandfather might never have left New Ross, and I might, if fortunate, be sitting down there with you. Of course, if your own President had never left Brooklyn, he might be standing up here instead of me.'

Kennedy was being light-hearted: it was one of his greatest gifts. The speech contained much that was his own work, this passage almost certainly.[2] It needed a touch of nerve, thus to speculate half-irreverently, half-admiringly, as to the alternative life of Eamon de Valera, and we may doubt whether his speechwriters would have known enough to risk it. His Irish visit was in any case unpopular with his court.[3] Everyone, including the Irish Department of External Affairs, had assumed before his election that he would be a little colder to Ireland than his predecessors, to show his credentials were American, not Irish-American. They thought it from their knowledge of his father.[4] But John Kennedy's Irish identity sat easily within himself, and he had been at variance with his father's social and political attitudes from his earliest published historical writing: *Why England Slept*, with its formidable critique of the diplomatic unfitness of Joseph P. Kennedy's patron and idol, Prime Minister Neville Chamberlain.[5] And he knew Ireland, and even Irish history, rather better than any of his servants seem to have done: he certainly knew de Valera better.

Both de Valera and Kennedy knew the wisdom of allowing myths to accumulate about them without gratifying their pedantry (of which each had his share) by correcting every record. For instance, Kennedy's entourage assumed that his only previous visit to Ireland had been in 1947 as the guest of his sister Kathleen, Marchioness of Hartington and her Cavendish in-laws of the Devonshire Dukedom.[6] But he had witnessed his father's honorary NUI degree conferred by de Valera in 1938. He had flown out of Foynes to resume his studies at Harvard in September 1939. He had visited Ireland and interviewed de Valera on the eve of the Potsdam Conference (where his father wangled his attendance) in July 1945. His chosen profession was not politician but journalist: he reluctantly accepted the political career because of the death of his eldest brother Joe (who would have been a predictable echo of his father as far as we can judge). His first newspaper story appeared in William Randolph Hearst's *New York Journal-American* for 2 February 1941.[7] It was an exceptionally fair-minded statement of the UK case against Irish neutrality, and of the Irish case for its maintenance, stressing that US evaluations were the more urgent if its own security depended (as Franklin Roosevelt said) on British survival and 'if Ireland's present policy weakens Britain's chances'. He stressed British fears of German seizure of Ireland with 'the Norway experience ever before them'. The story's headline declared that the Treaty ports were 'IRISH BASES VITAL TO BRITAIN' but Kennedy affirmed that the Irish 'presented an equally impressive case ... to give the British these bases would mean the involvement of Ireland in a war for which they are completely unprepared. The Irish government feels that its first and fundamental duty is to its own people. Except for extremists, of course, the Irish are completely sympathetic to the British cause.' This last depended on one's interpretation of 'extremist' but the article made a very friendly case both for Britain and for Ireland, in a journal whose proprietor's bitter Anglophobia had hitherto abominated sympathy for 'England' either from Ireland or from the US. And it concluded with a shrewd estimate of realities of anti-partitionism as a motive of the de Valera government:

Of course it must be pointed out that de Valera reportedly has stated that Neutrality for Ireland is now more important than Union. That he should reject an opportunity to fulfil his life-long ambition is, his supporters say, conclusive evidence of his deep sincerity.

When Robert Fisk reached the same conclusion in his *In Time of War*,[8] reviewers expressed a surprise which involuntarily paid tribute to Kennedy's hard youthful head (not that they knew of it).

War service took Kennedy away from both Ireland and journalism, but four years later he reported in the same paper on the anti-partition cause in July 1945. He singled out Dillon as the heart of ideological dissent from de Valera, but while seeing in him an advocate of 'co-operating and the building of mutual trust' with Britain, Kennedy diagnosed hope of pickings across the Irish spectrum if de Valera could be forced into a corner: 'Dillon is attempting to pin de Valera to being completely in or completely out of the British Commonwealth and thus make political capital, no matter what decision he makes.'[9] Evidently, Kennedy foresaw the possibility of unity across the board among de Valera's opponents, hopes of revenge and sweets of office outweighing ideological hostilities. He also noted that de Valera saw it too:

> De Valera's elaboration of his remarks left the situation to many observers as misty as this island on an early winter's morning. 'Ireland,' said de Valera, 'was an independent Republic associated as a matter of external policy with the states of the British Commonwealth' ... De Valera, realising how subtle his position is and not wishing to alienate those who advocate a complete break with Britain, yet conscious of the fact that only with Britain's support can partition be ended, is skating along thin ice successfully with his enigmatic reply.

Apart from interviews with Dillon, de Valera, and what pot-luck he could make of Dublin and other journalists, Kennedy's sources for the second story may well have been his obvious ones for the first: the Irish diplomatic corps. He had first encountered these islands as an appendage of US diplomacy or, as the Irish External Affairs officials termed embassy progeny in those days, 'a diplomatic brat'.

However we may evaluate Kennedy as President, he seems to have been a good journalist. His presidential zest for the press conference with its hazards of unexpected tripwires from old colleagues arose from that. And he evidently saw in de Valera a pragmatist operating amid ethnic totems and taboos. The obvious question he would have put to fellow-journalists at the time – a particularly natural question from an officer recently in war service – was why de Valera had expressed condolences to the German Embassy on the death of its head of state, Adolf Hitler. The most authoritative answer he would have received would have been that in this gesture, widely unpopular outside Ireland, he strengthened his political flank inside it against attack from Anglophobe republicans such as Seán MacBride. And in that cool, half-mocking, half-celebrating exchange of destinies with de Valera in 1963, President Kennedy was paying an informed tribute to the skills of the first head of government he had had a chance to assess at close quarters since the fall of his father's friend, Chamberlain. (Kennedy admired Churchill from afar, but had no chance for close encounter). This Irish eye of the young journalist might be forgotten by everyone else, but he might be expected to remember, with advantages, what deeds he had done in assessment of de Valera. And as a young aspirant for presidential office who read books and attended seminars on political power, he had more means of judging the success of de Valera's performance than that of any other comparable figure. He continued to read in Irish history, presumably some of it covering the twentieth century, such as the American writer Mary Bromage's life of de Valera.[10] What de Valera's influence on Kennedy may have been we cannot say: at all events it was more than that Edwin O'Connor allowed for the Irish in Ireland as far as Jimmy Kinsella, based on Joseph P. Kennedy, was concerned: 'I'm about fed up with these home-grown Micks: there's not a quarter in the crowd.'[11] Lord Longford briefly cast de Valera for Kennedy's alternative father.[12]

There was little more than a quarter (by Kennedy standards) in the crowd of de Valera's immediate relatives when he was born on 14 October 1882, in Manhattan rather than Brooklyn (still a city in its own right). The confusion may have arisen from Kennedy's own birth in Brookline, Massachusetts: the slip may perhaps be called Freudian. The birthplace qualified de Valera as eligible for the Presidency of the United States. Curiously enough the incumbent at his birth, Chester A. Arthur, was saluted by the Dublin *Nation* as 'America's Irish President', but is assumed by some historians to have been born in Canada (and hence ineligible) although he always assigned himself a birthplace in Vermont.

De Valera, excluded by his mother from her American home and her second marriage,[13] grew up dependent on his Irish relatives, without much status in the neighbourhood. In a famous passage, he declaimed on 6 January 1922, amid the Treaty debate: 'I was reared in a labourer's cottage … the first fifteen years of my life that formed my character.'[14] An illuminating anecdote with which Pauric Travers begins his dispassionate and briefly comprehensive life of de Valera and shows his subject as the boyhood friend and fellow-folklorist (amateur) of tinkers.[15] It certainly increased his credentials to speak for 'the people of Ireland'. It also left him firmly at the bottom of the social heap.

His upbringing seems to have been increasingly loveless with the emigration of his aunt, the death of his grandmother, and the late courtship of his Uncle Pat. In all of this the USA lay westward, a beacon to so many (especially those who never went there), for him perhaps a paradise, his mother at its centre and himself left like Peri at its closed gate. His recollection of the parish priest of Bruree, whose masses he served, the Rev. Eugene Sheehy, was that the Land League priest had taught him love of country. Sheehy had campaigned in the United States on behalf of Parnell, then imprisoned in Kilmainham. On 1 December 1881 (less than a year before de Valera's birth) he had thrilled a Chicago reception with: 'Nothing good – nothing great has ever been purchased without sacrifice. No birth – above all that of freedom – has been without pain' and: 'We wish to destroy landlordism only as the stepping-stone to a greater and higher end.'[16] America was the most obvious common ground between the two of them, and the most obvious place for that instruction on love of country to begin. It was the apogee of Sheehy's career: there, he was lionised as the spiritual father of his people; back in Ireland he had been thrown into jail before his departure, and thrown into ecclesiastical recrimination afterwards.

In Blackrock, de Valera was reprimanded for reading *Deadwood Dick* after hours. He would have heard some fragments of American news. In 1897, for instance, ex-Congressman Joseph McKenna of California, a Catholic, was appointed Attorney-General of the United States by President William McKinley: there was some controversy about it from anti-Catholic agitators who were annoyed at finding McKinley did not share their sentiments, and hence Irish news reports would have picked it up. It was a time of particular sensitivity to supposed job discrimination against Catholics in and out of Ireland; the outcry would have drawn Irish Catholic attention and the President's fidelity to his word would have strengthened American standing. The Tories were in power and the chances of Catholic appointment to such posts in Ireland had disappeared with the Liberal defeat in 1895.

McKinley sent the Kilkenny-born Archbishop John Ireland of St Paul, Minnesota, to represent the United States in France at a commemoration of Lafayette, and on the return journey Ireland spoke on 9 October 1900 to the boys of Blackrock, where de Valera was now a pupil. As a result of Ireland's visit, a prize for religious knowledge was instituted, which de Valera won: it was a Douai bible in which he entered what little he knew of his parents' history. He must thus have been deeply aware of the implication of the American constitutional separation of Church and State, meaning that an archbishop could be chosen as the envoy of a secular state, in contrast to what would obtain in his Catholic-filled but Protestant-ruled island bearing the archbishop's name. The prize was awarded by the President of Blackrock, the Rev. John T. Murphy, a friend of Archbishop Ireland from his own long pastorate in Pittsburgh. There he had gained experience of the St Vincent de Paul Society and introduced it to Blackrock, de Valera becoming President of the Vincent de Paul Conference.[17] The lesson would have been that ethnic and religious groups see to their own welfare (on which many US urban political machine bosses would have heartily agreed, having seen their machines fatten on such principles): it also bred suspicion of state charity or welfare obligations. The philosophy was better suited to a wealthier society with stronger traditions in organised private charity than Irish Catholicism had known. It also bred in de Valera the vocational ideal, the sense of citizenship as obligation more than right, once the state was representative in its government.

If he transmitted such views to the young John Kennedy in 1945, as in the context of national ideals, we might well have an origin for the famous cry in the Kennedy inaugural speech on 20 January 1961: 'Ask not what your country can do for you! Ask what you can do for your country!' It fascinated the listening Americans, but it would have been no surprise to constituents of de Valera, and its assumptions had turned Irish emigration into a haemorrhage over the previous ten years. The American antecedents of the Blackrock Vincent de Paul were further affirmed by the prominence in the body of an American schoolboy, John Junker of Philadelphia. De Valera was remembered at Blackrock defending the debate motion: 'The old monastic form of charity to the poor was preferable to the modern state social services'.[18]

'Blackrock was not America but was still a new world' observed de Valera's authorised biographer Tom O'Neill, presumably echoing a sentiment from his informant. Sometimes it induced contrary opinions. In the Literary and Debating Society de Valera declared, 'constitutional monarchy as a form of government' to be 'preferable to republicanism', asserting that 'constant elections disturbed the nation, and are not conducive to the prosperity of the people', and that 'there is no rule so tyrannical as that of them all'. This may have been a passing conviction, or one taken up to defend a motion in need of supporters (a useful mode of practice for a maturing debater). Whatever its origin he lived to revert to the republicanism of the land of his birth. It may also reflect the time that in 1903 he did not avail himself (presuming he had known it) of the usual procedure for a United States aspirant for citizenship, vis. to report to the Dublin consulate, with proof of his American birth or parentage, making oath of, or affirming, allegiance to the USA. Whatever his reasons, they did not include dedication to a future Irish state or to the former Fenian-proclaimed Irish Republic. He would take pride in being a stateless person in the future, limiting his allegiance to the once and future Ireland.

He may very well have been keeping his options open. Once he had followed Thomas MacDonagh into the Easter Rising in 1916, he was anxious not to be seen to hedge his bets. He himself assumed he would be executed when he had surrendered at the end of the week's fighting, but his wife Sinéad persuaded the US Consul, Edward Adams, to appear at de Valera's court-martial in recognition of a claim of American citizenship which it was impossible to verify or otherwise. Adams informed the State Department in the fullness of time that he had been responsible for the preservation of de Valera's life. We do not know when de Valera learned of Sinéad's action and its result, as officially assumed by US authorities, but he invariably denied that his American birth saved his life. To be the surviving commandant was one thing; to be the commandant who survived by special pleading of individual peculiarities was a very different one. De Valera was ready enough to let his American birth make him more than his contemporaries, born subjects of the British monarch; he was not prepared to let it make him less, the patriot privileged above his pledge.

His insistence on the point was greatly to influence kindly historians.[19] He did not want to be caught using the Stars and Stripes as a flag of convenience. Tom Clarke – whose widow had a powerful influence on de Valera – had been shot without making any claim of US citizenship, strong as it would have been. De Valera could not afford to live the imaginary life of an American when faced with that sacred precedent. So, the United States must not be seen to have been the cause of his survival, even though it probably was.[20]

But he had an American agenda to fulfil, responding to those yearnings from his childhood to be brought back with honour into his mother's household and affection. His new status as survivor/leader gave him his opportunity. Although he must never seem less than Irish, he could then make the most of his special relationship to America. The Irish expression *Cad as tú?* (which de Valera would have learned from Sinéad or from the Gaelic League) was rendered by the lexicographer Dinneen 'whence' or 'wherefore' 'are you'.[21] Dinneen might be pompous and prolix: a people dissecting each other with the brevity of *Cad as tú?* were not likely to stitch themselves up in legalistic archaism such as 'whence' and 'wherefore', meaning as they did, 'from what are you?, out of what are you?' Yeats would capture it in: 'Out of Ireland have we come/Great hatred, little room/Maimed us at the start/I carry from my mother's womb/A fanatic heart' and Thomas N. Brown (Copernicus of Irish-American studies) would apply it to the Irish-American nationalists.[22] But de Valera, austere pedagogue, brought other legacies from his mother. His American origin gave him high hopes of a future that never materialised, high romance as an alternative identity, low reproach as a reminder of his dubious status and questionable name, whence the lustre of his survival must now seek to escape. 'Whence' meant 'Wherefore'.

His practical training had in fact come from the spiritual arm: Sheehy, who had shown him how nationalism could be an escape from low status and dull poverty; the Christian Brothers, who gave him the necessities of bread-and-butter education; the Holy Ghost Fathers at Blackrock, who showed him the luxury of higher learning with its payoff as a clerical profession in the church or school. This last is fairly crucial. The Holy Ghosts gave de Valera his first serious political training: before he ever learned the science of lay politics, he witnessed the subtler and sometimes more ruthless delicacies of the clerical kind. It could be crude (especially in the hands of the more bovine bishops) but the regular clergy brought it to a fine art, perfected by the rivalries and antipathies honed in day-by-day community encounter.

De Valera's statement about coming from a labourer's cottage showed that he knew from the bottom of the social pyramid what discrimination and ostracism could feel like: the labourers perpetually suffered from the contempt of the tenant-farmers and their participation in the Land League struggles on the tenants' side won little thanks for themselves. But his 'I have not lived solely among the intellectuals' was (apart from its tender vanity) a tribute to the Holy Ghosts whose ranks he had sought to join as a priest and whose collegiality he was permitted to enter as a teacher. A boy, cut off from any family ties apart from remote replies from America, had the surrounding clerics with which to fill his mind in place of family feuds, rivalries and consolidations.

Before the Rising he never tried his hand at Sinn Féin politics, or at any involvement, apart from nominal membership, in the more shadowy politics of the IRB. He entered the Easter Rising as a teacher giving a class a drill with new equipment and the prospect of a more experienced rival school to face. His imprisonment taught him a little about the politics of the defeated, inching minute advantages from their victors, but he was hostile to talk of political activity. The Holy Ghosts graduated great men from de Valera's generation – the O'Rahilly brothers, Pádraic Ó Conaire, the future Cardinal d'Alton (whom de Valera defeated in theology)[23] – but, unlike the Christian Brothers and the Jesuits, the Holy Ghosts turned out few secular politicians. When their ugly duckling won swan status, Blackrock proved ready enough to make itself that kind of swan lake. But it was the USA which had to perfect de Valera in secular politics. His lake was the Atlantic, and his American past was shorn of its awkward ambiguities by immersion in an American future.

De Valera had, of course, won two elections and been chosen as head man for Sinn Féin, the Volunteers and Dáil Éireann, but his first election to parliament happened when he had barely come to terms with his own candidacy, and his second was won when he was once more in jail. People had manoeuvred and manipulated, some killing others off, still others killing themselves off, to make him president of organisations of whose origins he had little or no practical experience and whose metamorphoses were shaking its founders to the core. Being a schoolmaster no doubt helped. He was the unquestioned figurehead, and the schoolboys deferentially proceeded with their own self-rule. Masters should not concern themselves with responsibilities undertaken by prefects. One could particularly rely on the head boy, Michael Collins, who got things done such as elections, jailbreaks and meetings.

It was natural of de Valera to think in such terms especially since the politician who most filled his aspirant mind at this point was himself a teacher. Thomas Woodrow Wilson had been professor at Princeton and Eamon de Valera had been professor at Carysfort Training College: that was his official status albeit, as Seán Ó Faoláin would put it, 'the title professor is a trifle magniloquent in the connection'.[24] Then Wilson had become President of Princeton, and then of the United States. His hairbreadth re-election was drama enough to filter through to de Valera in Lewes Jail in November 1916, together with possible adverse British comment since Wilson's neutrality was seriously resented. That last point enhanced the attractiveness of the exemplar. That the exemplar wanted nothing to do with him was beyond his ken, and beside his point: 'The fact that Mr de Valera may be an American citizen constitutes no reason for clemency in his case, or for a request by this government for clemency on the part of the British government' sniffed Assistant Secretary of State Frank L. Polk on 14 July 1916, still unaware that 'this government' had, in the person of its consul, done exactly that.[25]

Wilson was simultaneously inactive in the cause of Roger Casement in face of domestic pressure, and in general wished to beg no favours from governments whose war he intended to arbitrate and whose postwar he wished to dominate. We cannot say how de Valera had regarded previous US Presidents: I leave to others the consideration of his possible links with Arthur, Cleveland, Harrison, McKinley and Taft. He certainly must have had some sense of Theodore Roosevelt, but to an Irishman in Ireland, Roosevelt would have had a very imperial sound (very different from the figure of gorgeous fun, flamboyance and finesse who transformed the presidency in the United States). Archbishop Ireland would have told him differently, but while he heard Ireland, there is no reason to believe he talked with him. Wilson, self-advertised as the scholar in the White House (though, in fact, a historian of far less originality than Theodore Roosevelt), was the President de Valera had been waiting for. If there was a case to be made for the elected head of government and head of state combined, he must be it.

Mr Ryle Dwyer deserves our gratitude for so thoroughly highlighting de Valera's becoming 'more Wilsonian than Wilson'.[26] It fell far short of idolatry. De Valera's view of Wilson was in some respects akin to Collins' of de Valera: that of school prefect or junior master (not widely separated categories in de Valera's experience) who might be both amused and, from time to time, irritated, by the peculiarities of a headmaster but who believes the headmaster's system is the right one, even when the headmaster seems to depart from it. That the parallel should be there so mathematically – de Valera:Wilson = Collins:de Valera – is simple enough. Having thus conceived his relationship to Wilson, de Valera then sought to act out Wilson's role as he saw it. Collins, who (as Lincoln Steffens said of Theodore Roosevelt) thought with his hips, slid into his role instinctively. Both men realised one another on levels they conceded to nobody else. Thus the Pact Election made sense to both of them, while bewildering and angering so many others. The thesis of de Valera's jealousy of Collins as his primary motivation says more about its perpetrators than about its subject. Of course Collins would not expect the headmaster to know much about rough work in the scrum or orchard-robbing after school hours, and indeed would feel the headmaster ought not to know it or act as though he did. Neither ever quite realised how much the other had grown up.

De Valera's Wilson fixation brought results good and bad, short and long term. In some ways, it was highly beneficial from the start. De Valera had nothing to do with the overtures to Germany involving Casement, Plunkett and, more indirectly, Clarke and MacDermott, or with Pearse's vague notions that the Republic might be set aside for a Princedom under Germany's Joachim. He took the earliest possible opportunity of setting himself up as independent before the world. During the East Clare by-election campaign of June-July 1917 he read the third paragraph of the Easter Rising Proclamation (that in which the Republic is in fact proclaimed) and endorsed it with a ringing assertion of his allegiance to the 'spirit' of 'that government'. But in so doing he avoided any endorsement of that government's 'gallant allies in Europe', as the German, Austrian and Turkish empires are termed elsewhere in the same document:

> … you men of Clare can assert it by your votes in the face of a world where millions are arrayed in the cause of freedom. I want you to declare it to Germany, to England, to Austria and to Turkey, to France, to Russia and to America what Ireland's claim is – absolute independence. We want Ireland a sovereign state, not a province in slavery.[27]

This was a declaration of independence from Germany as well as from Britain (or 'England' as he unthinkingly termed it, slavishly following English custom). America's triumphal place at the end salutes its normal status for Irish nationalists since Parnell appealed to it in 1880 as arbiter, although there was a touch of de Valera's own declaration of independence. He had got out of jail without official United States' intervention, and he probably did not know that he had got in with it. But it meant that he echoed the earlier Declaration of Independence of 4 July 1776 in whose inheritance he had been born, holding the rest of the world enemies in war, in peace friends.[28] It allowed for future tactical or strategic alliances, but no dependence such as Plunkett had sought and Pearse anticipated. In so doing he cut free from any existing IRB or Clan na Gael ties with Germany and the central powers, who had shown small justification for their maintenance. It meant an American focus, both in terms of Wilson's public statements, and with a view to Ireland's benefit from the peace settlement: failing that, it meant future appeal to America where Ireland was strong, as opposed to Germany, where it was merely (in every sense of the word) a convenience. As election victor, as surviving commandant, and as the bearer of a European name, he could take the leadership in world (if not always in domestic) policy.

This at once put him in an excellent situation for any future appeal to the USA, although he had to wait almost two years before personally making it. His constant thought of his birthplace, at least in terms of the recognition he sought from his mother there, meant that he thought of the American people at large, not simply a fraction of it. His name prevented his being wrapped up as Irish-American, and if it left him vulnerable to the more racist of them, it gave him a basis on which to appeal to the Americans at large beyond Irish-America's limits, as indeed Parnell before him had done. (In both cases their divergence from standard Irish-American patterns of ethnicity aided them: Parnell sounded English, to an American ear, de Valera looked Spanish, and interested non-Irish could thus feel more welcome).

De Valera gave an early taste of his remarkable international sense by recognising that in all the nations warring against one another in June 1917, millions among them were doing so 'in the cause of freedom'.[29] This was to stand above the conflict, and to understand it. But it distanced him from the traditional focus of Irish-American revolutionary nationalism, the Clan na Gael and its malevolent Methuselah, John Devoy. Devoy and his friend Judge Daniel F. Cohalan were bitter supporters of Germany in the First World War which made them hopeless conduits through which to appeal to the opinion of the United States, now a belligerent against Germany. Even when the war was over, there was much obvious difference between former supporters of neutrality and former supporters of the wartime enemies of the United States. Wilson could be vindictive: but his prejudice against Judge Cohalan was reasonable.

De Valera's pursuit of Wilson as saint whence to find inspiration, and stick with which to reprimand the British, produced much citation of Wilson's 'no people shall be forced to live under a sovereignty under which it does not desire to live.'[30] This linked them to the UK's associated co-belligerent (Wilson, keeping a free hand – which he would use – declined to be an 'ally'), but de Valera worked up his Americanisation of the Irish cause so that American observers would see counterparts. He insisted that 'international recognition for our Irish Republic' came first, and after it the time when 'the Irish people may by referendum freely choose their own form of government', republican or not.[31] The United States had first similarly decided on independence, secondly and thirdly on forms of government, respectively the Articles of Confederation and the constitution. The referendum was a clearer mechanism than had been open to the revolted colonies in 1777–81 or the independent states in 1787 and beyond, and it had won American popularity in many states throughout the preceding years of the twentieth century.

In May 1918 de Valera drafted an appeal to Wilson against proposed conscription in Ireland. Its opening was, if anything, over-educated:

> A century and a half ago, England strove by brute force to crush the nascent American nation because it dared to assert its rights. By brute force today England threatens to crush the people of Ireland if they do not accept the status of helots, suffer themselves to be used at her good pleasure, and, meekly bowing their heads, permit themselves to be quietly exterminated. A century and a half ago, the champions of American liberty appealed to Ireland against England, and asked for a sympathetic judgement. What the verdict was history records.[32]

This would naturally recall the Gettysburg Address with its similar opening allusion to the Revolutionary Era 'Four score and seven years ago': that reflected a life-long admiration for Lincoln on de Valera's part. He would have a portrait of Lincoln in his immediate surroundings, speak of him with authority as an opponent of partition, identify his role as 'liberator of a race' with the Irish struggle 'for freedom', applaud his readiness to endure civil war rather than let his country be truncated. It was a bit specious in places (though the identification of Irish and American black struggles was noteworthy, consciously or otherwise harking back to Daniel O'Connell).[33] Unfortunately it showed little awareness of Wilson the man, behind Wilson the statesman.

Wilson never forgot, either in racial attitudes, or in historical writing, that in his first decade of existence he had seen Union troops occupying his father's church in Staunton, Virginia: he might be publicly obliged to be civil about Lincoln, but he identified Lincoln's cause with repression as black as any de Valera might charge the 'English' of 1776 or 1918. (Clemenceau had been an enthusiastic witness of the liberation of the slaves and their attempted grant of equality in Reconstruction, and must have heartily despised the alleged liberalism of Wilson, who denounced equal rights for blacks as public corruption).[34] De Valera, a New Yorker however briefly, responded instinctively to Lincoln's as a sacred name and never shared in the Irish Cult of the Confederacy inaugurated by aged Young Irelanders.[35]

An American identity could be as geographically variable as an Irish one. But in his use of the Continental Congress' address to the Irish people in 1775, de Valera had been at his most exquisitely adroit. The Irish people were largely unaware of the Congressional Address prepared for them in 1775, and the Irish parliament after vehement debate had endorsed government policy: the Irish parliament was entirely Protestant but Irish Catholics of the day were more likely to sympathise with the British government than with the American rebels whose leading Irish allies were the noisiest anti-Catholics in the Irish parliament.[36] The smoothness of 'history records' is delicious. In fact, the language of the Congressional Address, mostly by the plain-spoken John Adams and his demagogic cousin Sam, showed its influence on the vehemence of de Valera's prose.

And if he was disingenuous on Irish history, he was apposite on British and American. He pointed out that the parliament of 1918 which had passed the Conscription Act 'has long outrun its course and has long ceased to be representative of public opinion', a cunning allusion to its prolongation for the duration of the war, in contrast to the US constitutional rule of a house election every two years, war (even civil war) or no war. Similarly he delicately suggested that any disagreement as to Irish unity (such as might be articulated by Wilson's ethnic group, the Ulster Protestants of Scots descent) could be likened to nay-sayers to the birth of the United States:

> We are, and always have been, united with more than that unity which was never challenged in the case of the new American commonwealth of the United States, despite the presence among its own people, and in every state, of active and coherent bodies of 'tories' and 'loyalists', estimated by modern historians as not less than a third of the whole population of the thirteen original states.

It grasped its nettles with enthusiasm. It not only showed that de Valera knew how to play an American card, but that he knew how to be the American card.

But this was still the schoolman at work. The practical laboratory closed around him when he set foot in the United States at the end of May 1919. From Lincoln Jail he had written to his mother with almost American infant copybook enthusiasm at the war's end:

> If America holds to the principles enunciated by her President during the war she will have a noble place in the history of nations – her sons will have

every reason to be proud of their motherland. These principles too are the basis of true statecraft – a firm basis that will bear the stress of time – but will the President be able to get them accepted by others whose entry into the war was on motives less unselfish … What an achievement should he succeed in getting established a common law for nations – resting on the will of nations – making national duels as rare as duels between individual persons are at present: if that be truly his aim, may God steady his hand. To me it seemed that a complete victory for either side would have made it impossible almost.[37]

Within this barely concealed heart-cry from him, the son expelled in infancy from the motherland – call him Ishmael[38] – sees salvation if the motherland – and the mother – prove true. It was the keynote statement of his future internationalism. He would show himself one of the great men of the League of Nations, one of those who would have made it work had the great powers not undercut the organisation and themselves at the same time. He based this now on the Fourteen Points, and by the time of his arrival in the USA was questioning the League now proposed at Versailles. But in the battle for Versailles Treaty ratification that followed in the USA and in which de Valera took some part (enlisted among the anti-Treatyites), he differed from his associates most of whom wanted the League dead and done for, while he sought a League true to Woodrow Wilson, with whom in prison and at brief liberty in Ireland, he had sought to identify. It was not the least of Woodrow Wilson's misfortunes that he created amongst his opponents such passionate Wilsonians.

As a role model Woodrow Wilson was dangerous, and the more de Valera learned about him the more dangerous he became. His reduction of colleagues to blind subordination, his utter refusal to tolerate disagreement, were lethal to himself and what he stood for. His errors in making and selling the Versailles Treaty haunted de Valera when confronted with the UK–Ireland one. Wilson weakened his bargaining position by going to Versailles, instead of remaining at home and pronouncing on the results. The USA had not been an ally, but an 'associated power': it was also a power in good financial standing where the Allies were bankrupt. De Valera had no such trump card as that: but he remained behind in October 1921, almost certainly to avoid Wilson's mistake. Lacking the clear directives of the United States' constitution as to how treaties would be ratified or rejected by the Senate, Dáil Éireann could only work by simple majority with no ultimate room for manoeuvre, while de Valera was evidently thinking of himself as a Senator Henry Cabot Lodge, hovering with reservations somewhere between irreconcilable anti- and pro-Treatyites.

De Valera was equally caught between the argument that An Dáil was a democratically-elected assembly expressing the popular will, versus that the Republic attested by the blood of some very unrepresentative martyrs of 1916 took precedence. Wilson had even compounded his situation by refusal to compromise, asking how could they reject this Treaty and 'break the heart of the world': rich rhetoric, but impossibilist. De Valera had not wanted a polarisation but events drove him towards it, and the Wilsonian precedent left him to play it out. And when polarised, de Valera became as intransigent about his Treaty as Wilson was about his, so much so that reconciliation between himself and his former friends and more recent opponents would never be possible.

This was natural to Wilson, a Calvinist by birth and conviction, ready to divide the world into good and evil. It was alien to de Valera's nature. He made the opponent of his first election his attorney-general in 1936. He had an old-fashioned, grievance-ridden, chip-on-the-shoulder history peddled (or piddled) for voter purposes in the *Irish Press*, but when confronted with professional historians he showed himself the good teacher wanting the latest materials, and backed them. In place of the vote-gathering legend of the Great genocidal Famine, he commissioned a study utilising modern techniques and committed as far as possible to objectivity, welcomed it warmly on appearance and hoped for a successor volume on Fenianism.[39] He invited one of its contributors, Thomas P. O'Neill, to become his authorised biographer, regardless of O'Neill's upbringing having been pro-Treaty, Fine Gael and Blueshirt: O'Neill had impressively defended the Famine record of the Tory prime minister Sir Robert Peel. De Valera wanted reconciliation but was trapped in an intransigence not his own. His psychological insecurity drove him back to his pitiless model.[40]

De Valera was the more ready to depend on the inspiration of Wilson, because Wilson had saved him from much. A world at war had despaired of democracy and the military ideal was asserted as superior on all sides of the global conflict. De Valera had felt a little of that in the months before the Easter Rising and afterwards, and he heard enough of it from former insurgents: Democracy, some of them would say, was English hypocrisy. Dermot Keogh, in his masterly *Twentieth Century Ireland: Nation and State*, brings home at the outset how close both sides on the Treaty split came to annexation by would-be military dictators.[41] De Valera's own collapse into something close to a nervous breakdown when faced by defeat on the Treaty made matters worse: he did not cause the Civil War, he did too little to prevent it.

But with whatever want of forgiveness for his opponents, he slowly worked his way back into democracy. For democracy was American, not merely British, and indeed much superior in the USA to what Britain had on offer. As a good American, de Valera identified democracy with motherhood. Equally, he had first come to know Wilson as a thinker during the days of American neutrality, much abused by the British press. That Wilson had been prepared to withstand such abuse for so long would give de Valera reassurance in the Second World War. That icy Wilsonian rhetoric, supreme in its righteousness, was not de Valera's style, but the conviction of justice amid the moralistic propaganda of critics he could and did articulate. The genuineness young Kennedy reported in the commitment to neutrality was reaffirmed by the most recent, and perhaps most objective, of de Valera's biographers, Pauric Travers:

> There is no question but that de Valera saw neutrality in terms of principle rather than opportunism. His success in maintaining neutrality was only possible because the people of the Irish state were similarly persuaded.[42]

The persuading of the Irish people raises another and less admirable American legacy: the *Irish Press*. De Valera deserves credit as the saviour of Ireland from fascism, if anyone does. In part he may have done so by containing political Catholicism which elsewhere in Europe facilitated a slide or a capitulation to totalitarianism. The varying fates of Spain, Portugal, Austria, France and Belgium are all instructive in this regard. One strength he had in state-building arose from his American experience, where his half-brother, whose friendship he had cultivated by correspondence long before they met, could inform him frankly as a priest how the American system of Church and State worked. We have no record of what was said in such talks during de Valera's long visit to America in 1919–20, but it is doubtful if Father Thomas Wheelwright differed from his brethren in holy orders.

People did not say so publicly, but the Roman Catholic Church was hopelessly if silently split on the issue as between the USA and the rest of the world. The Roman Catholic Church had suffered some degree of persecution in colonial America, above all in Maryland when it passed from the hands of its Catholic founders. The advent of the American Revolution offered what Catholics united with the new USA found an admirable solution. The separation of Church and State under the First Amendment to the constitution meant that nobody could persecute anyone else. The former Jesuit and future Bishop of Baltimore who advised the revolutionaries on Catholic questions, John Carroll, saw states under Catholic auspices as a potential danger to the Church: such states had persuaded the papacy to suppress the Jesuits. The growth of the Roman Catholic Church in the United States had been on that basis of separation, and the wealth contributed by American Catholicism to the Church across the world meant that it behoved Rome to walk warily in its criticisms of its most generous daughter. (This still applies today: Cardinal Ratzinger feels himself entitled to rebuke the makers of the European constitution for its secular character, but is very careful to say nothing of the kind respecting the 200-odd year old American variety. The Vatican is in no hurry to take the vow of poverty).

De Valera's constitution of 1937 followed a secular instrument created by London and Dublin in 1922. Historians have ably charted the pressures upon him and on twentieth century Irish politicians in general from advocates of confessional statism in Ireland, Dermot Keogh and Finín O'Driscoll are surveying Irish political Catholicism for a volume of European scope and hence comparative data.[43] They show a courteous patriarch, now thanking a self-appointed Catholic ideological lobbyist for the gift of a book which he deemed to be useful but whose author had hoped he would make prescriptive, now establishing a commission to investigate the possibilities of vocational organisation. Those sittings were protracted by its argumentative personnel and the report was ultimately set aside with ministerial contempt. De Valera in fact contained political Catholicism, partly by producing a constitution which opened with salutations to the Blessed Trinity and recognised the special position of the Roman Catholic Church as the majority religion (a feat well within the power of any individual of adequate vision), but which conceded little beyond existing usages such as the ban on divorce. De Valera listed several faiths also recognised by the state, including the Friends (non-Trinitarian) and the Jewish congregations (non-Christian), regardless of the Preamble. As Joseph Lee remarked, the recognition of the Jews is one bright moment in the bleak panorama of Europe in the 1930s.[44]

It was in fact a variation on the United States' separation of Church and State, but in a specifically positive fashion, one where de Valera could both protect the vulnerable and distance the clericalists. He would have liked Vatican endorsement which, having failed to make Roman Catholicism the state religion, he did not get: but that price he had no intention of paying. It kept at bay also the most sinister threat, one posed, for instance, by Professor Michael Tierney, seeking an Irish version of Mussolini's doctrines integrated with papal encyclicals.[45] De Valera was prepared if necessary to alienate bishops who sought to pressurise in favour of confessional or corporate states, and he made much of his friendship with his Jewish devotee, Robert Briscoe, TD, deliberately sacrificing any potential electoral gains from sectarian displays. This was not necessarily an American social legacy – Irish-American relations with Jewish-Americans could be very nasty, as the Kennedys knew and some of their associates showed. But it did adhere to American constitutional faith, which probably deserves the credit for de Valera's courageous and honourable stance. Daniel O'Connell had certainly been a crusader for Jewish emancipation after Catholic, but the physical force tradition in Irish nationalism which had produced de Valera showed no such ecumenism.[46]

27

Yet, in one respect de Valera may have prevented Irish fascism by diverting anger in a specific direction. Anglophobia may have been the safety-valve which enabled Ireland to escape other forms of nativism. The *Irish Press* pumped it up day after day. The wrongs of Ireland, real and imaginary, were forever paraded through its columns and those of its stable-mates. Akin to these themes was an unconcealed celebration of physical force over constitutionalism, which duly yielded its crop of IRA activists. Its sensationalism appears small by today's lack of standards, and even in its time it probably compared favourably to the *Daily Mirror*. But its inspiration is obvious: William Randolph Hearst, whose representative John Kennedy we met at the beginning. Hearst had been at the height of the anti-Treaty demagoguery during de Valera's eighteen-month stay in 1919–20. He was busily at work, for instance, denouncing Herbert Hoover as a British agent, and he had five million readers to whom to do it. De Valera, driven from his natural sympathy for Wilson's ideas, was forced to accept the alliance of the Hearst lynch-mob against him. It might be the better part of wisdom to make oneself the Irish Hearst, but it proved a Frankenstein monster, and it proved a long fuse with effects in creating the thirty years' war in Northern Ireland at the end of the century. All the more did de Valera see the need for such support in his future political career when the Civil War was over and his jail term had been served. He had learned what unscrupulous former supporters could do to his reputation when John Devoy started operations in his *Gaelic American*. He had seen something of the power of William Martin Murphy in questioning the Catholic credentials of his enemies, and Murphy's *Independent* would be his implacable enemy after 1922. Hence the *Irish Press*, and hence also the decision to have it out-Herod Hearst.

De Valera was Irish. His American origins, his American yearning, and – in 1919–20 – his American education made him wear his Irishness with a difference. It increased his sense of the effectiveness of public opinion and the marshalling of international sentiment. It showed him how to beware so-called friends of his country (the Devoy-Cohalan public fund-raising body was the Friends of Irish Freedom) with their own agenda (its funds went to finance their Republican party choices for office). It gave him a civic code in some respects superior to that on offer from the United Kingdom whence he hoped Ireland would escape. It supplied him with friends and funds, and sympathetic indignation from Americans as valuable as Collins' military victory. Although the greatest single factor in the Lloyd George government's discomfiture was the Sinn Féin newspaper briefing in London, from the richly English voices of Desmond Fitz-Gerald and Erskine Childers, probably the most insidious propaganda the UK ever faced in its own capital.

And it demands much further study.

Eamon de Valera and Blackrock 1898–1921

Seán Farragher, CSSp

The School Journal for 14 August 1898 has this entry: 'Fr Superior return-ed considerably refreshed by his holiday in Clare.' That holiday, in the plans of Providence, proved a deciding factor in Eamon de Valera's ca-reer, as the Superior in question, Fr Laurence Healy, spent his holiday at Lisdoonvarna in the company of Fr James Liston, curate at Bruree. When the intermediate results were published on 30 August, young Edward de Valera, as he was then known, learned that he had secured a £20 exhi-bition – or scholarship – in junior grade. As he had to travel seven miles to the nearest secondary school, namely the Christian Brothers' school at Charleville, necessitating much expenditure of time and energy, he hoped to be accepted at a boarding school on the strength of this £20 scholar-ship. He had lived with his uncle Edward Coll in a labourer's cottage since his return from New York in 1885, where he had been born of an Irish mother and a Spanish father. His uncle could not be expected to con-tribute much to the £20. As no reply was received from the colleges in the south to whom he had applied, Fr Liston advised him to write to Fr Healy. He was immediately accepted on the strength of his exhibition alone.

As school had begun on 1 September he was already a week late. So without any further delay he purchased a new suit for 16/– and the other items mentioned in the prospectus, and set off for Dublin, aged 16. Horse trams still operated from Kingsbridge to the city centre. He then had to walk to Merrion Square to board the electric tram. He asked the conduc-tor to let him down at Blackrock College but the conductor was at a loss to know whether he wanted to go to St Joseph's Vincentian College Black-rock or to the French College as 'Rock was still known locally; and in-deed it was still its official title for the intermediate board, as can be seen from the admission card supplied by them to Edward de Valera for his middle grade examination in 1899. That was the original official title of the college.

Fr Laurence Healy was in fact the first Irishman to be appointed President of the college, succeeding Fr Jules Botrel, a native of Brittany, in 1896. That year too saw the first Irish bursar, Fr Neville, take over from Fr Martin Ebenrecht from Alsace. Other links with the early origins of the college were snapping just then. Fr Jerome Schwindenhammer – one of the three founder members in 1860 – was to die in France shortly after Dev arrived at the college. The first ceremony he witnessed at the college would have been the funeral mass for Fr Huvetys, the first superior of Rockwell (1864–1880) and superior of Blackrock (1880–89).

New links with the future were being formed. The first phone was installed in the college just before Dev arrived. The first ever kinematic or movie shown in the college took place that year too. The past students were about to form their first union and their senior or 'Castle' team, as it was known, was about to apply for senior status, which was granted in 1899.

De Valera was quoted in his obituaries as saying he chose Blackrock as it was then the most competitive school. It was credited in fact with the highest number of exhibitions won by boarding colleges in the published results of that year. The college victory dinner was held mid-September to celebrate these results and de Valera often recalled the opening words of the dean of studies' speech: 'Who fears to speak of '98!' This quotation puts us in immediate touch with the competitive spirit and the ideals of that era, when each school had still to depend for its survival on the published successes of its students.

As de Valera began middle grade at Blackrock he felt himself very much of an outsider. Apart from his late arrival, most of his classmates had the advantage of being in the school for junior and even preparatory grades. He had to cope with the different text books and different methods and this he found disconcerting especially in Latin class where his teacher, Fr Keawell, was notorious for insisting on his method being followed. This resulted in a disheartening number of billets to see the dean of studies, so disheartening that Dev even contemplated running away from school. But the dean, Fr O'Hanlon, who was once described to me by Sr Manes of Sion Hill (recently deceased) as of the 'woolly sort', just said:

'De Valera are you doing your best?'

'I am Father.'

'Then go!'

Dev in fact very soon got to love the regular life of the college with its long uninterrupted hours for study, a luxury he had never known at his uncle's cottage. He soon found a kindred spirit in John d'Alton – later cardinal. His admiration for this student, whom he already sensed as marked out for the Lord's vineyard, is expressed in a letter written then to his half brother Thomas Wheelwright in America – a letter happily preserved. Dev himself found his mind veering towards the priesthood as his vocation but Fr Healy advised him against joining the junior scholasticate of the congregation until he gave the matter fuller consideration.

The Christmas of 1898 Dev spent with the scholastics who did not go home on holidays in those days. He was invited by the prefects to join them in a team to play the scholastics in the first ever rugby match they were officially allowed to play. Until then rugby was forbidden to the scholastics as being contrary to French clerical decorum. They followed more or less the form of football planned for their predecessors in 1874–76 by Michael Cusack.

Dev's first rugby match literally left its mark on him. Determined to halt his opposite number and not knowing how to tackle properly he went down between his opponent's legs to stop him, and as the player had hoops on his footwear Dev received a nasty gash in the lug! He seems not to have taken a very active part in rugby thereafter and never figured on a school's team. He was a keen supporter, however, of the 'Castle' or club team and liked to recall that he helped shoulder home all the way from Ailesbury the captain of the victorious Metropolitan side in 1899. Dev knew that for him studies were paramount as he had to pay his way by his success in the public examinations. Successful he was in the middle grade examination in 1899. He won a £30 exhibition and though he won no medals for individual subjects, as did several of his classmates, he secured the highest total of marks and was thus adjudged the best all round student in the school. One of the honours that went with this distinction was that he was chosen as reader of prayers – in church and study hall and at retreats for that year – a privilege that he appreciated highly. The manual of prayers that he used was treasured by him all his life and the prayers from it were among the last he heard being read for him by his devoted chaplain, Fr Willie O'Meara, at Linden. He was received into Our Lady's sodality on 8 December 1898, and among the souvenirs of his school days that he passed on to the college is the medal with his name inscribed that he received on that occasion.

Revolutionary, politician and highly controversial character that de Valera was, his name does not immediately jump to mind as a possible candidate for canonisation, though he has been recently described by one professor of history as 'a saint in politics'. In all interviews I had with de Valera himself and with others who knew him in his school days, including Cardinal d'Alton, his character comes through as that of one remarkably upright, honest and of truly noble cast, but by no means a plaster cast, as he had a remarkable sense of humour, enjoyed schoolboy pranks and took part in the usual student escapades.

Once, when work was going ahead on the early chapters of his official biography, he asked me were there any of his contemporaries alive who had given a personal appraisal of him as a schoolboy. I mentioned that one such appraisal that immediately came to mind was the opinion expressed by Joseph O'Kane, one of his classmates. 'He said you were the last boy he would have imagined in those days as being destined to be a successful politician.' 'Did he give any reason?' Dev laughed heartily – that almost schoolboy laugh that had endeared him to his close friends right up until his last days. 'I am afraid we cannot use that – as a lot of people might not believe it!' But it echoes the sentiments expressed by one of his teachers in the *Blackrock College Annual, 1932*:

> In character, too, he showed himself at that time what he is today. He had a certain dignity of manner, a gentleness of disposition, a capability of adapting himself to circumstances, or perhaps I should rather say, of utilising those circumstances that served his purpose. No one of his fellow-students ever heard him utter a harsh or unkind criticism of a fellow student. So with a full knowledge of his character, he began to glide gradually into the category of favourites, of those, that is, of whom men are inclined to trust because they are upright, honourable, trustworthy and sincere ... !

It is well to remember that these words were written before de Valera had made his mark as Taoiseach and as President.

Fr Healy resigned as President due to ill health at the end of de Valera's first year at Blackrock. He was succeeded by an outsider, Fr John T. Murphy, who though a student of the college, had spent long years in Trinidad and in USA where he had been rector since 1888 of Pittsburg College – now Duquesne University. A man big in body and in mind, possessed of boundless energy and a gifted orator, he set about galvanising Blackrock and restructuring its outward appearance. Clareville House and the property were purchased in early 1900, but this deal was begun and carried through by Fr L. Healy. The boarders' recreation was extended to its present limits by purchasing part of what was then Willow Park. In his grand strategy to improve the frontage of the college along the main road, Fr Murphy took advantage of the arrival in Ireland the following year (April 1900) of Queen Victoria. Tradition has it that he got the students to line the road to cheer as the queen's carriage passed, and then for another carriage, the signal for which was to be given by Fr Murphy raising the huge ceremonial hat he had brought with him from Pittsburg College. The carriage in question was that in which the Earl of Pembroke travelled. Whether the earl was so proud of being so cheered in front of the other notables, or so ashamed of the dilapidated condition of the houses along the front, he rose to Fr Murphy's bait and not merely settled the matter of leases to Fr Murphy's pleasure but made an official visit to the college. There is a tradition that only two students refused to salute the queen's carriage – and the name of de Valera is not among them!

De Valera had a great admiration for Fr Murphy and loved to listen to his oratorical *tours de force,* just as he remarked in later years he used like listening to Mr Dillon's speeches in Dáil Éireann.

Fr John T. Murphy's first year at Blackrock coincided with de Valera's year in senior grade. It was an eventful year. Apart from Queen Victoria's visit, that year was marked by the first ordination ever at Blackrock, that of Fr Joseph Shanahan, CSSp, later of Nigeria fame. The ceremony was performed by the first student of Blackrock to be consecrated bishop, Mgr Emile Allgeyer (1897). De Valera remarked on how impressed the students were by this solemn ceremony, as also by Fr Shanahan's first mass offered at the college the next day. Later that year Fr Murphy invited his friend, the then renowned Archbishop Ireland of St Paul, Minnesota, to visit the college and address the entire school. The press account of the visit put in bold letters that the archbishop stressed that he was:

> ... speaking to young men in whose hands were *the destinies of the Irish people.* Half a century hence those whom he addressed would be alive to see the fruits of their own efforts, and he trusted those efforts would be such as to place the Irish people in possession of all their legitimate rights and worthy of the possession of these rights ...

Fr Murphy was himself very much in demand as a speaker for the big occasion or for the furtherance of charitable causes. One such cause he espoused wholeheartedly was the Pioneer Total Abstinence Movement founded towards the end of 1898. That a branch was formed early on in the college is obvious from the portrait of de Valera taken 1899 in connection with his success in the public examination, as he is wearing what must have been one of the first PTAA badges. Soon lemonade was to replace the traditional whiskey or claret punch for the students on festive occasions. The invocation was not enthusiastically greeted by the 'Castle' or university students whose favourite bunking out place was to Keegan's licensed premises then adjoining the property.

Another cause adopted enthusiastically by Fr John T. Murphy was that of the revival of the Irish language, especially its upgrading in schools. The Gaelic League was actively campaigning for this cause at that time. At a major speech given in the Rotunda, October 1900 by the President of the Gaelic League, Dr Douglas Hyde, Fr Murphy was chosen to second his motion and explain the situation as then affecting secondary schools. Soon after he was called on to address the Gaelic League in Blackrock Town Hall on the subject 'Why we should study the Irish language'. Among those present as noted in the press was W. J. Pearse; Patrick Pearse was probably at the second such meeting. Little could Fr Murphy have foreseen that the conclusions to be drawn from these beginnings would lead some of his listeners to the 1916 Rising. His comments on the Rising take on a special dimension when one recalls his involvement with the cause of Irish language and culture in 1900.

When de Valera arrived in Blackrock he had no knowledge of Irish. He envied those who had. He recalled to me as he passed through the recreation in 1958, the very spot where he saw his classmate, Thomas F. Rahilly, reading one of the earliest issues of *An Chaidheamh Soluis* in 1899. He recalled how amazed he was that a student of his own age could read that strange script and translate the contents for the other students. Years later, when de Valera was Taoiseach, he set up the Institute for Advanced Studies, and he appointed Thomas F. Rahilly as director of the Celtic Studies Department.

Irish was being taught in the school by Tadhg Ó Donnchadh (Torna) but only to a handful of senior students for whom 'Celtic', as it was called, was a suitable subject for the combination most likely to win them the highest number of marks for a possible scholarship. What that class lacked in quantity it made up in quality: there was Thomas F. Rahilly the noted Irish scholar, Martin O'Mahony (later known as 'Suig' to generations of Irish students in Blackrock) and the well known Gaelic writer Seán-Phádraig Ó Conaire. There was no question of Dev attending these Irish classes even if he had some Irish.

He recalled other students in the 'Castle' preparing for higher civil service examinations and studying Fr O'Gowney's *Irish Grammar* as a relaxation from time to time, but he did not seriously attempt to learn the language till years later when his friend and tutor Michael Smithwick, who taught Irish and mathematics at Blackrock, introduced him to the Gaelic League classes.

When de Valera reminisced about his life at 'Rock it was really the years spent at the 'Castle' that came most readily to mind. He spent three years in all there as a student: 1900–01 (matriculation, which was then a separate course from senior grade) and 1901–03 (first and second arts). He then spent two years teaching in Rockwell, between 1903–5, returning to the 'Castle' at the end of the school year to prepare for the BA examination. Then, late in 1906, while professor in Carysfort Training College, he returned to the newly extended 'Castle' as a lodger for about a year and a half. As such, he was the last survivor of the old 'Castle' days, and because he made it as it were his home in those years, he was a store of anecdotes, facts and comments providing much material for recreating a living picture of that institution that he so much loved and admired. Not that he was blind to its limitations. He more than most suffered from one limitation after 1900, namely the lack of competent staff to teach mathematics and science at a university level; and mathematics was his speciality. Before his arrival in the college in 1898 the dean warned the other students of the impending arrival of a 'mathematical genius from Bruree' in order to stir up emulation.

When later Dev arrived in John Maguire's Greek class, the prime boys, knowing Maguire's often expressed contempt for mathematics, introduced de Valera as one for whom mathematics was the only subject worthy of his serious attention. Maguire ordered Dev to take out his mathematics exercise and dictated some sentences in Greek to be written across his mathematical notes in spite of Dev's protestations that he had a special exercise for Greek. 'There now,' said Maguire, 'you have at least one bit of Christianity in the midst of all that paganism.' Maguire did succeed in imparting a love of the Greek authors, especially the orators, and years later when de Valera was in the middle of a speech denouncing the Treaty in Killarney he was for a moment at a loss for words when he recognised his former Greek professor among his audience. He was conscious that he was using the yardstick of Demosthenes in judging his performance. The only comment Maguire made afterwards was: 'De Valera, I admire your oratory but disagree with your politics!'

In the 'Castle' those studying for a university degree in mathematics or science and even those sitting for the civil service entrance examinations had often to depend on crash courses or grinds on a part of the syllabus from a university lecturer who came along for a number of classes; then these students who could afford his fee coached other students for a lesser sum. Michael Smithwick for example, was among those coached by John Hooper, later director of statistics in the Free State government, and Smithwick in turn coached de Valera and others. They had their own teachers, of course: Johnny Haugh, the author of a famous arithmetic text and Fr Hugh O'Toole their science teacher; both were competent in their subject but lacking drive as teachers. In modern languages and the classics, 'Castle' students were well served.

The students were lodged in houses acquired by the college along the old Williamstown Avenue. These houses they dignified by the high sounding names: 'Grey's Inn', 'Lincoln Inn' and the favourite more prosaically know as 'Piggeries'. The 'Piggeries' was favoured by the students because it was most remote from supervision. De Valera was assigned a room there, junior though he was, as being one of the more solid sort. The senior and tougher set sized up the situation. Dev woke up in the middle of the night there to find himself being lifted out of bed by four of those seniors who told him to keep quiet while they extracted twelve large bottles from beneath the floor and replaced them by twelve others. The ones replaced were full of wine bottled that evening by Brother John from a cask that had arrived from the college cellar. The empties were placed in their stead! Next day claret, mulled over the gaslights, was the treat for those 'in the know'.

Apart from class and study hours, life in the 'Castle' was to a great extent organised by the students themselves, under a benign dean, Fr Downey, and a prefect. They had their various societies for which they drafted the rules and enforced the penalties for misconduct. De Valera figured prominently in some of these societies. His first post was librarian and as such he was vested with the power of search when any of the regular magazines they contributed to disappeared from the reading room. He was not long in the job when he used this power on two seniors, rightfully suspected as it happened. He recovered the magazines but was almost 'sent to Coventry' for his pains.

They had also a thriving Literary and Debating Society and we find de Valera's name in time on the organising committee, and his contributions to the debates recorded in the minutes. On the subject 'That the policy of free trade is preferable to protection' (13 February 1901), the minutes read: 'Mr de Valera was in favour of a little of both.' More interesting perhaps was the stand he took on the motion 'That a constitutional monarchy as a form of government is preferable to republicanism': 'Mr de Valera maintained that constant elections disturb the nation and are not conducive to the prosperity of the people.' Another reason why he preferred constitutional monarchy was that 'there is no rule so tyrannical as that of "them all"' (27 November 1901).

De Valera's major contribution to the Castle Literary and Debating Society was (significantly for a future chancellor of the NUI) a paper read by him (18 February 1903) on 'The Irish University Question'. This was no mere academic subject. It was hotly debated at the time and the 'Castle' students and staff felt the injustice of their position under the old Royal University where they had to sit for an examination set by those who taught in certain other colleges and then examined their own and all the other students as well. There were other grounds of complaint all outlined in this paper which took him weeks of research in the National Library and elsewhere, to prepare.

When I detailed the main points of the paper to him some years ago, I mentioned that he ruled out the Queen's Colleges as a practical solution because they were condemned by the Catholic bishops. He laughed and said 'Let it be put in my biography some day that I rejected something because I had been told to do so by the Irish bishops!'

The solution he favoured was the foundation of a New University of Dublin with three constituent colleges, one for Catholics, one for Presbyterians and Trinity College, all common matters such as examinations and exhibitions to be dealt with by a senate composed from all three colleges.

The practical relevance of the matters being discussed can be gauged from the attendance of the staff with Fr John T. Murphy in the chair. The closely written twenty foolscap pages were preserved by de Valera and presented by him to the college, as was the copy of the bible he was presented with by the college President Fr Murphy, on securing first place in the test he set on the series of lectures he gave the 'Castle' students on Apologetics and Christian Philosophy.

Consequent to a lecture given by Fr Murphy under the auspices of the Society of St Vincent de Paul, a branch of the Blackrock parish conference was founded at the 'Castle' in 1901. At first it would seem there was some reluctance on the part of the senior parish members of the conference to allow students to carry out the delicate work of visitation of homes in the locality, but their minds were soon put at ease. The first secretary to be appointed was E. de Valera and the following year he was the obvious choice as President, a post he held as long as he remained in the 'Castle'. The students took their work seriously, most of all their President, as can be learned from the reports of that period (see, for example, *Blackrock College Annual 1936*).

One of the places de Valera recalled visiting the aged in those years was Linden Convalescent Home where he himself was to end his days, happy to be in such familiar surroundings. Less happy memories were connected with a visitation involving a house in Booterstown where it transpired that there was a case of smallpox. He felt obliged to have himself immediately vaccinated resulting in his being very ill. As he was sitting on the roof of the old 'Castle' where he had his room in the tower during his final year, he realised that he could not identify the fathers as they walked along the avenue. He dated the commencement of the deterioration of his vision to that period, but he also realised that he had profited from the experiences gained through this intimate contact with the poor and the aged during these formative years of his life.

De Valera had asked specially to be allowed to use the mere lumber room in the old 'Castle' tower in preference to a more comfortable room along Williamstown avenue, as he thought it would help him to study better. He was plagued by a tendency to fall off to sleep while reading. The change of room seemingly did not make much difference. Finally, he decided to climb a tree near the 'Castle' in order to remain alert while studying, and indeed the most vivid image that some of the junior students of that period recalled when they spoke of Dev at Blackrock, was seeing him perched on that tree with a book in his hand. Incidentally, a snapshot of him at this period taken by an American boy, John Junker, shows him with a relaxed group of students some of whom are holding footballs; De Valera alone is holding a book with his fingers marking the pages as if ready to return to what was his priority.

De Valera in fact took little active part in football games at this period. He was interested in athletics but even here one got the impression that his main aim was to maintain physical fitness. He prepared seriously for the annual sports with almost the same approach as to solving a problem in mathematics. He weighed up the possibilities open to him knowing the other contenders in each event. Having opted for what he had the best chance of winning he sized up the most formidable challenger, planned to keep close behind till the moment when the final spurt was called for. But reality did not match the theory. On one occasion, he stopped to attend a casualty and forgot that it was a race. On another occasion, this time the two mile cycle race, he thought he had all planned to perfection following as he imagined the likely, and in fact the eventual winner, but his defective eyesight played a trick on him as two competitors wore the same colour singlet and he kept behind the wrong man losing almost a lap before he realised his plans had miscarried. The official photographer has left us a good record of the start of that race with Dev being aided by his friend Jim Sweeney who afterwards wore the green jersey for Ireland. That same day Dev's tactics did work out as planned. He beat Paddy Cahill in the senior mile.

By now the image of de Valera to have emerged is the serious, aloof, austere figure that many have imagined him always to have been. That was certainly not Dev's idea of himself in those student days. Right up to the end he used to delight to relive the pranks and the escapades he took part in. One cannot easily imagine him gate-crashing a fashionable ball, but this indeed happened when both he and R. Manning stuck on false moustaches to give themselves the appearance of added years and respectability. Unfortunately for them the moustaches dropped due to the heat and they were summarily expelled. Raiding the Clareville orchard was a temptation he could not resist, though he found it was extremely difficult to see the apples at night, so he concentrated his attention on the Virginia plums instead.

Their outings on Sunday to Blackrock Park under the pretence of being interested in the band were really an exercise in 'dolly twigging'. Sensing that I was out of my depth at this stage he laughingly explained that the word meant 'admiring the girls that were out to be admired!'

The most frequent breach of rule by the 'Castle' students was going 'over the wall', which being interpreted meant bunking out to Keegan's licensed premises which in those days, and indeed away back in 1798 (when a man called Kinshellagh was the proprietor) was very conveniently on the college side of the main road. Fr Murphy, as might be expected from an ardent apostle of temperance, was mainly responsible for having this public house transferred to the opposite side of the road in 1904. Of course, there were delicacies even for the teetotaller to be had at

Keegans, as snacks, pastries, etc., were served. Dev recalled clearly his very first bunking 'over the wall'. He was introduced there by 'Bugler' Dunne. The name recalled to his mind how much their nicknames and slang in those days were coloured by the Boer War, then in the news. Their favourite drink, 'coffee with a shot of the hard stuff', was known as a Khaki. There was always an element of risk involved in 'going over the wall', as if caught you were called out at the Monday night 'session', and so much was deducted from the £5 deposit that each student had to lodge with the director as a guarantee of good conduct throughout the year.

It was the prefect's duty to keep an eye on students' movements. Their prefect one year was James Burke, later author of the 'Missionary Hymn'. Being a keen musician he once thought to slip out quietly to the Theatre Royal for the Halle Orchestra's visit. The word went round and all adjourned across the wall – all but one tall man among them who could easily be mistaken in the moonlight for Mr Burke, if he were only dressed in a soutane and biretta, and especially if the biretta were worn at the unmistakable Burke forward tilt. De Valera had no difficulty in convincing the dodgers on the way in that they were being spotted by their prefect, that they had been tricked and were all in for a fine at next session. Mr Burke was at a loss to explain why he was greeted on several occasions in the next few days by the students whistling the 'Keelrow' as a protest against something mean. And Dev thought it wiser at this stage to sing dumb till the matter could be taken as a joke – until later years in fact!

Dev had a fund of such anecdotes which, though they help recreate the atmosphere of those days, would be devoid of any further significance were it not that they may help in some degree to understand how his own personality ticked, as it were, before he became deeply committed to the national movement. One is left with the impression that whereas he was a good mixer and was readily accepted in all company, he was never immersed in the crowd, that he held himself consciously or otherwise in someway apart and was given to calculating many of his incursions. Sometimes that was influenced, it would appear, by the fact that he had less pocket money at his disposal than most of his associates and that he had to be more cautious in order to pay his way.

An anecdote helps illustrate this. Many contests the students indulged in ended up in the loser having to stand a treat in Keegans. One such contest was a burst for the old 'Castle' gate when it was locked. The last to hit the ground on the far side had to stand the treat. Dev was challenged and the following evening was fixed by the three involved. In the meantime, Dev went along and examined the gate minutely sizing up what portion gave the best leverage on the way up. Needless to add he had not to foot the bill. Dev actually became an expert in climbing the present college gate when locked against his homecomings in later years. When his brother, Thomas Wheelright, visited him in the 'Castle' in 1907, in order to impress junior, Dev successfully got over the gate in three moves carrying his bicycle on his shoulder. When he mentioned jokingly to his 'Castle' dean in later years that he had been well prepared for prison life while in the 'Castle' he may not have amused Fr Downey as he soon realised, but he was really referring to no more than his methods of getting in and out of institutions!

When his second class scholarship in mathematical science in the Royal University examination only netted him £15, to defray the expenses of his board and tuition at the 'Castle' he volunteered to take part-time class in the college in order to make up the difference. He offered to take all the classes, hitherto taught by Patrick Kelly, later Sir Patrick, Chief of Police, Bombay, who had just qualified for the Indian civil service; but he was instead assigned two students who had failed their solicitor's preliminary examination and he had to coach them in all five subjects. They were successful this time and as a token of appreciation they presented Dev with a ticket for the Welsh-Irish international match, 1902. He preserved this souvenir from his first students, Florie Green and Donegan, and it is now among his own souvenirs in the college archives.

He was also asked to stand in for other teachers during periods of absence, notably Johnnie Haugh for long years teacher of mathematics in Blackrock. A class of 'chicks', as the youngest juniors were then called, liked to recall in later years their reactions to this youthful and rather over-gentlemanly stand-in for Mr Haugh, whose threats of dire punishment invariably ended up in a few 'biffs' with a shoe lace. They, too, decided to collect to make him a present but when the wags in the 'Castle' told him they were going to present him with a needle and a spool of thread he dropped a word to the class indicating that he was not in favour of students making presentations to teachers. However he readily accepted the ebony walking stick they had in fact procured for him!

At the end of the school year in June he decided that the time had come to accept the first full time teaching post offered. The offer came from Rockwell where the teacher of mathematics, Robert Walker, wanted to come to the 'Castle' in order to study for his degree in mathematics. So Dev moved out of the 'Castle' to Rockwell in September 1903, but he was back again at Blackrock from June to October 1904 studying for his BA examination. A snap taken of him during that period with Fr Botrel shows him dressed in knee breeches, already clearly recognisable as the tall distinctive figure that was to appear in so many historic moments for the next seventy years.

Due to his lack of time and tuition throughout that year de Valera secured only a pass degree in mathematical science. This was a big disappointment to him and was to militate against his chances of securing a first class post in the teaching profession or in the civil service. He had put away all idea of the Indian civil service, having first-hand evidence of the colonial mentality at its worst induced in one of his acquaintances after a few short years in India.

With his degree came de Valera's final break with the student life in the 'Castle', though he was to return for a year and a half again as a lodger while teaching in Carysfort Training College. Those who wondered in later years at his repeated requests to have the 'Castle' re-opened, as a hostel for students from all the colleges run by the Holy Ghost congregation, had probably no idea of how deeply he felt about the sterling educative value of the old 'Castle' system. He was himself the last survivor of a whole generation moulded there since its inception in 1875, first as a training school for entrance into the civil service and then as a university college to prepare students to sit for the examinations conducted by the Royal University. Dev was also very conscious of the sizeable and sterling contribution made by so many of the products of the 'Castle' to the formation of a native Irish administration, which took over smoothly and efficiently from the British in later years.

At the end of the school year June 1905, de Valera decided to resign his post in Rockwell, much to the regret of all there, and seek fortune nearer the centre of things as he had planned to continue his studies. The only post available was that of teacher in a Catholic school in Liverpool, with the prospect of attending the university there. He was so depressed however with the alien atmosphere in Liverpool that he returned immediately to Dublin where luckily he got a part-time post in Belvedere College, supplemented by classes in Clonliffe College and at Eccles Street.

At the end of the year he was contacted by Fr Baldwin, CSSp, whom he knew well at Rockwell to tell him that the superioress of Carysfort Training College (where he was now chaplain) was looking for a mathematics teacher. Dev gladly accepted the post even though it was only for two hours each day. He soon applied to be allowed to board at the 'Castle', which in the meantime had been greatly enlarged in the expectation of favourable developments in the sphere of higher education.

Dev spent some eighteen months in residence in the 'Castle' going out to teach at Carysfort Training College and at St Mary's Rathmines, where his former dean of studies Fr O'Hanlon was the superior. He also gave grinds to individual students studying for university examinations. Among them was his former student Paddy, later Monsignor, Browne, who from de Valera's class in Rockwell got second place in Ireland in mathematics in senior grade; and Cornelius Gregg of Blackrock, who beat Paddy for first place! Another of his students at this period was

Dick Butler, past-pupil of Blackrock, who is reported to have similarly coached the Prince of Wales, later King Edward VIII. Gregg, incidentally, who was later to be rated as one of the great minds of the British civil service, was highly valued by Churchill as chancellor of the exchequer, and later with his mathematical acumen, was invaluable in cipher-breaking during the war. He was later knighted.

One feature of this period vouched for by Bishop Heffernan, then prefect in the Castle and a life-long friend of Dev, is worth recalling as Dev never denied it. His overcoat was used regularly by the Castle students and the girls in the Training College as their mail bag. All Dev had to do was to hang his coat in the same spot each day in both venues!

During this period, 1906–09, Dev took an active part in the Blackrock Club or 'Castle' teams as they were still known. He had begun to play senior football while in Rockwell and was now chosen occasionally to play for the firsts, but more often for the Metropolitan side which he preferred and which he captained in 1908. His team was narrowly defeated in the final. He served as secretary to the club for one year and helped at the running of the annual sports each year in the college. With regard to schools rugby at this time it is interesting to learn that the minutes of the schools' rugby committee record that E. de Valera was one of the two members present at the Gresham Hotel in October 1905 at the annual general meeting, representing Belvedere College; and that in the following year, October 1906, and again in 1908, he was one of the two who represented Blackrock. And in this connection it is worth mentioning that the first ever fixture between Blackrock and Belvedere took place in January 1907, shortly after de Valera moved into residence in the 'Castle' after his first year teaching at Belvedere.

Fr Downey resigned as dean of the Castle in 1908 and a special function and presentation was arranged by a number of his friends including de Valera. That was the signal for Dev to pull up his roots finally and move to outside accommodation, having spent most of his life from 1898 to 1908 in such close association with Blackrock, Rockwell and St Mary's. At a special reception given by him as President of Ireland in Áras an Úachtaráin in 1960 in connection with the college centenary, he paid a moving tribute to those formative years to which he admitted freely he owed so much. At the college centenary he and his classmate Cardinal d'Alton were obviously the central figures. Fifty years previously they were also among the special guests at the golden jubilee celebrations of the college although they are out at the edge of the photos then. But that was away back in 1910!

Next came 1916. The then Castle students, now reduced in numbers, mixed with the Sherwood Foresters as these consulted their obsolete maps looking for Williamstown Avenue, demolished in 1906, as a suitable stopping place. They were on their way to face Commandant de Valera's men at Mount Street Bridge. When the fighting was over and it was learned that de Valera was among those condemned to death, Fr Downey, then President of the college, contacted the attorney general, Sir James O'Connor, who happened to be a past student of the college, to pass on the word that de Valera was American-born. He passed the same message on to James McMahon, secretary of the GPO, another past pupil of the college.

Fr John T. Murphy, who was then provincial superior, wrote just after the Rising to inform the superior general in Paris on what had happened in Dublin. In his report he deplored the imprudence of the leaders of what he considered a misguided rebellion but paid tribute to their sense of honour and their Christian piety. He had of course known de Valera as a student and Thomas McDonagh as a prefect in Rockwell (1896–1901).

When de Valera was elected President of Dáil Éireann in 1919, it was decided that he should go to the United States as soon as possible in that capacity. Very shortly after his secret arrival, and before he made his first public appearance at the Waldorf Astoria, Fr William O'Donnell, CSSp, who knew him personally and was deeply involved in the Irish movement in the United States, arranged that he should visit the Holy Ghost community at Cornwells Heights, Pennsylvania, composed as it was of past Blackrock and Rockwell men known to the President. Realising that it was a historic occasion they improvised a battery of lamps to take a time-exposure photo of the group that night. Seated beside the youthful looking President is one of Blackrock's earliest students, Fr William Healy, CSSp. He it was who was responsible away back in 1865 for erecting the first (home made) green flag over the college, on St Patrick's Day 1865. He was described by his French director as 'outre en politique, comme arch-Irlandais'. As he sports his Irish colours here again, for the last time as it transpired, one can imagine him saying that he could well sing his 'Nunc demittis', now that Ireland seemed to be on the threshold of being a Nation once again.

After his return to Ireland, the residence provided for the President was at 'Glenvar', just across the road from Clareville. It was in an outhouse in Clareville that Eoin MacNeill's men were screening the intercepted mail-bags. In an effort to trace them down, a military cordon was thrown around the area. The college and Clareville were searched with no result, but de Valera was accidentally arrested at 'Glenvar'. When his identity was confirmed at the Bridewell the news was flashed to London and the instructions from there were that he was to be released immediately. He was released, much to his surprise, at Portobello Barracks. Having procured an old bicycle he cycled back to Blackrock. He ran in to his old friends Fr Larry Healy and Fr James Burke, who were amazed to see him again. As he ate a hasty meal they tried to puzzle out the reason for his sudden release. In the event of his being around on Sunday it was arranged that he and his secretary, Miss O'Connell, could have mass and dinner at the college. They both arrived and at dinner with Fr Downey and Fr Burke, de Valera produced an envelope with a special seal that had been handed to Miss O'Connell the previous day by Bishop Mulhern on behalf of Lloyd George. The letter signalled the start of the Truce negotiations. That was Sunday 26 June 1921.

Eamon de Valera and the Civil War in Ireland, 1922–1923

Dermot Keogh

Eamon de Valera, unlike most members of his political generation, has not lacked biographers. They range greatly in quality, objectivity and professionalism. As a general comment, I have long since come to hold the view that de Valera is more in need of being rescued from the un-critical prose of his admirers than from the vituperative attacks of his most ardent critics. Even hyper-critical work has not done nearly as much damage to de Valera's reputation as the perfumed praise of his hagiographers.

Broadly speaking, it is possible to divide such works into categories, one of which comprises studies that move from hagiography to the warmly positive. This work ought not to be dismissed as being of little scholarly use. The studies vary greatly but many of them make indispensable reading.[1]

A benign view of de Valera's role during the Civil War is to be found in Bromage, Macardle, MacManus and both of Seán Ó Faoláin's two biographies. The latter was a veteran of the War of Independence and an anti-Treatyite during the Civil War, who rejected the view that de Valera could be blamed for 1922:

> But in his case it is most cruelly unjust to blame him for the events of 1922. He was not then the leader of the people, but the leader of a minority, and a political minority at that. Over the militarists he had no control, and they avoided or rejected his influence, so that when he issued his Cease Fire Order in May 1923 he only did so because the chastened militarists were only too glad to accept his control that they once rejected, and to accept his magnanimous offer to try to pull together the scattered remnants of republicanism in Ireland. There is not another man in Ireland who would have so unselfishly taken up the Lost Cause, with all its opprobrium and all its associations of defeat. But this man would go, and has gone, to almost any length to bring about the unity of his people, so woefully divided in the hour of apparent triumph.[2]

In O'Faoláin's second biography in 1939 – as hostile as the first was idolatorous – he maintained that interpretation of de Valera's impotence during the Civil War:

> De Valera lived in those days through his Inferno. Like Dante he descended into Hell, and his face began to show the marks of his journey. All that he had fought for, all to which he had devoted his life, was in ruins. He was now forty years old – an age at which a man knows that the next round figure will put him among the elderly men. He was powerless. To use his own despairing words he watched from 'behind a wall of glass'. He was repudiated as leader by the majority of his people, not acknowledged as leader by the remainder. Not until the soldiers began to realise that the game was up did they think about him, or turn to him and then they turned to him only to give him the task of announcing defeat.[3]

M. J. MacManus, who published his biography in 1944, proved to be an even more vigorous defender. He wrote: 'The biographer of de Valera is not required to linger over the actual period of the Civil War. De Valera had tried to prevent its coming and he had failed; he was equally powerless to shape its course.'[4] MacManus entered into the most vigorous defence of his subject of study. He provides the following portrait of de Valera on the eve of civil war in June 1922:

> Once again, because de Valera had not taken the easy way out, because he had had the moral courage to do the hard and the bitter thing, he was made the chief target for opprobrium and abuse. He, and almost he alone, was held up to the people of the two islands and to the outside world as the man who had plunged Ireland into civil war. He was stigmatised as vain, fanatical and obstinate, as a man who had broken all the rules of fair dealing, as one who should be outlawed forever from the councils of statesmen. In Britain, the old jibe, applied in other years to Parnell and O'Connell, was revived: 'He doesn't know what he wants and won't be happy till he gets it', and that in spite of the fact that no leader had ever stated what he wanted more consistently or more lucidly. Such attacks were the measure of his enemies' fear. They dreaded lest he should succeed in re-uniting the forces of the Republic and in giving public opinion the sense that resistance to the new oppression was morally right.[5]

That view is very much out of favour at the beginning of the twenty-first century. Criticism of de Valera has grown. The range and quality of the work on the adversarial side of the argument also ranges greatly in quality and in professionalism. Many of the texts are very hard-hitting. A minority, I regret to say, might be described in modern-day popular language as 'hatchet jobs'.[6] But, as with the other category, the work is worth examining in detail.

The flavour of the writing of those historians most hostile to de Valera and to his reputation may be judged by quoting from the work of Tim Pat Coogan. He has written perhaps the most popular and widely-read biography in recent years. Coogan is merciless in his criticism. In relation to de Valera's failure to lead the Irish negotiating team to London in autumn 1921, he writes: 'The question which will forever hang over his reputation in Irish History is: would he have been on that road if his rivalry with Collins and his fatal streak of "cute hoorism" had not made him shirk the responsibility of going to the London negotiations.'[7] Coogan presents him as being myopic and strangely resilient to accepting the inevitable: 'The policy he said he intended to pursue was, in the conditions of the time, akin to the captain of the *Titanic* deliberately deciding to ignore the existence of the iceberg.'[8]

One of de Valera's favourite disguises during the Civil War was, according to Coogan, the garb of a priest which, he argues, was 'symptomatic of the atmosphere of intrigue and unreality in which he increasingly operated during those tragic days.'[9] Coogan writes of 'de Valera speak'[10] and of a 'de Valera fact'[11]. In other words truth, to him, was relative. He was also a man of exaggerated self-importance, according to the same author: 'His American-inflated ego made him impervious to the feelings of the majority of the Irish people, whose wishes he professed to be able to divine through his own unique process of vascular oracularity.'[12] He is depicted by the same source as being a disciple of Machiavelli[13] who was always in quest of 'extremist support'[14] during the Civil War. There is even a reference to a rumour of gossip concerning his relationship with his secretary, Kathleen O'Connell.

In fine, the thesis presented in Coogan's volume argues that the 'cute hoor' de Valera – a pupil of Machiavelli – partially driven by jealousy of Michael Collins fomented and then prolonged the Civil War. That thesis does not diverge significantly from the cruder versions of Cumann na nGaedheal propaganda of which the election poster in 1932 given on the next page is an example.

There is a middle ground of professional scholarship. This is a growing corpus, some of which is cited in the endnote. It is by far the most useful category of work on de Valera's life and times.[15]

There is a fourth category of publications that is indispensable for the study of de Valera: collections of his speeches, statements and sayings have been published since the 1920s. There is a reference to the publication of his early correspondence on Anglo-Irish relations in 1922.[16] As a student at UCD in the late 1960s, I discovered under the direction of Dr Maureen Wall a pamphlet entitled *The Hundred Best Sayings of Eamon de Valera*. Published in 1924, it had collected together in abbreviated form a range of political observations and comments. The editor of the pam-

1932 Cumann na nGaedheal election poster

phlet was not identified.[17] When de Valera came into office in 1932, the first collection of his speeches to the League of Nations was published in book form.[18] A selection of his speeches for the war years was also published.[19] Maurice Moynihan has produced by far the most impressive and comprehensive compendium to date of de Valera's speeches and writings. This is useful for scholars not only for the texts chosen but also for the commentary that Moynihan has added in introducing many categories of documents. These are critical notes carrying with them the authority of one who worked closely with de Valera in office for over two decades. Moynihan is a fair-minded observer/participant.[20] Proinsias Mac Aonghusa has both written about de Valera and published a collection of quotations.[21]

Although I would place de Valera's officially sanctioned biographers, Lord Longford and Professor T. P. O'Neill in the first category – the sympathetic/partisan – I feel that this choice may require further explanation. In the first line of their acknowledgements, they write: 'This book could not have been written without the co-operation of President de Valera himself.' They record that he had 'steadfastly refused to write an autobiography, but once he had agreed to the suggestion that an authoritative biography be written, he could not have been more helpful.' The work was not an official biography. It was to be, in their own words, 'an authoritative biography'. In the completion of their task, both authors expressed their gratitude to de Valera 'not only for making his huge library of private papers freely available to them, but giving them the benefit of his personal recollections of the great events in which he has played so prominent a part.' He was President of Ireland at the time and those consultations took place in the official residence in the Phoenix Park.

There was a further important fact recorded in the acknowledgements. De Valera interacted with the two authors in the writing of the text: 'But he made it clear at a very early stage that, if they ever found a discrepancy between his memory of events and contemporary documents, it was the documents that must be trusted.' But for a man who was thirty-three years old when the 1916 Rising took place, the next line in the acknowledgements is of great methodological significance: 'The authors would like to record that such discrepancies were almost non-existent.'[22] There was an almost perfect match between de Valera's personal memory and what was in the archives. The 'almost non-existent' phrase is not explained. Neither is there an explanation as to what the 'almost non-existent' might have been. Was it the case that the discrepancies between memory and documentation – no matter how marginal – were recorded in the footnotes?

Other sources reveal that Lord Longford, who had been an admirer of de Valera since the 1930s, was only brought into the writing of the biography late in the proceedings. O'Neill, with a considerable advance from Hutchinson, had been in a position to work on the research and writing for three years.[23] There was also a parallel process. De Valera's biography was being written in Irish by O'Neill and Fr Pádraig Ó Fiannachta. The only two volumes to appear were published in 1968 and 1970.[24] Covering the period until 1937, and encompassing the Treaty negotiations and Civil War, it was designed to be a very detailed life of its subject. The tragedy was, however, that the much more detailed multi-volume biography in Irish never materialised. Read side-by-side with the relevant section in the single-volume English edition, the historian may speculate on what might have been. In the English edition, 344 pages, out of 474 in total, are devoted to the period of de Valera's life up to 1939. Some 50 of those pages focus on the Civil War (pages 181–234) and are given the chapter titles: 'The Drift to Disaster' (January–June 1922), 'The War of Brothers' (July–October 1922), 'The Emergency Government' (October 1922–February 1923), 'The Darkest Hour' (March–May 1923) and 'De Profundis' (May 1923–July 1924). Both authors provide the reader in these pages with a minimalist interpretation of de Valera's ability to influence events during the lead-up to the Civil War and during its progress. Rather than allow the documents in the de Valera archives to reveal the tortuous path to Civil War, the 'authoritative biography' seeks to defend his actions. His series of speeches in March 1922, referred to below, receive thirteen lines to describe their content. Longford and O'Neill continue:

> These awful warnings were quickly seized upon by the *Irish Independent* and others, not as prophecies but as incitements. Mr de Valera described the paper's editorial as villainous and went on: 'You cannot be unaware that your representing me as inciting to civil war has on your readers precisely the same effect as if the inciting were really mine.' For fear of future misrepresentations, however, he left aside this argument in later speeches.[25]

Evidence for this last critical line is not cited in the volume. It remains undocumented. Did the authors simply make that surmise based on their reading of the documents? It must also be asked whether that last line was added following discussion with de Valera while the book was being written? The answer to those questions would have a critical bearing as to how that particular sentence ought to be interpreted. This points to the great difficulty of using the Longford/O'Neill life in a classroom or as a source.

Both authors describe de Valera's great dilemma in March 1922. They interpret his refusal to condemn the use of arms as an effort to preserve the fragile unity of the republican side. Both authors also argue that de Valera's failure to denounce the leading militant anti-Treatyite Rory O'Connor's repudiation of the authority of Dáil Éireann as being 'for reasons alike of honour and prudence'. Longford and O'Neill continue:

> He was, in fact, in a nightmarish position, with little influence on events in practice. On the one hand the pro-Treaty government authorities held the initiative. On the other, the republican section of the army, composing probably more than half the Volunteers, were taking independent action.

They argued that de Valera, apart from a few meetings with Liam Mellowes and Rory O'Connor, 'had little relationship with republican members of the army and little information about them.' The occupation of the Four Courts on 14 April came as a complete surprise to him: 'He had no part whatever in this step. But he felt that the dispute was a matter for the Minister for Defence and any interference by him would be unwelcome to either party.'[26] None of those statements are footnoted and must have been the memories of an elderly de Valera.

Longford and O'Neill quote de Valera as writing towards the end of the Civil War to Ms Edith M. Ellis in London on 26 February 1923:

Alas! Our country has been placed in a cruel dilemma out of which she could be rescued only by gentleness, skill and patience, and on all sides a desire for justice and fair-dealing. Instead we find ourselves in the atmosphere of a tempest – every word of reason is suppressed or distorted until it is made to appear the voice of passion. I have been condemned to view the tragedy here for the last year as through a wall of glass, powerless to intervene effectively. I have, however, still the hope that an opportunity may come my way.[27]

Opportunity did come his way in the mid-1920s after the closure of a civil war that was low in casualties by comparative international standards but that left a legacy of bitterness with which de Valera had to struggle throughout his political life. One must be grateful to Longford and O'Neill for helping to construct – over forty years after the end of hostilities – Eamon de Valera's perceived record of the Civil War and of the part that he played in it. Therefore, having read that biography, the historian is equipped with a highly personalised and very subjective account of the origins and development of the Irish Civil War.

When the biographies of de Valera are assembled together, as I have done above, it becomes very clear that much remains to be done in order to address the most basic questions about his life and times. Despite the many tens of thousands of words written about the most important political figure in twentieth century Ireland, a critical mass of scholarship is still missing to explain the role of this enigmatic personality in the development of the history of twentieth century Ireland. De Valera awaits his biographer. The first task facing such a person will be to deconstruct the work of earlier historians, political scientists, journalists and popular writers. I am convinced that the historian must begin work on de Valera and the Civil War by questioning the reliability of every printed source until proved otherwise.

Let me draw attention to the manner in which, for example, the unfootnoted Bromage biography is used to build an historical narrative. The most substantative problem with this work and with other early biographies is the degree to which the narrative is woven from a series of quotations not based on primary sources. This technique has the effect of placing the unsuspecting and uncritical reader close to the events. It is like listening to live radio coverage of the Civil War. The microphone or short-hand taker always appears to have been there at the critical moment to capture the contemporary reaction of Eamon de Valera. Many of those quotations – if they are to continue to be used – require to be sourced with the greatest of care.

There is another problem associated with the study of de Valera and the Civil War. Contemporary anti-Treatyite commentary on de Valera was robust and that remained the case throughout the early decades of the young state. His supporters wrote 'corrective' narratives and biographies, helped considerably by his arrival in power in 1932. Now, in the early twenty-first century, over eighty years later, de Valera's Ireland has become synonymous with social deprivation, economic stagnation, high unemployment, emigration, censorship and sexual repression.

In the wake of the popular success of the Michael Collins film in the 1990s, the climate of prevailing political correctness has become even more unfavourable than before to the personality and the political career of Eamon de Valera. The dashing Michael Collins, after all, was the hero of the hour. De Valera was the villain. Hollywood has spoken, and very powerfully so in Neil Jordan's fine film. But cinema is not necessarily reliable history. It will be difficult to replace such an emotionally satisfying interpretation of the Civil War. But the task of doing so requires to be tackled in a comprehensive manner.

There is not the space here to review the new historical scholarship based on archival work in Ireland and abroad. Books by Hopkinson, Garvin and Regan among others are providing a range of new questions that throw light on the world of Eamon de Valera in the Civil War years.[28] Excellent work is being done and usually in less than ideal circumstances, as I found when I went to research this article. Key archival collections remain closed to researchers. In the case of one collection, it was withdrawn without warning and remains closed as this article goes to print.[29] What follows is an attempt to raise a series of questions about de Valera and the Civil War.

One theme dominated de Valera's discourse throughout the early months of 1922 – his unshakeable belief that the Treaty was not the best possible settlement on offer to the Irish government. In a private session of Dáil Éireann on 14 December, he used an interesting mixed-metaphor to describe his disappointment at a job only half-completed:

> I was captaining a team and I felt that the team should have played with me to the last and that I should have got the last chance which I felt would have put us over and we might have crossed the bar in my opinion at high tide.[30]

His imagery was more biblical when writing to his close friend and unofficial adviser, the rector of the Irish College, Mgr John Hagan, on 13 January 1922:

> A party set out to cross the desert, to reach a certain fertile country beyond – where they intended to settle down. As they were coming to the end of their journey and about to emerge from the desert, they came upon a broad oasis. Those who were weary said: 'Why go further – let us settle down here and rest, and be content.' But the hardier spirits would not, and decided to

face the further hardships and travel on. Thus they divided – sorrowfully, but without recriminations.[31]

But there were recriminations aplenty between January and June 1922 and de Valera's role during those months has been described as ambiguous at best and devious at worst.

Maurice Moynihan, a critical admirer and friend who came to know de Valera very well as a senior civil servant from the mid-1930s to the end of the 1950s, edited the collection of his speeches and statements referred to above. But Moynihan, in his work as editor, also undertook to write an informative personal introduction to each document or collection of documents. His observations on those critical months in early 1922 are particularly interesting.[32] De Valera's rhetoric, particularly in March, is very familiar to many informed readers. The words that he spoke in the months following the acceptance of the Treaty on 6 January 1922 by Dáil Éireann returned to haunt him throughout his long political career.

Moynihan has gone to great lengths to trace some of his most controversial speeches to their sources. I have covered this above in another context. But I wish now to address the matters raised in greater detail. Moynihan writes that 'those historians and commentators who tend to lay on him the major blame for the outbreak of the Civil War tend to place a heavy reliance for their proof on that cluster of speeches from March 1922.'[33] On 16 March de Valera was quoted as saying in Dungarvan, County Waterford: 'the Treaty did not make the way to independence easier; it barred the way to independence, so far as one generation can bar another.' He was opposed to the Treaty 'because it barred the way to independence with the blood of fellow-Irishmen.' He was quoted as saying further that 'it was only by civil war after this that they could get their independence.' On 17 March, de Valera spoke at three venues – Waterford, Carrick-on-Suir and Thurles. In Carrick-on-Suir, Moynihan quotes him as having said that 'if the Treaty was accepted, the fight for freedom would still go on, and the Irish people, instead of fighting foreign soldiers, would have to fight the Irish soldiers of an Irish government set up by Irishmen.' He added, according to what Moynihan quotes, that 'if the Treaty was not rejected perhaps it was over the bodies of the young men he saw around him that day that the fight for Irish freedom may be fought.' In Thurles, Moynihan quotes de Valera's most famous remarks from those months, that if the Volunteers of the future tried to complete the work the Volunteers of the previous four years had been attempting, they 'would have to wade through Irish blood, through the blood of the soldiers of the Irish government, and through, perhaps, the blood of some of the members of the government in order to get Irish freedom.'

Moynihan took each of the above quotations from the *Irish Independent*. That paper carried editorials on 18 and 20 March condemning the content of those speeches. The *Irish Times* spoke of de Valera's 'gospel of hatred'. De Valera, in a letter published in the *Irish Independent* on 22 March, described as 'villainous' the interpretation of him as 'encouraging' and 'preaching civil war' and of engaging 'in the language of incitement' and 'violent threats'. The editor of the paper added a note to the end of the de Valera letter. He vigorously denied that his

> newspaper had made an attempt to distort the plain meaning of Mr De Valera's speeches, and, taken with certain concurrent circumstances, we believe it is the construction which would be placed on them by thousands of others … We hope that in view of the above letter Mr de Valera will use his best efforts to discountenance any attempt at civil war in the future.[34]

While reference will be made to those speeches again later in this article, I wish to point out that historians operate with the gift of hindsight and the knowledge that the Civil War broke out on 28 June 1922. Despite the ominous signs, the inevitability of civil war may not have been that apparent to major actors such as de Valera in March 1922. His rhetoric reveals the confusion, the hurt and the fear of many people as they were turned to face each other in those months which have been described as the 'ante-chamber of Civil War'.[35] I don't feel that it is possible to improve on Professor T. Desmond Williams' description of the origins of the Irish Civil War:

> All wars are the product of indecision, chance, misunderstanding, and personal will. They come from the environment in which people work and the conviction of those in power … Perhaps the extremists on both sides alone knew their own minds and the contingent situation better than those of more moderate opinions. But moderation, reluctance to engage in a war with one's own countrymen may be of greater value than the confidence and arrogance of those who see right and wrong too clearly. The balance between the forces of liberty and order may have depended upon those who found it hardest to decide between black and white, even if muddle and panic deriving from these decisions greatly contributed to the origins and conduct of this particular war. A full state of war lasted for nearly a year, but its after effects for much longer.[36]

Given the importance of those speeches delivered around 17 March 1922, it is very important to search the contemporary press accounts in order to determine the extent to which the reports in the *Irish Independent* were an accurate statement of what de Valera actually said on those occasions. How many journalists covered those events? Is it possible that one might find different versions in the provincial press? Or was it a member of the provincial press who was also filing the copy on the speeches to the *Irish Independent*? I don't know the answer to these questions. But a textual analysis of those speeches might reveal that de Valera was more cautious in his fiery rhetoric than was revealed in the national press. That point has been made earlier in this article. But it requires to be restated even if I don't hold any great expectation that the record would be substantially changed by cross-textual analysis. De Valera appeared to be less than his cautious self in March 1922: nowadays, his condition might be diagnosed as a nervous breakdown.

De Valera was more conscious than most of the polarisation that was taking place in Irish society during those weeks. While two distinctive camps had yet to be formed, many people remained confused in their own minds. However, there was no mythic line in the sand. Yet the march of events propelled even the most reluctant towards having to make a decision. That loss of unity was a source of bitter disappointment for de Valera. His political rhetoric in the United States and at home had stressed the national unity of Irishmen and women determined to achieve independence. The prospect of open division was a source of personal disappointment to de Valera. He had come to symbolise that unity of purpose. He had worked to achieve it. Now, on 14 April 1922, he was not even consulted by the military leaders of the anti-Treatyites when they occupied the Four Courts and other buildings in Dublin. Despite his rhetoric, de Valera did not act as if he believed that civil war was inevitable. The bombardment of the Four Courts by the national army under the leadership of Michael Collins on 28 June had not been preordained. The evidence does not support the claim that de Valera worked to foment civil war. However, his hagiographers also fail to prove that he does not hold any personal responsibility for the outbreak of violence. While working for a political outcome, de Valera failed to break ranks with the 'anti-Treatyite' militants even when they repudiated the authority of Dáil Éireann and of the democratic system.

The working out of the details which led to the 'Pact Election' on 20 May provided a false hope that de Valera and Collins together could stop the slide towards civil war. The 'pact' provided a panel of pro- and anti-Treaty Sinn Féin deputies to contest the 16 June general election. This was yet another attempt to rebuild the national consensus that de Valera believed was central to the success of the struggle during the War of Independence. The electoral outcome was an overwhelming endorsement for the Treaty and for peace. The result weakened de Valera's capacity to bargain with his own militants and with the Irish Provisional Government.

Two events precipitated the turning of the armed stand-off between Treatyites and anti-Treatyites into civil war. On 22 June, an IRA unit murdered Sir Henry Wilson in London. Responsibility for the killing was correctly laid at the door of the IRA. But the question remains as to whether it was actually Michael Collins who, many months before, had given the order to the unit who carried it out. The background to the killing is not important in this context. But the outcome was to bring British government pressure on the Irish Provisional Government to dislodge the anti-Treatyites from their positions around the capital city of Dublin. The second event to force the Irish government to change policy was the kidnapping on 26 June of General J. J. 'Ginger' O'Connell by the anti-Treatyite garrison at the Four Courts. That was seen as an act of provocation. The Four Courts were bombarded. Civil war was unavoidable.

De Valera, who said in response to the news of Wilson's death that it was only necessary for statesmen to have the will to be fearlessly just in order to find peace, found himself taken completely by surprise by the action of the Four Courts garrison. It is clear that the anti-Treatyite military leaders had not kept him informed of their plans. This is of importance as de Valera was the sole surviving commander of the 1916 Rising. It may have been that the military leaders did not think highly of de Valera's skills as a commander in the field. But more than likely the military leaders saw him as a temporiser and as somebody who did not have the stomach to go through with military action. When the time arose, he found himself isolated by the military people on his own side.

The Provisional Government did not trust him enough to seek him to intervene in a last-minute effort to pre-empt armed combat. De Valera was seen as being an intransigent anti-Treatyite. That was a mistake. But de Valera's powers of intervention and persuasion were irrelevant once Michael Collins had decided to use force to dislodge the anti-Treatyites from the Four Courts and other vantage-points in the capital. Paradoxically, de Valera's first instinct was to attempt to halt the fighting. This view is supported by an eye witness, Robert Brennan, who recorded that de Valera's first response when he got to his headquarters in Suffolk Street was to ask of Stack and Brugha: 'Well, will we try to stop it? ... I was thinking of trying to get hold of the Lord Mayor.' How reliable is this as a source? According to O'Faoláin, Childers rushed around to de Valera for a message on the new and terrible situation. 'What shall we do? We must attack them', Childers said, to which de Valera replied: 'No! No! No! Don't say a word. I'll settle it. I'll settle it.' O'Faoláin continues:

> Thinking, as always of peace and unity, he may in that moment have gone too far in his efforts to conciliate Rory O'Connor. He confessed almost as much later, and afterwards he had to bear the blame and brunt for Rory O'Connor's action in hastening, if not originating that awful conflict.[37]

Returning to the Brennan version, de Valera said to Brugha and Stack that he was going to issue a short statement.[38] He finally felt obliged to side with 'the best and the bravest of our nation' who had been unwilling to abandon Irish independence 'under the lash of an alien government'.[39]

De Valera's influence on the course of events during the following days was negligible. He rejoined the Dublin Brigade's Third Battalion and was present for a time in the Gresham and Hammam Hotels. With the fall of the city to the Provisional Government, he went on the run. Dressed as a priest, he hid out in Rathgar.[40] He left 11 Upper Mount Street and made his way south on 11 July via Wicklow where, according to Bromage, a contingent of Liam Lynch men heard he was in their area, picked him up and brought him to Clonmel.

His personal papers reveal in very great detail his movements during July, August and early September when he returned to Dublin. Two months in the field illustrated how severely he had been marginalised by the militants. The following list, probably a contemporary note in his own hand, shows his itinerary.[41]

There is a detailed note, probably dictated to his biographer T. P. O'Neill, of his activities during that period:

I left Dublin for the South on July 11th or 12th 1922. I was still in Callan on July 11th and probably reached Clonmel on July 12th. Liam Lynch and others were there. I heard news of how Jerry Ryan had outwitted our people at Thurles and that Major Prout in charge of the Free State troops was advancing from Kilkenny. I had news, also, of some truce arrangement that had been made at Limerick. As a result of news about Prout, Lynch and his officers decided to take the headquarters to Fermoy. I accompanied them to the new barracks. Shortly after my arrival there, it occurred to me that it was most unfair to leave Seamus Robbinson to face the Prout onslaught and I asked permission to go back to be with him. This was granted.

He then goes on to point out:

On the way back I was told that the barracks at Cahir, Tipperary, Carrick, Clonmel had been set on fire. I felt this was a mistake, and rushed to Clonmel where I succeeded in persuading Seamus Robbinson not to go on with the burning. I pointed out that the burning of the barracks would be an indication that we had left these areas and it would be an enemy advance by the Free State troops to take these towns. A substantial portion of the Clonmel barracks was, accordingly, saved, but when I went to Tipperary and Carrick I found the barracks had been destroyed ... I stayed for a few nights in Cashel barracks and then went back to the headquarters at Clonmel. From Clonmel some of our men went out to hold Carrick-on-Suir.[42]

Aug. 11 —

Waiting in F. barracks to leave. One of the most ignoble the most miserable days I ever spent.

Thoughts! Thoughts!

arrived at night at Queenstown near Mallow —

Slept at O'Connor's County Surveyor,

Aug 12.

Saw Comdt O'B. He thought that not concentrating on Partition & later on breach by Collins of pact we lost our chance of bringing the country with us. He did not know how closely my endeavours had been to his ideas.

Had a ride with Hyde on "Charger". Slept at "Kilfeadar House"

Aug. 13. Sunday.

Went for a walk in the field — Meditation. Any chance of winning? If there was any chance duty to hold on to secure it. If none duty to try to get the men to quit — for the present.

The people must be won to the cause — before any successful fighting can be done. The men dead & gloomy. — just holding on. How long will it last?

Heard H. G. dead.
He was I believe unselfishly patriotic — & courageously. I thought he had not stooped to the methods he employed to win.

Tu 15 Gougane.

W 16 — Left Gougane for H. on Hill tried guns.

Th 17 — Shrout day "doing nothing"

F 18 — Got some mail.

Sat 19 — A few shots — Reading

20 — Reading.

M. 21 — Left afternoon for Cúl na matha & then on to Sullivan near Boneraw — Newestown

T 22 Very near rencontre with Mick at Bealy Bheith Ballyvourney to Mhynne Abbey

W. 23 — To Ardarough, Ghenville, Geo P's column,

Aug 22

Tu 22 — Mineral rencontre Ballyspar — M'Abbey. M. killed.

W 23 — M. Abb. via Skenvivea Kenworth, Dr Barry

Th 24 — Araghin, Tubrid, N'castle. Meadonn.

F 25 — "Meadonn" — Shapstown mountainside.

Sat 26 — Shantonroe. the old loughlin, Loughlin Nurney,

27 — Nurney —

M. 28 — 3f. Nurney

De Valera, assigned as adjutant to Commandant General Seán Moylan, had little success when he talked of peace to an intransigent, Liam Lynch.[43] He learned in early August of the death of Harry Boland. In his diary he recorded on 11 August: 'Waiting in F[ermoy] barracks to leave. One of the most if not the most miserable day I ever spent. Thoughts! Thoughts!'[44] On the day that Arthur Griffith died in Dublin, de Valera was visiting the retired veteran member of the Irish Parliamentary Party, William O'Brien, at his home near Mallow. While there is an extensive account of their conversation in Bromage,[45] his diary recorded:

> He thought that not concentrating on Partition and later on breach by Collins of pact, we had the chance of bringing the country with us. He did not know how close my endeavours had been to his ideas. Had a ride with Hyde on 'charger'. Slept at Kilpeadar House.[46]

He learned of Griffith's death the following day. Bromage records how a woman in the house where he was hiding found him sobbing when she brought him food. He had just read the news of his death in the paper.[47] De Valera left the house without eating anything. He recorded in his diary:

> Went for a walk in the fields – meditation. Any chance of winning? If there was any chance duty to hold on to secure it. If none duty to try to get the men to quit – for the present. The people must be won to the cause – before any successful fighting can be done. The men dead and gloomy – just holding on. How long will it last. Heard A. G. dead. He was I believe unselfishly patriotic – courageously. If only he had not stooped to the methods he employed to win.[48]

The following day he asked the question in his diary: 'I wish I could know his [Griffith's] ideas when he signed that treaty – Did he think when it was signed I'd accept the *fait accompli*?'[49]

These were not the thoughts of a man in battle command of the anti-Treatyite forces. He was a political leader being passed – at considerable risk to local anti-Treatyites – from one safe house to the next until he found himself in west Cork *en route* to Kerry. But de Valera changed his mind and made his way back towards Dublin. He made his way to Miss Barry's of Ballylegan, near Glanworth. Crossing the ford there, he heard of the death of Collins. Taken to Dr Barry's of Kilworth, he stayed the night of 23/24 August. He made his way through Callan and Fr Kelly of Rathoe, where he stayed from Saturday 26 to Monday 28 August.[50] Lynch, in a letter of 30 August, turned down the idea of a meeting of IRA commanders with de Valera.[51] The forces of the anti-Treatyites were not under de Valera's control. According to Macardle, de Valera wanted the TDs who supported him to enter Dáil Éireann.[52]

Part of de Valera's problem was that a number of those most likely to exercise a moderating influence over the anti-Treatyite militants were in jail – Seán T. O'Kelly being among them. In Kilmainham, O'Kelly wrote that it would be far better 'for the good of the country' to try to end the hostilities. He prevailed upon Oscar Traynor and Tom Barry to contact the Provisional Government authorities.[53] Barry made the contact and Liam Tobin was sent to interview him. But the meeting ended 'in hot words on both sides', according to O'Kelly, after Tobin tried to 'bully' him and place obstacles in the way of the talks. He added:

> If they adopt bullying or hectoring manners and raise all sorts of petty quibbling points, such as that our people must write their notes only on paper headed 'Provisional Government', they are going the right road to secure a continuance of the war till the very last bit of ammunition of the republicans has been expended and the last of their men imprisoned or shot.[54]

O'Kelly suggested that one of the bishops ought to be approached to act as a mediator. O'Kelly felt that Traynor and Barry were willing to go to talk with O'Connor and Liam Mellowes in Mountjoy. The rector of the Irish College, John Hagan, arrived in Dublin towards the end of August. He approached Mulcahy and put O'Kelly's ideas to him. Mulcahy was not very enthusiastic but he sought to facilitate the monsignor. A letter from Mellowes and O'Connor to Hagan on 6 September 1922 demonstrated only intransigence. Both men joined in the 'passionate longing' that:

> the section of the countrymen now in arms against the Republic should end the senseless and criminal sterile and unite with us in its defence against the common enemy whose devilish machinations have, by the aid of the powerful and corrupt press in this country, stampeded them into continuing the war which the British forces hitherto failed to make effective.

They promised Hagan, however, to hand on his letter to their superiors outside the prison. Hagan wrote that the communication did not show 'anything like eagerness to arrive at an understanding'. He urged both O'Connor and Mellowes to meet the two men from Kilmainham (Barry and Traynor) as they would be 'giving away no principles'. On 11 September, Mulcahy wrote to Hagan that he had given permission for the meeting. But in the meantime, Barry had escaped from jail while a note to Mellowes and O'Connor had gone unacknowledged.[55] It appeared that the minister's instincts about the lack of will for peace were the more accurate.

Hagan made one final bid to salvage the peace move by contacting de Valera. But the limitations on de Valera's power to influence the military wing of the anti-Treatyites were evident in his reply. He suggested to the rector that he should see the prisoners first as 'nothing will be gained by seeing us at the moment.' He recommended that he see an unnamed friend in O'Connell Street who would be 'able to give all necessary information from our point of view.'[56]

The initiative foundered as had a peace move initiated by another clergyman who was working in San Francisco, Mgr John Rogers. De Valera had agreed to meet Richard Mulcahy in Dublin on 6 September. Both forces issued safe conducts to the other side. However, Mulcahy was advised by the anti-Treatyites to travel in civilian clothes.[57] Mulcahy was giving the anti-Treatyite leader a last chance before he set out on a definite course. Mulcahy took the meeting sufficiently seriously to issue an order which reduced routine raids as much as possible, limited the movement of troops and sought to avoid military activities. But the meeting with de Valera was not successful.

Further peace efforts by the leader of the Labour Party, Tom Johnson, and the trade unionist, William O'Brien, did not meet with success. Dáil Éireann met on 9 September. Despite his personal wish to take part in the debate, de Valera and his associates were not present. Mulcahy requested the cabinet, in mid-September, to introduce emergency powers establishing military courts for soldiers or civilians found guilty of crimes ranging from armed attacks on the national forces to being in possession of arms or explosives or taking part in looting, arson and destruction of private property. Dáil Éireann approved the draconian proposals on 28 September by 48 votes to 18.

Instead of calling off the futile struggle, de Valera and the anti-Treatyites attempted to regroup. A meeting of the army executive was held on 17 October and a decision was taken to set up an 'Emergency Government' of the 'Republic' with de Valera as President. Austin Stack was nominated Minister for Finance, P. J. Ruttledge was given Home Affairs, Seán T. O'Kelly got Local Government, Robert Barton was given Economic Affairs and the jailed Liam Mellowes was made Minister for Defence. It did not appear to the reasonable observer that de Valera and the anti-Treatyites were prepared to end hostilities at the earliest time.

Convinced that de Valera was not going to sue for peace, the Executive Council met on 4 October 1922 and took a decision to approach the Roman Catholic hierarchy to secure a condemnation of the anti-Treatyites. The bishops did not disappoint. On 22 October a statement was published condemning the campaign of destruction which had resulted in murder and assassination and 'wrecked Ireland from end to end'. Those involved were 'guilty of the gravest sins, and may not be absolved in confession, nor admitted to holy communion, if they propose to persevere in such evil courses.'[58]

Crestfallen, de Valera wrote apologetically to his friend, Archbishop Daniel Mannix of Melbourne, on 6 November 1922 that he had often wished 'but had not the heart to write you.' He said:

> The last pronouncement of the hierarchy here is most unfortunate. Never was charity of judgement so necessary, and apparently so disastrously absent. Ireland and the Church will, I fear, suffer in consequence.

He spoke about the fait accompli of the Treaty agreement:

> The tactics subsequently resorted to were still more unworthy and made inevitable the existing situation which, once the document was signed, could have been averted only by the most delicate tact and rigorous straight dealing. I am convinced that the Free State Agreement must go. It has brought nothing but disaster so far, and promises nothing but disorder and chaos. It gives no hope whatever of ordered stable government. Human nature must be recast before those Irishmen and Irishwomen, who believe in the national right and the national destiny as in a religion, will consent to acquiesce in the selling of the national birthright for an ignoble mess of pottage, as they regard it. Think then of the prospects of a government which can only exist by outlawing the most unselfishly patriotic citizens of the state.

He added that party feeling was 'running rather too high now for calm dispassionate thinking, or for real statesmanship to have any opportunity.' He held the IRB as being most responsible for the present situation but added:

> The people everywhere, young and old, are beginning to realise that the only salvation for the nation now is a return to the old Sinn Féin principle of cleaving to their own institutions, whilst ignoring the authority and the institutions which the foreigner has tried to impose.

Returning to an old theme of his, de Valera wrote:

> I cannot but think of the hopes of this time a year ago – the almost certain prospect of a settlement which all could have accepted or at least acquiesced in, leaving us a united nation with a future to be freely moulded under God by ourselves. It is sad, but chastening to realise how rudely they were all blasted within a month ... and I assure you of the affection and esteem of all who are striving now that the way may not be closed for those who may be destined to complete the work towards which the hopes of the nation have been set definitely since Easter 1916.[59]

The Bishop of Galway, Thomas O'Doherty, expressed the anger of many when he wrote on 11 November to Mgr Hagan in Rome:

Things are not very hopeful here. De Valera has allowed himself to be hoisted into the 'Presidency' on the remaining bayonets of Rory O'Connor's squad. It is not a very dignified or comfortable position now. The Republic is out now for victory or extermination and the women are screaming or fasting.[60]

The day before this letter was written, 10 November 1922, Erskine Childers was arrested at Annamore, County Wicklow, the home of his cousin, Robert Barton. He had been making his way to Dublin – probably at de Valera's request – where, it was believed, he would be made secretary to the anti-Treatyite 'government'.[61] Childers was sentenced to death on 18 November and he was executed by firing squad four days later.[62] The debate which followed the sentencing of Childers was marked by a certain Anglophobe vindictiveness on the part of a small number of government ministers.[63] De Valera must have silently blamed himself for what had befallen Childers.

The grief of a number of prominent Irish bishops was revealed in their private correspondence. The auxiliary Bishop of Armagh, Patrick O'Donnell, wrote to Mgr Hagan:

No event of recent years has saddened me in the same way as the execution of Erskine Childers. Since I heard of it I think of little else. I knew him some years ago and derived much friendly assistance from him during the Irish Convention [1917]. I think I was the first to suggest that his services would be sought at that time. So, much as I disliked intervening in any way, when I saw a few days ago that he was in jeopardy, I wrote to the Law Adviser suggesting that he should be spared. Plainly I had nothing for my pains. All the executions are deplorable especially that of poor Childers. I said mass for him today ... Up to then the Irish government seemed to me to have done well on the whole and then, I can judge, wisdom left them. I trust it may soon return ... Our cardinal and the Archbishop of Dublin are against the executions.[64]

The Archbishop of Dublin, Edward Byrne, wrote in protest to Cosgrave. John Hagan wrote to say that he was glad to know that there was at least one voice raised on the side of mercy: 'unfortunately deeds like this are bound to awaken distant echoes, and only one endowed with the gift of prophecy can venture to foretell where it is going to stop.'[65]

De Valera had no control over the decision by Liam Lynch to issue an order on 27 November that all TDs who had voted for the 'Murder Bill' were to be shot on sight.[66] On 30 November, three other executions were carried out. Shortly after that a copy of an order, purporting to be signed by Tomás Derrig as 'adjutant-general' of the anti-Treaty forces, was found in the possession of a prisoner on his arrest. A copy was sent

to Cahir Davitt who was in the Army's Command Legal Staff. It provided for the 'execution' of all members of the Provisional Government,
all members of the Dáil who had voted for the Army (Special Powers)
Resolution, the members of the Army Council and most if not all of the
Army's Command Legal Staff. Davitt recorded: 'We were generally sceptical as to whether this wholesale "execution" order was to be accepted
at its face value when our doubts were tragically resolved on 7 December.'[67] Seán Hales, a distinguished west Cork military leader in the War of
Independence, was shot dead leaving the Ormond Hotel in Dublin on his
way to Leinster House. Another deputy, Padraic Ó Maille, who was travelling with him in the same sidecar, was seriously but not fatally wounded. This crisis completely eclipsed the formal coming into being of Saor-
stát Éireann (Irish Free State) on 6 December 1922.

Davitt was summoned to the adjutant-general's office where the
Army Council had been meeting on the evening of 7 December. Mulcahy
told him that they had decided to set up a system of military committees
to deal summarily with persons arrested in possession of arms, ammun-
ition or explosives, while retaining the military courts to deal with cases
other than those of persons caught red-handed. Any such person arrested would be brought as quickly as possible before a committee of officers. They were to investigate the circumstances of the arrest and report to
the Army Council recommending a punishment. Mulcahy wanted Davitt
to draft regulations for such a committee and have them ready that
night. Davitt saw the committees as something in the nature of a drum-
head court-martial. He said that they could have no judicial function
since they could decide nothing but only make a recommendation. Each
committee would have to include an officer from Davitt's Command
Legal Staff. He could ensure that the committee's investigations were
properly conducted and its report properly presented. But with regard
to the un-judicial character of the proposed committees, Davitt said he
would prefer that he should be requisitioned solely in his military capacity and that neither he nor any member of his staff would have responsibility for the military committees. He agreed to draft the communiqué
which appeared under Mulcahy's name the following day in the press.[68]

At a meeting of the government that evening a decision was taken
to execute four prisoners. The men were Rory O'Connor, Liam Mellowes,
Dick Barrett and Joe McKelvey. Archbishop Byrne had spent a number
of hours on the eve of the execution trying to persuade Cosgrave against
taking the action. To compound the tragedy Rory O'Connor had stood as
best man for Kevin O'Higgins. Mulcahy and Eoin MacNeill were believed
to have proposed and seconded the motion for execution. Kevin O'Higgins accepted the decision with great reluctance. The following day the
four men were executed in Mountjoy without due process as a 'reprisal'

for the assassination of Hales and a 'solemn warning' to those associated with the four executed men who were 'engaged in a conspiracy of assassination against the representatives of the Irish people.' These were the terms used in the official communiqué.

Archbishop Byrne wrote to Cosgrave on 10 December expressing his dismay that the term 'reprisals' had been used in the army communiqué announcing the executions:

> Now, the policy of reprisals seems to me to be not only unwise but entirely unjustifiable from the moral point of view. That one man should be punished for another's crime seems to me to be absolutely unjust. Moreover, such a policy is bound to alienate many friends of the government, and it requires all the sympathy it can get.[69]

The superior general of the Calced Carmelites, Peter Magennis, wrote to John Hagan from the United States:

> I received the news of the shootings of four amongst which was dear friend Liam. That has given me a turn I am almost afraid to contemplate. I know those fellows [ministers] were contemptible curs, but it never occurred to me they were such vampires. Drunk with this sudden greatness their one idea is to revel in human blood.[70]

The death of Seán Hales provided a good insight into what the tragedy of civil war had brought to many families. His brother Donal, who lived in Genoa, remained on the side of the anti-Treatyites. His sister Madge wrote to him:

> Our home is now a lonely one. Oh Dan it is heart-breaking to look back on poor Seán's life and all he suffered for the cause of Ireland. I would give anything to know if the hearts of the men who took that noble life had one spark of pure love for their country. I am sorry Dan to say that there is more false passion on the Irregulars' side than love of their country.[71]

Saddened by his brother's death, Donal nevertheless felt obliged to write to the *Cork Examiner* to protest over the 'reprisal' killings of the four anti-Treatyites in Mountjoy:

> Shocked at the violent death of my brother John I feel it however my duty to raise my voice in terrible protest against the cruel reprisal on the persons of the innocent prisoners shot by the authorities of the Free State in a Dublin prison, 8th Dec. 1922. My brother would be the last to tolerate the inhuman act and in life affirmed the heads of the republican movement to be men of high and pure ideals, disinterested in purpose, without personal ambition and like himself struggling for the complete independence of their country.[72]

But that was not how Cahir Davitt saw events. In his memoir, completed in 1958, he remained equally resolute. The government had accorded the anti-Treaty forces belligerent rights up to 15 October 1922 when the period fixed for amnesty expired:

> I have, I believe, already indicated that I was not in favour of the execution policy; but I never doubted the right of the government to adopt and enforce it … I was not in favour of executing anyone if it could be avoided; but if anyone were to suffer death it was they who deserved it most [the members of the Four Courts Executive] as a punishment for bringing about the tragedy of fratricidal strife. The reprisal execution of O'Connor, Mellowes, McKelvey and Barrett was not merely the most justly deserved of all the executions it was also the most justifiable. As a drastic means of ending the incipient campaign of assassination of Dáil deputies its success was immediate and conclusive.[73]

While there were no further 'executions' of Dáil members, further research will determine the nature of the impact of the executions on the anti-Treatyite forces. De Valera had been numbed by the deaths of close friends at the hands of former political colleagues and comrades. But what latitude did he have to act to restrain the anti-Treatyites?

Liam Lynch had a sanguine and very unrealistic view of the military and political struggles. On 21 December he had written that the 'home situation generally is very satisfactory, and generally is immensely improving from week to week.' He felt that the anti-Treatyites now believed that the 'the situation is already saved, at least, as far as the present enemy is concerned.' Lynch was hoping for a large supply of arms from Germany which would give his forces the decisive advantage. That was to be organised by Seán Moylan who had been sent in November to the United States because he was in very bad health to act as a liaison officer for the anti-Treatyites.[74] His departure was a serious blow to those who favoured an end to the war among the anti-Treatyite military.[75]

In December 1922, the war entered a new and dangerous phase. There was a new-found ferocity and ruthlessness in the activities of the anti-Treatyites. The property of prominent government supporters was destroyed. On 10 December the home of Seán McGarry was set on fire by a party of armed men who failed to allow the family time to reach safety. His wife and two children suffered from burns, one of the children dying later as a result. The premises of Mrs Nancy Wyse Power in Camden Street were set on fire. The offices of two firms of Dublin solicitors were also destroyed in December. Lord Glenavy's oldest son, Gordon Campbell, had his home burned down on 18 December. Bombs were thrown at the offices of the *Independent* in Middle Abbey street. On 20 December a party of armed men seized the Dublin to Belfast mail train, forced the passengers to leave and set it on fire. They then compelled the driver to crash his train into another train carrying government troops and military supplies. Two unarmed soldiers were fired on in Dublin. One was killed and the other was seriously wounded. An explosion wrecked the premises of Denis McCullagh. Many other acts of wanton vandalism were committed throughout the country.

Amid such mayhem came news on 20 December of seven executions. In some cases, the tactics chosen by the National Army to fight against the anti-Treatyites did not come out of a textbook. In Kerry, in particular, the methods chosen to prosecute the war require scholarly investigation. One officer who served in the south, Lieutenant Patrick Quinlan – a veteran of the War of Independence – has left the following account in his diary for 14 December:

> Was Orderly Officer today. Same old ding-dong again. Nothing but [?] as to how I got on. Of course A.1. was the formula of the report I had to give everyone but it cut me that I could not open up about some of the things that I had seen and learned during the tour. I could not very well say 'this fellow is a waster, or that fellow is a dud, a fool or a featherhead', and in cases where you would least expect it, but mum is the word. I compare some officers of the National Army to a beautiful fruit or [?] which grows in the cooler season in the vicinity of the Dead Sea. It grows very rapidly flowering into a most dazzling display of gorgeous petals ripening slowly into a lovely fruit like a tomato but breaking into dust and generating an obnoxious and pungent odour when touched. Thus it is with the bogus patriotic Dandies who grew up and blossomed during the Truce but they are bursting under the test like the fruit one by one but they leave the pungent odour which is obnoxious to the taste of public opinion. It ill becomes me to entertain thoughts of kicking up a row about the state of affairs in this army but when there is a grievance where is the remedy to be found. The authorities must be fully aware of the state of affairs or if not they are to blame.[76]

Cahir Davitt, an unimpeachable source, has written in his memoirs of an incident which occurred towards the end of December. A party of armed men, who described themselves as 'the authorities', called at the lodgings of Francis Lalor and took him away by force. His body was later found near Milltown golf course. Davitt commented: 'This killing had all the appearance of being an "unofficial execution" carried out by some members of the government's forces.' It was in that fashion, he added, 'we saw the old year out.'[77] The Irish Civil War, comparatively speaking, was not characterised by a systematic policy of widespread extra-judicial killings. As Todd Andrews wrote in his memoirs: 'In Civil War, alas, there is no glory; there are no monuments to victory or victors, only to the dead.'[78]

Despite the routing of anti-Treatyite forces in different parts of the country, de Valera told McGarrity in a letter on 20 January that:

> there will be much bloodshed and suffering here before this conflict is ended. The worst of it all is that England is having the laugh at us, and that there is no peaceful method of solution in sight. The people are dispirited and it is impossible to get back the vim and dash of a couple of years ago. We are however doing our best.

He felt that there was now no alternative but to continue the struggle – a belief he still held, however half-heartedly, as late as 5 February:

> Some more of our good men are falling by the way, but there can be no turning back for us now. One big effort from our friends everywhere and I think we would finally smash the Free State. Our people have a hard time of suffering before them, and we have of course to face the possibility of the British forces coming back and taking up the fight where the others lay it down – but God is good.[79]

He told McGarrity that he felt 'if this war were finished Ireland would not have the heart to fight any other war for generations, so we must see it through.'

But the Civil War on the anti-Treatyite side had deteriorated into a series of skirmishes and attacks on soft targets. The family home of the Minister for Home Affairs, Kevin O'Higgins was attacked by 'Irregulars' at Stradbally, County Laois, on 11 February 1923. The haggard was set on fire and the raiding party then entered the house and shot dead Dr O'Higgins, the minister's father, in the presence of his wife and daughter. In that climate, anything other than total victory was unacceptable to Cosgrave and his ministerial colleagues on the Executive Council. He told a delegation, representing neutral IRA on 27 February 1923, that that objective would be secured even if it meant having to kill 10,000 republicans.[80]

Among the anti-Treatyites to die was Charlie Daly from Knockane, Firies, County Kerry. He had joined the Irish Volunteers in 1913 where he rose in the ranks to adjutant. Arrested and returned for trial in summer 1917, Daly refused to recognise the courts and went on the run. In September 1918 he received a two-year jail sentence. Released in 1919 he took up his old position in the IRA and was elected to the Kerry County Council. He served as a brigade quarter master in the south until he was sent to Tyrone by headquarters in August 1920 as an organiser. He was arrested in Dublin and spent a few months in jail before being released. He was immediately appointed by Michael Collins as officer commanding the Second Northern Division in May 1921. Daly opposed the signing of the Treaty. He remained in Tyrone until April 1922. He was then sent by the anti-Treatyites to Donegal where he was subsequently arrested on 22 November.[81] He was arrested with two Listowel men, Timothy O'Sullivan and Daniel Enwright, and another man, John Larkin, from Derry. Found guilty by court martial of being in possession of firearms and bombs, they were sentenced to death and jailed in Drumboe Castle, Stranorlar, County Donegal.[82]

Daly wrote on 7 February to his friend, Fr Brennan, of Castlemaine in Kerry, who was also his parish priest. He took advantage of the fact that he was writing to a priest to unburden himself and the letter went uncensored:

> I would never have thrown away the prospects which were mine twelve months ago and gone through all this painful business with the knowledge of possibly meeting a fate such as mine may be without having been actuated by the purest of motives. I hope, Father, that you don't think that I've said all this as an argument or in a spirit of opposition. Neither argument or opposition would do me any good situated as I am now. I am but as a man faced with probable death explaining my feelings and convictions to you and that only from the moral and religious point of view apart altogether from political arguments. You will, I am sure, understand my intention all the more readily as you happen to hold opinions different to mine.

Daly regarded the last war as a having been a glorious one: 'Everything – patriotism, glory and the popular support of the people and clergy, impelled every Irishman worthy of the name to do his part in it.' He regarded the Civil War, however, as being 'that most horrible of all wars' and were it not

> ... for my strong convictions as to its morality and righteousness I would never have taken part in it, or persisted in it afterwards, not against the common enemy but against our own comrades and dearest friends we have been compelled to turn our arms. This was repugnant enough in itself but was much more so when we had to do it at the cost of forfeiting the sacraments, which every Irish Catholic cherishes so much, and also with, to some of us, the thought of possibly imperilling our souls.

Daly found it particularly difficult to cope with the condemnation of the bishops. He had seen Bishop O'Sullivan a year ago and had not been persuaded by him that he was wrong in his judgement. He regretted that all the more because of the active role the bishop had played in the War of Independence. But as regards the stance of the hierarchy on the Civil War, Daly observed that 'both national and church history of many countries – our own in particular – record similar parallels in the past and time has since shown that mistakes were made.' But Daly remained on the anti-Treatyite side 'which was not alone up against the power of a mighty empire, but was opposed by a power which, with me, counted far more – the power of the bishops' opposition.' That fact might have had the effect of keeping him neutral, 'but then I am not one of those who can stand idly aside when a great national issue is at stake.'[83]

The four were told that they would be shot on 14 March 1923. The common local belief was that was a reprisal for the shooting of a Free State officer, Captain Bernard Cannon, at Creeslough on 10 March 1923, who was killed by a bullet to the heart fired during a raid on the local barracks. Writing to his father within hours of his execution, Daly had little doubt that he and the other executed men 'will be with God in a couple of hours from now.'[84] His farewell letter to his mother was very devout and reassuring. Daly had no doubt about the morality of his actions or the justice of his cause. The local parish priest, Fr P. B. McMullen wrote to Daly's friend, Fr P. J. Brennan on 21 March 1923. He asked the priest to contact Daly's mother and explain that, although he had only known her son for a short time 'I learned enough of him to see that he was far above the average and to respect him highly though in politics we stood far apart.'[85]

Bishop Patrick O'Donnell in Armagh, who also stood far apart from him on politics, spent 'the entire evening' trying to get through to Dublin. He got through after a few hours and sent his 'most earnest representations against the executions.'[86] But the mercy plea did not prevail. Ironically, when the anti-Treatyites took local reprisals after the executions, among the large houses burned down were Bishop O'Donnell's family home just outside Glenties.[87] Donegal, which had been relatively quiet, became involved 'in grim earnest in the turmoil of the Civil War.'[88]

Military victory was in sight for the government forces. Peace initiatives, from whatever quarter, failed. The Archbishop of Cashel, Harty, did not meet with success and neither did the ill-fated representative of the pope, Salvatore Luzio.[89] He arrived in Ireland on 19 March. The hierarchy treated his mission with great suspicion. He was snubbed by the government and almost arrested when he went to meet Eamon de Valera at a secret rendezvous. The government sent an emissary to the Holy See and he reported on 24 April that Luzio was being recalled. The monsignor left for Rome on 7 May, glad to get away from the cold of the climate and the heat of the politics. He is believed to have remarked in disgust that he had come to meet the bishops and met twenty-six popes.

There had been considerable activity within the ranks of the IRA men in the south to secure a negotiated peace, with Tom Barry prominent among them. Despite the danger, a decision was taken to call a meeting of the army executive of the anti-Treatyites. They met on 24 March in a cottage in the Nire valley, County Waterford. During four days of discussions, de Valera placed peace proposals before the meeting based on three principles:

1) the inalienable right of the Irish people to sovereign independence;
2) recognition that the Irish people were the ultimate court of appeal;
3) no oath or test would debar a person taking a full share in the nation's political life.[90]

A divided executive agreed to meet on 10 April. But news of that meeting leaked to the government side and large numbers of troops were deployed in the area. Liam Lynch was fatally wounded on 10 April in an engagement with government forces in the Comeragh mountains, County Waterford. Further arrests were made of senior IRA leaders in the days that followed.

At a meeting of the anti-Treatyite military executive on 20 April, Frank Aiken was elected to succeed Lynch. An Army Council of four was also appointed. It met in Dublin on 26 April together with de Valera and three members of his 'cabinet'. A unanimous decision was taken to sue for peace, and to suspend all offensive action effective from 30 April. Both de Valera and Aiken issued statements on 27 April to that effect. De Valera then used the good offices of Senators Andrew Jameson and James Douglas to make contact with the government. They met on 1 May and took de Valera's message to Cosgrave. The latter, however, refused de Valera's request for personal negotiations. Instead, he gave Jameson a document for de Valera which set out the terms for surrender.[91] De Valera, countering, drafted another document which was rejected by Cosgrave on 8 May. The anti-Treatyite cabinet and Army Council met on 13 and 14 May. They took a decision not to surrender but to dump arms. That order was given on 24 May and it was accompanied by a statement from de Valera addressed to the 'Soldiers of the Republic, Legion of the Rearguard'. The Civil War was over.

Writing to Mrs Jim Ryan on 26 December 1923, Mgr John Hagan, who had remained on the republican side, reflected on the events of the previous two years and wondered if they justified his 'theory that there was never such a thing as genuine Irish nationality, and that we really are an amalgamation of clans, each well pleased with itself if it secures a job or prevails in some similar way over the other.'[92]

A general election was held on 27 August while the country was still in an unsettled state. Sinn Féin got 43 out of 153 seats. The Labour Party retained only 14 seats. The government party, Cumann na nGaedheal, which had been founded in March 1923, took a disappointing 63 seats in a Dáil which had been enlarged from 128. That was a gain of only five seats. Eamon de Valera had been arrested on an election platform in Ennis on 12 August 1923. He polled 17,762 to his Cumann na nGaedheal opponent's 8,196. In jail, he joined about 10,000 anti-Treatyite internees, some of whom went on hunger strike. There was no official willingness, despite protestations from prominent clergymen, to allow an early mass release. De Valera was to be kept in jail until his release on 16 July 1924.[93]

Why did the Free State forces wait until August 1923 to arrest de Valera? He had been quite visible during the Civil War, spending most of the time in Dublin shifting from one safe house to the next. It was not beyond the wit of Free State intelligence to track him down and to arrest him if they had wanted to do so.

Unfortunately military archives, which ought to be able to provide the answer to this question, do not have a file on Eamon de Valera. Neither is that missing file – or related files – to be found in the de Valera papers. Could it have been that he was seen – for all his faults – as a restraining influence on the anti-Treatyites and left in circulation for that very reason?

While the Civil War was not de Valera's finest hour, he had the imagination and the constitutional subtlety to propose a compromise which was employed by a more flexible generation of English politicians in India in 1947. De Valera was not the revolutionary die-hard depicted in Free State and British propaganda of the time. He was a politician who, during the early months of 1922, continued to believe in his ability to rekindle the spirit of national unity fostered during the War of Independence. Naively, he did not believe that civil war was likely. But he did fear the 'malevolent' hand of the British and the ability of London politicians to interfere in Irish affairs. The outbreak of the war took him completely by surprise. His early impulse may have been to hold the field for a time until honour had been settled. But the adoption of guerrilla tactics, against his wishes, determined that the conflict would not be over in a few weeks. The war dragged on and de Valera found himself marginalised. He may have hoped that the Catholic hierarchy would intervene and bring about an end to the fighting. His hopes of that were dashed following the October pastoral. The bishops of his church had sided with 'the enemy'. His efforts to bring the anti-Treatyite military under effective political control failed. The shooting of Erskine Childers and the policy of executions further removed any remaining possibility of a cessation of violence. Each side had its own new martyrs. The actions of the respective sides provided the rationale for their opponents to continue the fight. De Valera was sustained in his view by the belief that the British were to blame. It was his role to restore national unity and bring about national regeneration.[94]

Nicholas Mansergh has written that de Valera was:

> at heart something of a Gandhian looking back in his case to the hard, independent country life of his childhood at Bruree, freed from foreign influences, its indigenous character reinforced by the use of the indigenous

tongue, as the source of national virtue and the ideal of national regeneration.

Owen Dudley Edwards is more inclined to see de Valera as a Nehru. I am also reluctantly inclined to agree with Owen Dudley Edwards' judgement:

He was Jeremiah. He was Jonah. Above all, he was Pilate.[95]

The aftermath of the Irish Civil War

Tom Garvin

The Irish Civil War resembled others of its kind in its viciousness and in the enduring hatreds that it generated. In this paper I would like to suggest some effects on the structure of Irish politics and even society that were consequent on the Civil War.

The first point that I would like to make is that it is probably not true that the conflict was triggered off by the actual terms of the Anglo-Irish Treaty or by any public actions of de Valera. During the Truce period of July 1921 to December of the same year, it was obvious to many observers that some elements of the IRA, now fortified with armaments acquired in relative 'peacetime', were determined to use physical force against any compromise settlement short of a republic. Behind them again were others who were equally determined to push Ireland the whole way to a perhaps vaguely imagined socialist republic dominated by the self-declared representatives of the small farmers and the workers rather than by what were thought of as the electorally chosen minions of national capitalism.[1]

The fact that the Treaty was an extraordinary concession was scarcely understood by some IRA soldiers and radical ideologues, galvanised as they were by the expectations raised by the emotional rhetoric of the time. The fact that it marked the final defeat of Anglo-Ireland was also not fully grasped, partly because some among the nationalists could perhaps be seen as trying to step into the shoes of the ascendancy. Collins' desperate plea that the Treaty offered the 'freedom to achieve freedom' was not always believed, and was sometimes denounced as a device to camouflage a continuation of ascendancy Ireland under green symbols. This noisily-expressed perception of the Treaty settlement as a sell-out was not just shared by extreme republicans or bolshevik sympathisers of the time, but even by later 'bourgeois liberal' commentators such as Seán Ó Faoláin in old age, at least in his more acidulous moments.

This mentality persisted for many years, and perhaps still is amongst us: the proposition that 1922 was a defeat rather than a victory or, at least, was not much better than an ignoble compromise. The 'Free State', it was felt, was a disappointment. The horrors of civil war made it worse: a military and psychological defeat for the ideals of the national revolution that was total.

This mentality persisted despite the fact that the Treaty was given huge majorities in the general elections of both 1922 and 1923. Republicans knew, in fact, that the vast majority of the population was in favour of the settlement, but rejected this popular will as being illegitimate, the product of clerical and press propaganda and an expression of the enslaved minds of the vast majority of the Irish people; the majority were ignoble and unworthy of the glorious destiny republicans offered them. In the eyes of republican purists, not only did northern unionists suffer from what Lenin would have termed 'false consciousness', but so did the majority of southern nationalists. Republicans were actually pleasantly surprised to find that they actually received about one-quarter of the votes in the first Free State election of 1923.[2]

The personal hatreds and distrusts that surfaced among the leaders in 1921–2 cast a revealing light on the tensions which had been inside the separatist movement and had lain buried there most of the time during the War of Independence. It was in part a division between administrators and fighters, and in part a division between groups of comrades, loyal to one or other of the groups of leaders on the pro- and anti-Treaty sides. In part again it was, indeed, between socialist and republican radicals and 'national bourgeois' leaders allied with Redmondite and ex-unionist elements.

There was a clear correlation between social class and support for the Treaty, with employers, big farmers and many urban middle- and working-class people supporting it, while other workers, small farmers and inhabitants of more remote areas opposed it. At the elite level, however, there was little obvious correspondence between social origin and position on the Treaty: many scions of the 'Big Houses' took up the anti-Treaty cause, while many young men of humble origin followed Collins, Griffith and local IRB leaders such as Alec McCabe in County Sligo.[3]

One of the reasons why the split took place so slowly and reluctantly between mid-1921 and mid-1922 was the vivid folk awareness the actors had of the destructive impact the Parnell split had had, a generation previously. Even in advance, the leaders feared the bitterness of a new one. Splits were dreaded, and were seen as a cardinal political sin, but disloyalty was also a cardinal political sin in the secret societies of the nineteenth century; fundamentally it was disloyalty which each side imputed to the other. The mind-set which labelled the other side as disloyal to the national cause created a mutual contempt which still, I would suggest, residually poisons political relationships in the politics of the Republic two generations later.

Republican purists developed a conspiracy theory about the split, one that still survives in republican folklore. Collins was, it was held, seduced by the bright lights of London and the flattery of the English aristocracy; absurdly, offers of marriage to a royal princess in return for national apostasy were alleged. In turn, it was alleged, Collins and his lieutenants had used the secret network of the IRB to cajole, bribe and bully TDs and IRA leaders to support the Treaty.

In fact, Collins signed the Treaty in good faith, but the purists needed a *Dolchstosslegende*, rather like that of Joseph Goebbels: a myth of the glorious IRA betrayed foully in mid-fight by internal betrayal and the preternatural cunning and corruption of the British political establishment.[4]

THE FIGHTING

The very term 'Civil War' may be a somewhat grandiloquent misnomer for the fighting that occurred in the twenty-six counties between June 1922 and May 1923. In part, the anti-Treaty IRA had local roots in a tradition of local solidarity, much as had the pre-Treaty IRA. However, during the Civil War both sides had local contacts; the rather bewildered British, with their massive armaments, were replaced, from the IRA point of view, by men with local knowledge and almost equally impressive armaments. Local men faced local men, often wearing similar uniforms and often even having bonds of affection. On the Free State side however, was an army drawn from ex-British veterans, IRA veterans and the apolitical youth of the towns. The old local cunning of IRA leaders was in vain against the Free State's combination of similar cunning, weight of armaments and men.[5]

An example of this is afforded by the capture of Liam Deasy by the Free State in January 1923. It was decided to execute him. In return for a stay of execution, Deasy eventually was to consent to sign a circular letter calling for an immediate end to the hopeless resistance to the Free State. Before this 'treasonous' act, Deasy was seen as a potential martyr by the republicans. Denis (Dinny) Lacey of South Tipperary IRA arrested five farmers who were brothers of the local Free State army's ex-IRA commanders in the area. If Deasy were executed, Lacey announced, all five would be killed by the anti-Treatyites. Tom Ryan, the senior Free State officer involved, recalled fifty years later:

> I knew that it was possible to contact Lacey urgently, through a sweetheart Miss Cooney, a Flying Column comrade of mine pre-Truce, who became Irregular and was at this time one of Lacey's key men [sic] ... She was at

business in Clonmel and was known to be doing Irregular work. I called to her address and gave her a dispatch to be delivered in haste to Lacey. The wording of the dispatch was as follows: 'I understand that Liam Deasy will be executed tomorrow. Should you, following on the event, carry out your threat to execute the five prisoners now held, inside twenty-four hours of execution confirmation – every male member of the Lacey family in South Tipperary will be wiped out.

Signed Tom Ryan, Vice Brigadier, National Army

Deasy was reprieved. The point is that the closeness with which the leaders of the two forces knew each other gave the conflict a peculiar intimacy and intensity that made its occasional viciousness even more unforgivable, as perpetrators and victims commonly knew each other and had roots in the same localities.[6]

Hideous murders occurred on both sides, and the hideousness was intensified by the fact that the killers and their victims commonly knew each other. Young Protestant men in west Cork were taken out and murdered by local IRA; their neighbours, Free State soldiers, chained IRA prisoners to landmines and blew them up. It seems that the murderers and victims at Ballyseedy knew each other and had a common background of local agrarian differences. IRA attempts to kill Free State TDs were followed by a terrible retaliation against republican leaders and IRA prisoners. The Civil War ended in a whimper rather than a bang, and no formal surrender was either offered by the republicans or insisted upon by the Free State.

A little remembered aspect of the conflict was cost. The Irish Civil War involved the hiring of fifty thousand soldiers. It also involved the systematic wrecking of the country's infrastructure by the IRA. The war was estimated at the time to have cost about £50,000,000. In our money that would be close on three billion euro. As the GNP of the country was perhaps less than one-third of what it is now, it possibly represents the equivalent today of nine billion euro, all taken out of the country in eight months, possibly a quarter of a year's GNP, or the equivalent of the entire EU tranche for Ireland for this decade. This crippling blow to the infant state was to make the penny-pinching traditions of the new Department of Finance institutionalised at the moment of birth.

CONSEQUENCES

The consequences of the Civil War for the minor European democracy that emerged from its ashes were so multifold as to defy any brief listing. However, in the rest of this paper I will try to list what seem to be some of the major consequences of the split and conflict that wrecked the national liberation movement of 1916–21. I suggest that these consequences fall

conveniently under four headings:
a. north-south and British and foreign relations;
b. the structure of the party system and of democratic politics in the state;
c. social and political culture;
d. the structure of public policy.

The permanent partition of Ireland
The partition of Ireland was, as we all know, institutionalised a year and a half before the signing of the Anglo-Irish Treaty in December 1921. Some partition under some constitutional formula was foreseen years earlier, but it was by no means clear that the 'deep partition' of 1922 was inevitable. The collapse of public order in the south of Ireland had various incidental effects. One effect that, I believe, has been inadequately commented on, was the weakening of anti-partitionist purpose among both Free State and republican elites. After Collins' death, solidarity between the Free State and northern nationalists weakened, and clear signs of accepting the north as a separate entity, perhaps to be negotiated with, but not to be absorbed, appeared among Free State leaders. The unionists' political hand was immeasurably strengthened by the much-publicised spectacle of disorder in the south, the apparent uncontrollability of the IRA and the equally apparent willingness of the Provisional Government to bring it to heel. It was easy for London newspapers to speak of the inability of the 'native Irish' to govern themselves; to ask how could anyone ask 'Ulster' to permit itself to be swallowed up in such a squalid, post-revolutionary and backward state. All the traditional stereotypes of the backward, superstitious and murderous 'native Irish' could be wheeled out, and were, by the *Morning Post* and other newspapers. The fact that the Civil War was rather short and was rapidly replaced by a return to civic peace was less emphasised.[7]

The Treaty settlement had been warmly supported by the 'Old Dominions,' in part because Ireland's energetic striving for an ever fuller measure of independence reinforced Canadian and other similar strivings. In mid-1922, for example, Canada legislated for the right of the federation to declare war independently of the imperial parliament; India watched attentively as the Irish blazed a trail which she longed to follow. Sympathy for the idea of a united Ireland existed in both the Canadian Federation and in what might be termed the 'latent federation' of British India. The violence in Ireland strengthened those in the Dominions who accepted Irish partition as acceptable and even natural, as against those who felt that Ireland, like Canada, South Africa or India, was somehow a 'natural' historic entity which should not be carved up at the whim of the imperial parliament. The diplomatic kudos of the Free State, very considerable in January 1922, was far less in May 1923.[8]

The party system

Irish political parties derive, in the main, from the divisions of the Irish Civil War, as we know. Only the Labour Party and the Farmers' parties have other structural origins. The opposition between de Valera and Cosgrave became one that still structures Irish party politics two generations later. The hatreds are now faded, but strange residues still persist of certain mutual perceptions.

These hatreds persisted for an extraordinarily long time, and seem to have partaken of a characteristically Irish persistence. As Helen Litton has commented, this persistence has sometimes been attributed to the small size of the population, which would have intensified the effect of personal relationships to people killed on both sides. However, Finland, with roughly the same population, suffered a ferocious little civil war in 1918, 25,000 people being killed, many of them murdered in concentration camps. The Irish conflict involved perhaps 3,000 killings at most, in the twenty-six counties. In Finland, former enemies were sharing government by 1937.[9]

In Ireland, the bones of the Civil War dead were rattled for forty years. Noel Browne remembered as a young politician in Leinster House (in 1948):

> I recall my shock at the white-hot hate with which that terrible episode had marked their lives. The trigger words were '77', 'Ballyseedy', 'Dick and Joe' and above all 'the Treaty' and 'damn good bargain'. The raised tiers of the Dáil chamber would become filled with shouting, gesticulating, clamouring, suddenly angry men.[10]

It is often lamented that the Civil War deprived Ireland of conventional European 'left versus right' politics, in favour of two factions based on ancestral hatreds. I would suggest that even without a civil war, Irish society did not naturally lend itself to this kind of polarisation. To imagine the impossible, had there been no civil war and had Collins succeeded in uniting both wings of the army as one force and had accepted that it could not be used to destabilise Northern Ireland, presumably Sinn Féin under Griffith, Collins and de Valera would have governed as a centre-right party, with farmers on the right and Labour on the left. Sinn Féin would have probably divided into two main groups, the one more republican and separatist, the other more 'commonwealth' and rightist. Both groups would have been rather loose and perhaps undisciplined. Irish politics would have been deeply centrist, although in a different form than was eventually to emerge under a centrist Fianna Fáil after 1937.

A likely contrast with our reality would have been the failure of a

Sinn Féin government ever to forge the kind of internal solidarity which Fianna Fáil did succeed in forging eventually. Fianna Fáil was the child of the Civil War; it was created in the prison camps of the Free State, much as Sinn Féin had been reinvented a few years earlier in British prison camps. The bitterness of the split and the comradeship of the defeated made possible the creation of an extraordinary political party under de Valera, whose unwritten motto might have been 'Never Split'. No matter what disagreements there might be within the party, Fianna Fáil generally has shown a bland face to its external public. Divisions between left and right, between industrialisers and traditionalists, between localists and national interest politicians, Catholics and secularists all have been consistently subordinated to the overall interests of the party, or national movement. Intellectual discussion suffered because its potential for division was seen. An almost Soviet habit of solidarity and intellectual conformity, combined with a great practical political skill, characterised independent Ireland's greatest political party.

Fianna Fáil could almost be characterised as the anti-Treaty IRA in civilian form. Old local commanders were converted into cumann secretaries and other key figures, aiming to rule Ireland by ballots rather than bullets. The seed of Fianna Fáil lay in the surprisingly large vote the republicans got in 1923. The voters seemed to be saying: 'If you accept the Treaty, there are those among us who like much of what you stand for. Act accordingly.' The vote tended to be in poorer and more remote areas, and in places where IRA presence had been strong. In particular, areas that had seen Black and Tan atrocities seemed particularly sympathetic.[12]

Republican prisoners in jail in 1923 were fascinated by the mechanics of proportional representation and were, in a grudging way, impressed by the pedantic fairness of the PR-STV system of voting devised by the Free State Government. The possibilities of Free State democracy were a shock to many republicans, persuaded as so many of them were by de Valera and Frank Gallagher that electoral democracy in the new polity was corrupt either in the sense of the ballot being interfered with or in the voters themselves being venal or cowardly.

In Newbridge military camp prisoners were being taught courses in constitutional law, local government, and Irish history, under the aegis of Dan O'Donovan, a well-known Dáil civil servant who went anti-Treaty, by September 1923. He and other lecturers suggested that the military victory of the Free State could be reversed by peaceful means. Non-violent penetration of the local government apparatus would, in the long run, deliver the new polity into the hands of its enemies. Local organisational centres were already being set up all over the twenty-six counties. This mixture of the military and the political, a central characteristic of Fianna Fáil, was a prime result of the Civil War. If there had been no conflict, Irish party politics would have been very different, almost certainly even more localist than it actually became.[12]

One could indeed argue that one of the reasons for the extraordinary tolerance which the activities of Charles Haughey and others received within Fianna Fáil was a long-term effect of the conflict. The party's internal solidarity was taken advantage of, and its internal discipline metamorphosed, for some, into a mechanism of intimidation and the enforcement of conformity. The party's most central strength was used against it by its own leaders.

Social culture and social control

A consequence of the conflict, it could be argued, was an effort to intensify Victorian aspects of Irish social culture. In particular, women, partially mobilised by the suffragette and nationalist movements, found themselves thoroughly subordinated by the events of 1922–23. The allegedly extravagant and extremist behaviour of many women leaders was used as an excuse to discourage the participation of women in political life after 1923. Although many women were politically effective in trade unions and professional associations, by and large Irish politics remained very much a man's world until the 1970s. Similarly, young boys and men were subjected to a neo-Victorian discipline of Spartan proportions in the schools of the Christian Brothers and similar orders in the decades after the Treaty. The genies of adolescent sex and violence had been let out of the bottle in 1919–23. The stopper was firmly put back again afterward, not to be taken out again until the 1960s.

The conflict also probably strengthened the power of the Catholic Church, at least temporarily. The Church had supported the Treaty, but rather conveniently many individual clerics had been vehemently anti-Treaty. The Church came to be seen as the only organisation capable of taming the animal instincts of Irish people. Film and book censorship, laws against dancing and policies designed to segregate the sexes were vigorously pursued by Church and State. The puritanism and repression of Irish society may have been aggravated by the aftermath of the conflict.

A less quantifiable cultural consequence was the death of idealism. The Irish state was founded in a wave of genuine idealism and enthusiasm that survived the Black and Tans and the British campaign. It did not survive undamaged the devastating psychological impact of the Civil War. Enthusiasm for the Irish language dried up and the task of reviving the old language was put on to the children. Many old revolutionaries later wondered privately whether the whole business had been really worth it. These questioners included such diverse people as James Dillon, David Neligan and Eamon de Valera. The perceived failure of revolutionary enthusiasm made many sceptical of all political action, and impelled many to enter the religious life in part, perhaps, seeking the fulfilments of the next world in reaction from the disappointments of this one. Others emigrated, some being effectively pushed out of the country because of their non-conformist political or religious views.

The structure of public policy

The split and the Civil War also strengthened the hand of the public service, central to Irish politics since at least the 1870s and now to be more central still. William Cosgrave leaned heavily on the wisdom of civil servants after 1922, and it is striking how quickly de Valera was to evolve a similar relationship with them in the 1930s. The systematic subordination of police and army to the central civil service, which still exists, is a direct legacy of the state-building process that was rushed through in 1922–23. Civil service 'conservatism' has been blamed for many policy failures since independence, but it could be argued that civil service prudence also prevented some wilder experiments dear to the hearts of old revolutionaries. The present-day Irish Republic is, perhaps, the most centralised of the older western democracies; this is in part a result of the British colonial inheritance, but is also a consequence of the Civil War; local government in particular was seriously weakened by the conflict, as central government came to see local councils as rivals for political authority rather than allies in government.

A little-commented-on effect of the conflict was the delivery of the main universities into the hands of the pro-Treatyites. Fine Gael had, for a long time, a preponderance of power inside UCD and the other NUI colleges. This had the unfortunate effect of alienating the natural governing party, Fianna Fáil, from much of what existed of academic intelligence in the new country. What price, if any, was paid for this divorce between dons and politicians is hard to say. I would guess that Irish anti-intellectualism and public philistinism, always likely to be strong in the early decades of independence, was mightily strengthened by the conflict. A certain anti-rationalism of style, always noticeable in Irish public policy, may have been aggravated.

CONCLUSION

The Irish Civil War had a profound effect on Irish political development, in ways that have been so pervasive and deep as to be taken for granted by we Irish who grew up in the world created by that war. North-south relations, relations with Britain and the commonwealth, attitudes toward veterans of the Great War, Church-State relations and the entire fabric and quality of public life were affected by the conflict to an enormous extent. While a superficial recovery occurred between 1932 and 1945 under de Valera, it was in many ways a hollow thing, a pretence that the events of 1922–23 had not really happened. A crippling of Irish public political culture occurred which necessitated an exaggerated reliance on Church and central State structures for the supply of political and cultural coherence. The historical dependence on the overarching structures of the Church, the State, the Fianna Fáil party and the GAA only began to fade in the 1960s, as a general social pluralism began to melt the sociological glaciers generated by the Great Freeze of the post Civil War period. This historical crippling is one which, I believe, we are still trying to overcome.

De Valera imagined and observed

Ged Martin

When Sir Ian MacLennan became British ambassador in Dublin in 1960, his mental picture of Ireland's President, Eamon de Valera 'was not necessarily attractive'. The 'trepidation' that he had felt at meeting such an ogre was swept away as soon as he presented his credentials:

> I was completely taken by him as a personality. He is one of the few people I have ever met whom you are convinced from the beginning that he is, was a great man, quite irrespective of what his beliefs or philosophy or politics were.[1]

As Tim Pat Coogan has pointed out, de Valera defined himself as 'the symbol' of the Irish Republic that struggled to emerge after 1919, a status admiringly conferred in several hundred pages of Dorothy Macardle's narrative of its history.[2] To his admirers, de Valera could do no wrong. To his antagonists, especially those associated with the British government, the official de Valera with whom they had to negotiate was 'austere, rigid, obstinate and very much with a one-track mind.'[3] To assess de Valera's role in Irish politics, both friend and foe had to commence by imagining him. Outsiders, at least, could be pleasantly surprised to find the man himself infinitely more attractive than both the principles that he embodied and the personality they had pictured.

Unfortunately, the discovery of a personal de Valera by cross-Channel and overseas visitors does not seem to have occurred until the 1930s. In the crucial period between 1916 and 1921, observers tended to project and impose a de Valera shaped by their own requirements. The 'de Valera devil', Tim Healy remarked in August 1921, was one of the 'inevitable products of political romance'.[4] As a result, there were in fact two contradictory but overlapping imagined de Valeras. One was a strong man in ruthless charge of an incomprehensibly wicked war against Britain, 'an unscrupulously mischievous enemy of my country' as Malcolm MacDonald put it.[5] The other was an idealistic schoolmaster, caught up in events that he could not control and dangerously out of his depth. The shortest way to solve the Irish problem was to construct de Valera as both simultaneously: the naïve de Valera might be moulded and tamed, so that the satanic de Valera would command the wild men to compromise. De Valera's rejection of the Treaty did not resolve the conflict between innocent and devil, but it did remove the man himself from the forefront of Irish politics for a decade, and so rendered it possible for outsiders to ignore him. Poor relations between Dublin and London during the first years of Fianna Fáil government merely extended the period of chill to the eve of the Second World War.

According to J. J. Lee, no fewer than four Irish political elites were swept away in the six years after the Easter Rising, although de Valera remarkably survived both the firing squad in 1916 and the Civil War of 1922–3.[6] For British political leaders, the Irish Question had acquired not only a new intensity but a new and puzzling practical aspect: with whom could they deal to reach a solution? Their two-fold reaction was characteristic of major powers dealing with either sudden revolution or mass colonial nationalism: they listened to the familiar old-guard nationalists who were being brushed aside, and hoped to identify a large-spirited superman in the emerging leadership. Dillon and Healy were to be their guides; de Valera was to be the Nehru or Kaunda, although in the short-term he proved to be a cross between Lumumba and Khomeini.

Unfortunately, Dillon and Healy did not know de Valera and both were tempted to fill the vacuum of their own ignorance by using him as a weapon in the mutual character assassination endemic to old-style nationalist politics. Healy admitted in 1921 that he had met de Valera just once, in 1918, when they had both taken part in the anti-conscription conference at the Mansion House.[7] At the time, Healy had privately described him as 'a fine fellow', but three years later he could not resist the side swipe that 'it was easy to discern that in his nature there is a strain of simplicity quite lacking in the Irish politicians with whom Mr Lloyd George was familiar'.[8]

Dillon had been a shade more generous. Although 'unacquainted with Mr de Valera,' he wrote in August 1917, and fervently disagreeing with his republican principles, Dillon took him 'to be a brave and honourable man', to be admired for having 'risked his life and suffered imprisonment for the cause of liberty'.[9] It is tempting to suggest that Dillon rarely spoke well of anyone whom he regarded as a serious political rival. The withdrawal of the old-style nationalist MPs from the House of Commons in protest against conscription in 1918 – a manoeuvre that dangerously conceded the electoral initiative to Sinn Féin – made it all the more necessary for politicians like Dillon to lay claim to superior political skill and mediating wisdom in their dealings with the British.

'The Sinn Féin leaders were not nearly so dangerous as they seemed,' Dillon assured C. P. Scott of the *Manchester Guardian* in August 1918. De Valera 'was a schoolmaster pitch-forked into a position of extraordinary prominence and power and nervously conscious of his own inadequacy'.[10]

It may not have been only the British elite that Dillon hoodwinked into believing he could manage the new dispensation. In May 1918, William O'Brien had described de Valera as 'personally a charming man, but he is too good for this rough world', predicting that he 'will no doubt subside into a meek instrument of Dillon's'.[11] Any such fantasy was swept aside at the general election of December 1918 when de Valera roundly defeated Dillon in East Mayo.[12] Dillon continued to believe, as he assured T. P. O'Connor in May 1921, that de Valera was 'not a strong man', and that although 'very much alarmed at the situation' and ready to compromise, he was 'completely under the control of the secret executive'.[13]

British politicians were always inclined to simplify Irish complexity; whether favouring concession or repression, they found it easier to assume that de Valera was indeed in control of his own movement. After a visit early in 1919, the minor conservative peer, Lord Newton, acknowledged that each time he had visited Ireland, 'I have come away feeling that I understand the country less.' He did, however, interpret the republican movement in highly personal terms. 'I never cease to wonder why we tolerate the persistent hostility of de Valera, as if we were in a perfectly helpless position.'[14] A former Liberal cabinet minister, Lord Haldane, placed a similar emphasis but drew a diametrically different conclusion. Invited to advise by the Lord Lieutenant, Lord French, Haldane abandoned the Viceregal Lodge to discuss the possibility of dominion status with Eoin MacNeill. He concluded that the Sinn Féin leaders were fanatical idealists whose principles were 'tempered by a shrewd recognition of realities and of what is practically possible.' Haldane proposed that French establish a triumvirate through which both sides in Ireland could determine a constitution. He agreed to serve as chairman, provided that 'my nationalist colleague should be de Valera himself ... de Valera would certainly be prime minister in an Irish parliament and was indispensable if the plan were to go through.'[15]

De Valera's eighteen-month American mission coincided with the country's slide into guerrilla warfare and counter-terrorism. His prolonged absence led some British politicians to question the extent of his control over the republican movement. Lloyd George concluded in January 1921 that de Valera had returned 'because he felt that the militant Sinn Féiners had been beaten' and he sought to claim credit for a political settlement.[16] In April, the prime minister planned to deal direct with Collins, 'the head and front of the movement'.[17] Others took a different view: 'there is only one man to see and that is de Valera', wrote the influential conservative, Lord Derby in March 1921,[18] a principle upon which he acted by making what de Valera later called 'the first important contact between the British and ourselves' a month later.[19] These initial feelers were not encouraging. In late June 1921, Austen Chamberlain commented that 'de Valera is a child without any experience of the world, without courage and without judgement.'[20] De Valera's judgement might be open to criticism, but denigration of the courage of one of the most notable commanders of 1916 presumably reflected a pejorative assessment of his absence from Ireland throughout the worst of the Troubles.

Among the confused multiple contacts that followed was an approach by de Valera to the southern unionists in June 1921. On receiving a telegram inviting him to peace talks, Lord Midleton at first assumed that it was 'a hoax, as I had never had any dealings with Mr de Valera and did not suppose that he even knew my name.' The assumption that the President of the Irish Republic might not know the name of one of the most prominent southern unionists reflected an unusually unworldly construction of de Valera, but Midleton and his associates equally subscribed to the satanic view of the Sinn Féin leaders. 'It was with difficulty we could bring ourselves to meet de Valera or Collins at all.' None the less, at the urging of Lloyd George, the unionist delegation arrived in Dublin on 3 July. 'As it was doubtful at what hour we were meeting the next morning', the delegation called to the Mansion House and were given to understand that the Lord Mayor's secretary would see them. They received a friendly welcome from 'a tall spare man with spectacles' who shook hands warmly on their departure and thanked them for agreeing to participate. When formal talks began the next day, the unionists were surprised to find that the helpful secretary had in fact been de Valera himself. Midleton decided to put to the test de Valera's claim 'that he had complete command of the rebel forces, and that General Collins would respond to any order he gave' by insisting on the release of the Earl of Bandon, who had been taken hostage in County Cork. Lord Bandon was duly freed, and Midleton noted that de Valera 'showed a business-like and reasonable spirit' throughout the negotiations.[21]

By this stage, the priority for the British was to persuade de Valera to come to London. Their chosen means of persuasion was the South African prime minister, Jan Christiaan Smuts, who had just arrived in Britain to take part in an Imperial Conference. Smuts had begun his career as state attorney of the South African Republic (Transvaal) on the eve of the Boer War of 1899–1902, in which he was a distinguished military commander. His political responsibilities had included the marshalling of propaganda against the British, and the title of his 1899 pamphlet, *A Century of Wrong*, had distinct Irish overtones. However, he had accepted defeat in 1902, and worked for reconciliation of South Africa's white communities within an enhanced commonwealth. Rewards came quickly. The conquered Transvaal Colony acquired self-government in 1906, and Smuts took a leading part in drafting a constitution to unite the defeated republics with Natal and the Cape Colony in the Union of South Africa that came about in 1910. When war broke out in 1914, Smuts fought for the empire, helping to over-run Germany's African territories. In 1917, he represented South Africa at the Imperial War Conference, and Lloyd George drafted him into the small executive body called the Imperial War Cabinet that had assumed temporary control over the British war effort. It was not surprising that when he returned to England in June 1921, he found 'that people of many points of view are looking to you to help us about Ireland.'[22] The second pronoun was as significant as the first: the British elite had come to see Smuts as their own miracle worker.

In relation to de Valera, this was a dangerous assumption. Like de Valera, Smuts was a formidable intellectual, but their mental processes were markedly different. Although detractors charged both with masking personal advantage under analytical complexity, Smuts saw himself as a philosopher, espousing a system of 'holism', through which apparent opposites were reconciled on a higher plane, a theory which lesser minds associated with his personal project of accommodating Afrikaner nationalism and imperial loyalty within the evolving structure of the British Commonwealth.[23] This was not an approach to the cosmos that was likely to chime with the mathematical mind of Eamon de Valera. Nor indeed, was it universally shared by his fellow Afrikaners, some of whom had risen in armed revolt in 1914 seeking to recapture their republican independence.[24]

Indeed, the strange personal ascendancy that Smuts had established within British politics was something of a smoke and mirrors exercise manipulated by Lloyd George. A radical liberal, Lloyd George had become prime minister in December 1916 in an unlikely alliance with the conservatives. A. J. P. Taylor unkindly suggested that Lloyd George brought Smuts into the Imperial War Cabinet because he had once run rings around the British generals who were now failing to defeat the Germans.[25] A more likely explanation is that a prime minister who lacked a firm party base himself had an interest in adding to the political plot a player who was even more disembodied than himself. An example of the role attributed to Smuts was George V's speech inaugurating the Parliament of Northern Ireland in Belfast in June 1921. It was Smuts who drafted the royal appeal for peace, thereby further adding to his stature as a problem-solver. Of course, the well-known story obscures the basic fact that the king spoke with the approval of his prime minister: Lloyd George, the first occupant of 10 Downing Street to adopt a presidential style, was not the man to allow his sovereign free rein in a major constitutional issue. The Belfast speech enabled Lloyd George to open talks with Sinn Féin in a manner to which his conservative followers could not object, by implying that responsibility for the olive branch rested with two great institutions, Smuts and the crown, the one beyond and the other above domestic politics.[26]

Naturally, it seemed a short step from Belfast to Dublin. 'If de Valera won't come over, I hope Smuts will go to him and make him come,' noted the king, in a typically bluff simplification.[27] The problem was that if de Valera refused to be cast as a second Smuts, he would by implication be discrediting the original, an outcome that the South African statesman could only accommodate by denigration. Moreover, it was all too easy, especially after the triumph of the Belfast speech, for Smuts to see himself as the true authority on Ireland's destiny, and mentally to marginalise de Valera as the impractical school-master in need of instruction by superior wisdom. His comrade in the East African campaign, Tom Casement, brother of the executed Sir Roger, lobbied him on behalf of the nationalist cause, acting with the unofficial approval of de Valera, while Horace Plunkett assured him that a solution on Dominion lines was possible.[28] Significantly, Smuts refused to travel to Dublin until he could claim to have been invited in his own right, and not as a British representative, although to the South African leader's embarrassment, Lloyd George subsequently published his correspondence with de Valera to put further pressure on the Irish leadership to come to terms.[29] The talks immediately followed the Mansion House conference with Lord Midleton.

Although the mission was widely reported in the press, Smuts travelled under the unlikely incognito of 'Mr Smith'.[30] On arrival, he evaded St John Gogarty who had been commissioned by Arthur Griffith to collect him from the ferry, apparently because Gogarty was the only person known to the Provisional Government to be in legal possession of a Rolls-Royce.[31] It was an appropriately unpromising prelude to talks with de Valera.

Smuts had been a student in Cambridge in the early 1890s, and the Second Home Rule Bill remained his implicit starting point for evaluating any Irish settlement. The major complications to the Irish question that had emerged since 1893, Ulster separatism and the proclamation of the Republic, could easily be brushed aside. Ireland had not been partitioned at all; it was 'merely that Ulster, which has always proved the obstacle, is now out of the way.'[32] The only credible interpretation of this curious statement is that Smuts assumed that unity would be maintained by the Council of Ireland. In his subsequent letter to de Valera, Smuts shifted his ground. 'Ireland is travelling the same painful road as South Africa'; self-government for southern Ireland would be the first stage, 'and the inclusion of Ulster and the full recognition of Irish unity will be the last.'[33] Not only would the British people never agree to an Irish Republic, but South African experience proved that it was not a good idea anyway. While theoretically independent, the Transvaal had been bound to accept British supervision by the 1884 Convention of London, and it had been from disputes over its interpretation that war had arisen. Thus Smuts directly challenged de Valera's favourite ploy of an Irish Republic bound by Treaty to respect Britain's interests. 'We in the Transvaal have worked both systems, and look at the result ... As a friend, I cannot advise you too strongly against a republic.'[34]

On a less elevated plane, the South African analogy created political problems for de Valera. Smuts felt that Griffith was sympathetic to his argument,[35] and Griffith was not only temperamentally inclined to subsume the Republic within a commonwealth solution, but had worked for a time in the Transvaal himself. Although de Valera left Smuts with the impression that he would put an offer of dominion status to the Irish people, he had no personal motive for shifting the basis of debate towards the ideas of Arthur Griffith. His own position as the symbol of the Republic owed much to the mystique of executed leaders of 1916. Among them had been John MacBride, who had fought against the empire in the Boer War, and had memorably dismissed his death sentence with the comment that he had looked down the barrels of British guns before.[36]

Smuts had travelled to Dublin backed by George V's confidence that 'you of all men will be able to induce Mr de Valera to be reasonable.'[37] The outcome of the Smuts mission is summarised by Macardle in a typically bleak sentence: 'President de Valéra [sic] explained to him how the position of Ireland differed from that of South Africa.'[38] Smuts was not used to being on the receiving end of other people's explanations. He reacted by belittling de Valera for undermining the myth of his own omniscient wisdom. 'A big man in Ireland will pull them through, but I did not see him in my negotiations with the Irish leader.'[39] With de Valera on the point of accepting Lloyd George's invitation to London, it was an unlucky moment to have so influential a voice denigrating him in the corridors of power. C. P. Scott recorded Smut's account of the Dublin talks. 'Was not impressed by any of them. No big man among them. De Valera was a romantic, lacking in practical sense and capacity of handling affairs. Very difficult in consequence to deal with.'[40]

The Smuts mission was thus an unhelpful preliminary to de Valera's visit to London ten days later, in mid-July 1921. Frances Stevenson, Lloyd George's secretary and mistress, had never seen the prime minister 'so excited as he was before de Valera arrived' at Downing Street. His negotiating strategy owed more to brainwashing than to diplomacy: de Valera found himself alternately wooed with the prospect of a seat at the imperial top table and threatened with renewal of repression. Lloyd George's conclusion that his visitor 'was the man with the most limited vocabulary he has ever met!' must be ranked as a highly unusual view of de Valera, but in the intimidating circumstances it was an understandable response; every time Lloyd George felt that he was getting through '& De Valera appeared to be warming, he suddenly drew back as if frightened and timid.' The voluble Welshman complained that de Valera 'was very difficult to keep to the point – he kept going off at a tangent, & talking in formulas and refusing to face facts.' One of the few moments of thaw in their talks came when Lloyd George, deduced by analogy from his native Welsh that 'Poblacht', the term used in the Proclamation of 1916 for 'Republic', simply meant 'people'. 'Isn't there another word?' he asked, and de Valera supplied 'Saorstát'. Why insist upon 'Republic', Lloyd George demanded, when Saorstát was 'good enough'. De Valera saw the funny side of the intrusion of Celtic linguistics into the politics of the island group and 'simply roared with laughter'.[41]

'I liked de Valera', Lloyd George told C. P. Scott.[42] Unfortunately, the warm personal impression did not oust the image, so determinedly endorsed by Smuts, of a naïve visionary. Invited to London as 'the chosen leader of the great majority in southern Ireland',[43] de Valera found himself expected to conduct himself as just another element in British domestic politics. Smuts, for instance, sought to impress upon de Valera the government's 'great difficulty with Ulster', only to find that de Valera 'doesn't really appreciate that the gov. have any real difficulty, & thinks that they are just using Ulster to frighten him.'[44] It was rather that de Valera saw himself as a head of state negotiating with a foreign power, and that the internal political difficulties of that power were none of his business. This may have been an unrealistic stance, but Arthur Griffith's subsequent promise not to rock the British political boat over Ulster robbed the nationalist cause of some freedom of manoeuvre.[45] There was a similarity of approach between the tough-minded Smuts and the more pacific C. P. Scott. The *Manchester Guardian* abhorred all violence. When he interviewed de Valera at a London hotel, Scott found the Irish leader aggrieved 'that we had denounced some of the Sinn Féin outrages as murders on a par with the murders committed by the agents of the government'. De Valera's position was that killings authorised by the Republic were legitimate, while those of the British were not. Scott was horrified and concluded that de Valera had 'a closed mind'.[46] When de Valera terminated the first phase of talks in August 1921 with an insistence on complete separation, the king summed up the British view that he was simply 'a dreamer & visionary'.[47] Thus when de Valera declared against the Treaty, the British were neither very surprised nor conscious of any special need to understand his point of view. Churchill's view of the anti-Treaty case was that 'Mr de Valera was still maundering about Poynings' Act, and that his view of Anglo-Irish relations and of the griefs of Ireland had not yet reached the sixteenth-century part of the story.'[48] In British eyes, the devil and the dreamer had fused into one.

For Tim Healy, the split was 'something out of dreamland', and he clung to his notion that de Valera was an earnest citizen of that realm. Still anxious to carve a political role for himself, in late December 1921, Healy tried to speed up the appointment of the promised Boundary Commission, seeking to persuade de Valera through the Archbishop of Dublin that Carson could not object to the appointment of 'an Impartial Colonial Statesman', that any such arbitrator was bound to make substantial territorial transfers to the Free State and that the necessary outcome had to be that 'the Belfasters are burst'. The archbishop despairingly reported that he had seen de Valera but 'cannot even understand the dialect he speaks.'[49] De Valera's refusal to bow to Healy's superior political wisdom merely confirmed that he was out of his depth. 'Poor man,' Healy wrote patronisingly, 'I think he has done his country more harm even than Parnell, with the very best intentions.' Surrounded by the wild men and women of extreme republicanism, 'he resents too touchily the supposed slur on his position.'[50]

The Civil War only gradually destroyed the new governor-general's view of de Valera as an innocent out of his depth. 'I can't believe the fellow as cracked as your informants seem to think', Healy wrote to his brother in February 1923, speculating that de Valera was perhaps 'browbeaten and bullied by Lynch'. When Lynch's death failed to liberate de Valera's strain of simplicity, Healy concluded that he was 'an unscrupulous man, prepared to sanction any mischief to gain his ends'. While condemning de Valera's 'futile wickedness', Healy was inclined to take the philosophical view that by removing de Valera from Irish politics, the Civil War had been a blessing in disguise.[51] Unfortunately for Healy, the Civil War proved to be only a brief setback, and de Valera was soon back in the Dáil, and Healy himself eased out of the Viceregal Lodge.

The Civil War encouraged a new construct of de Valera, one which unfavourably emphasised his American birth and Spanish origins. If the responsibility for opposition to the Treaty could be solely attributed to de Valera, and if de Valera could be re-classified as 'a half-breed Spaniard', then the Civil War could be explained away as an alien aberration and Ireland itself acquitted of the sin of fratricidal conflict. In an interview with a British journalist in 1928, Healy denounced the leader of Fianna Fáil as 'a barren impostor' with a foreign father, 'a vain, shallow man without a shred of ability', motivated solely by jealousy. One of St John Gogarty's cronies referred to de Valera as 'the Dago', while John Devoy discounted the claimed Hispanic parentage and referred instead to 'a Jewish bastard'.[52] Gogarty himself retorted that because the Irish refused to be ruled by one of their own, they were 'culture-beds for any political microbe'. The fact that de Valera was 'unreckonable' merely added to his mystique.[53]

To outsiders, who had less need to explain away the innate violence of the Irish Civil War, de Valera's origins merely added a bizarre touch of the exotic: to Britain's outspoken Dominions Secretary, Jimmy Thomas, he was 'the Spanish onion in the Irish stew'.[54] In noting that 'Eamon de Valera was not born a citizen of the country he rules' the American journalist John Gunther drew a parallel with two other outsiders by birth, Hitler and Stalin.[55] On one occasion, de Valera himself rescued an over-enthusiastic visitor from an embarrassing moment. The Canadian journalist Grattan O'Leary had been reared in a remote part of Quebec by a father who lived exclusively for the politics of the distant homeland. O'Leary himself was not only intensely proud of his heritage, but subscribed to the fashionable myth that the essence of Irishness was to be combative. When the Taoiseach greeted him in Dublin in 1941 with the words, 'I presume you're of Irish descent', O'Leary was moved to a reply more notable for pride than discretion. 'Mr de Valera,' he proclaimed, 'there isn't one drop of blood in my veins that isn't Irish.' 'Well,' replied his host, 'you have the advantage of me there', good-naturedly putting his visitor at ease by thanking him for 'a story to amuse his colleagues'.[56]

The more genial side of de Valera's personality only became apparent to outsiders very gradually during the decade after Fianna Fáil came to power in 1932. Smuts was almost certainly not alone in continuing to brand de Valera as 'a mad fellow'.[57] It was not simply that Ireland had largely fallen off the British political agenda, but rather that the country and its new rulers no longer figured large in British social itineraries. At a personal level, the commonwealth framework had helped some British leaders to get to know O'Higgins and McGilligan in the 1920s, but murder and electoral defeat had put an end to these contacts. In 1932, personal relations had to begin all over again.[58]

When John Maynard Keynes lectured on 'National Self-Sufficiency' at UCD in 1933, he was in full retreat from the Victorian ideology of *laissez-faire*, and shocked some of his audience by expressing sympathy for Fianna Fáil economic policies. Although privately regarding the new government's drive to grow more wheat as 'insane', Keynes was attracted to its other developmental plans. He met de Valera 'who impressed me distinctly favourably', and helped pave the way for a visit by Josiah Stamp, a retired senior British civil servant who was an expert of debt negotiations. Stamp in turn found de Valera 'very charming'.[59]

It is ironic that it was the abdication crisis of 1936 that formed a landmark in the improvement of British assessments of de Valera. By November 1936, Baldwin's government was privately facing the fact that Edward VIII would have to go. Among the many sensitive elements in the situation was the complication that the Statute of Westminster of 1931 had given the dominions a right of veto over any change in the succession to the throne. Thus de Valera, who fifteen years earlier had refused to accept the crown, now found his consent required to get rid of the king. Naturally, a desire to oblige the British formed little or no part in de Valera's handling of an issue that he found an 'acute embarrassment'.[60] However, the abdication provided a direct opportunity to distance Ireland from the crown by passing the External Relations Act, and eased the way for the adoption of the 1937 constitution. Given the gains on offer, there could be little incentive for de Valera to muddy himself in the technical handling of issues as alien as monarchy and divorce. Securing Irish acquiescence was the responsibility of Sir Harry Batterbee of the Dominions Office. Not surprisingly, it required a personal visit to confirm that de Valera would agree to ratify Edward VIII's departure, if only to prevent Wallis Simpson from becoming queen of Ireland. In his desperation, the British prime minister, Stanley Baldwin, had refined the idealistic headmaster into yet another de Valera: 'he is such a gentleman he won't kick an enemy when he is down.'[61] Baldwin was full of gratitude when Batterbee returned with the news that Dublin would co-operate. According to Whitehall folklore, Batterbee suggested that the prime minister should direct his thanks to divine providence. 'De Valera has always counted on winning any argument by towering over his adversary. As you know he is 6 feet 1. But the good God made me 6 feet 4!'[62] As an analysis of British-Irish relations, the story was otiose, but it does suggest the beginnings of a view of de Valera as a personality in his own right.

Part of de Valera's projection of Ireland as an independent state was his use of the League of Nations, a stage handily provided for him by the Cosgrave government decision to seek election to the League Council in 1930. Paradoxically, Geneva also provided de Valera with an environment where he could temporarily be free from the overwhelming baggage of Irish nationalism. Gunther reported that although a teetotaller at home, 'an odd point, he drinks wine or beer when he is on the continent. He likes nothing better than to sit in a café ... sipping a glass of beer and watching people.'[63] It was partly through the League of Nations that de Valera established an extraordinary but unfortunately short-lived measure of understanding with Baldwin's successor, Neville Chamberlain.

This rapprochement certainly helped to bring about the wide-ranging settlement of differences between the two countries in 1938. British civil servants regarded de Valera as 'stubborn, almost fanatical',[64] but the Dominions Secretary, Malcolm MacDonald, was anxious to establish a personal relationship. Unofficial talks were held on several occasions in 1936 at a London hotel while de Valera was on his way to visit an eye specialist in Switzerland. MacDonald was 'taken by surprise' at their first meeting: he had expected the 'tall, austere figure' of press photographs, but instead of the 'prim, stern countenance' that he had expected, there was a 'friendly smile which lit his face as he greeted me'. Indeed, de Valera occasionally 'revealed a pleasant sense of humour which was inconsistent with the grim image of him portrayed in the British press.' The Irish leader was 'courteous and considerate', 'a quietly charming man' who 'never stood on ceremony … no doubt because of his absolute confidence in himself and the rightness of his cause'.[65] More formal discussions followed from the autumn of 1937. At one point, MacDonald appealed to de Valera 'as a realist' to recognise that Britain as well as Ireland faced political difficulties in reaching a settlement. To J. J. Lee, those three words 'spoke volumes': 'adult' politicians in Britain were beginning to recognise de Valera as 'a practical politician of uncommon capacity'.[66] This may make more of the phrase than is fully warranted: the British in 1921 had consistently demanded that de Valera prove his realism by endorsing their view of their own internal difficulties. In 1937–8, the British government was prepared to make extensive concessions, but de Valera was prepared to concede little in return, beyond explicit acceptance of membership of the commonwealth now that he had effectively emasculated the crown. MacDonald himself complained that de Valera was 'unyielding' and expected 'us British to do almost all the giving; and to hope only for the gift of Irish goodwill.' The Irish leader was 'a transparently honest and sincere man' who 'repeatedly and fervently' urged an end to partition. When arguing his case, his face became 'unchangeably solemn', while his 'quietly reasonable voice' was 'sometimes vibrant with intense emotion'.[67]

The prime minister, Neville Chamberlain, backed MacDonald in taking a chance on the goodwill of de Valera. 'I am satisfied,' Chamberlain wrote in January 1938 'that, queer creature as he is in many ways, he is sincere, and that he is no enemy of this country.'[68] When the agreement was finally signed at 10 Downing Street three months later, it was in a far more relaxed atmosphere than that of December 1921. Chamberlain announced that he wished to return an item of lost property; twenty-two years earlier, de Valera's field glasses had been impounded following his surrender at Boland's Mills. 'The recipient examined them carefully when they were handed across the table and agreed that they were his.' It was a gesture that could succeed only within an atmosphere of goodwill: de Valera had told Smuts in 1921 that he was reluctant to go to London and be placed in the position of an errant schoolboy.[69] Yet if the act of restitution suggested a new chapter in British-Irish relations, it also carried with it final overtones of the belief that de Valera, like Smuts, might tread the path of Smuts from defeated foe to loyal ally. In this, the British were to be disappointed.

The warm relationship between Eamon de Valera and Neville Chamberlain was unlikely but genuine. The British prime minister was the son of Joseph Chamberlain, the radical whose defection to unionism had helped kill Home Rule in Parnell's day, and the half-brother of Austen, one of the signatories of the Treaty of 1921. Lee suggests that the two were drawn together by the features that they shared, including 'their headmasterish temperaments … and their intimations of personal infallibility'.[70] One can only comment that such personalities rarely manage to co-exist, as de Valera had shown in his dealings with Smuts. Rather, they were drawn together by another quality identified by Lee, their commitment to peace in Europe. When news broke during the Munich crisis of September 1938 that Neville Chamberlain was to fly to see Hitler in person, de Valera was attending an official dinner in Geneva, in the remarkably unlikely company of the socialite, Diana Duff Cooper. She recalled that it was de Valera who broke the solemn silence with the words: 'This is the greatest thing that has ever been done'.[71] Sadly, the Munich settlement unravelled within a matter of months, but the beleaguered Chamberlain continued to draw encouragement from the support of his Irish counterpart. They held a two-hour meeting at Downing Street in March 1939, and Chamberlain reported in a family letter: 'He is strongly of opinion that I have been right all through & am right now.'[72] When Chamberlain fell from power in May 1940, one of the most glowing tributes that he received came from Eamon de Valera.[73] So ended the brief period when *Dublin Opinion* believed that 'Nev and Dev understood one another'.[74]

John Gunther provides a sketch of de Valera as head of government in the 1930s. In the summer of 1937, the American journalist was permitted 'a brief chat' on the understanding that nothing would be quoted on Irish affairs. Gunther outlined a conventional profile – American birth, Boland's Mills, de Valera's family, his enthusiasm for mathematics, his indifference to money: 'rigid self-control; fanatic faith in his duty to Ireland; extreme seriousness of mind; complete unworldliness; a certain didacticism; stubbornness, humanity.' His 'single-track mind' made him work hard: 'one may see lights in the President's quarters till after midnight. He has bread and butter for supper. He has never, except for reasons of illness, taken a holiday.' At weekends, followed by an official car and a private detective, he walked energetically for exercise in the hills near Dublin, to preserve 'the spare but rugged frame that fanatics need'. To lighten the picture, Gunther added that 'when he laughs, he laughs very heartily.' While de Valera was 'extremely religious … his Catholicism is neither ostentatious nor bigoted; several of his friends are Protestant'. One member of his staff commented that de Valera's 'whole life is a prayer'.[75]

Despite himself, Gunther was impressed. He had come to Dublin intending to fit de Valera into a pattern of fanatical leaders who were keeping the margins of Europe aflame with petty nationalisms: 'In Jugoslavia, in Bulgaria, in Syria and Egypt and Palestine, I have met young de Valeras of various breeds.' Given his preconceptions, he found it difficult to accommodate the fact that he had encountered 'an alert, interested and extremely courteous' man, eager to quiz his visitor on his impressions of continental politics and quick to pounce good-humouredly on an unguarded allusion to 'the British Isles'. 'De Valera looks less severe than his pictures. The long nose and the deep lines to the mouth are his most characteristic features.' When, however, his host turned to Irish issues, Gunther's doubts returned. 'He was patient, explicit, and formidably, sombrely reasonable. But in that gaunt face I saw the eyes of a fanatic.'[76]

Gunther was especially struck by the distance that de Valera maintained between himself and his people. Everyone in Ireland referred to this 'tall, gaunt man' as 'Dev', but few dared to address him so to his face. At public events, 'he does not smile or nod to the crowd. He walks straight ahead, very reserved, and seems to pretend that the crowd is not there.' Perhaps only an American observer would have commented that de Valera was 'very attractive to women ... They follow him about at functions; he is smiling and reserved, and, without ever being rude or pompous, manages to create a sense of distance between himself and them.'[77] Another visitor, the Australian prime minister, Robert Menzies, noted a less attractive aspect of the isolation of 'the Chief'. 'The very clerks in the offices stood promptly and rigidly to attention as he strode past. His ministers ... spoke with freedom – but with no disloyalty – in his absence, but were restrained and obedient in his presence.'[78] Malcolm MacDonald once asked what happened if the Executive Council disagreed with the Taoiseach. A laughing Seán Lemass replied that a decision would be taken 'by a minority of one'.[79]

By contrast, de Valera seemed indifferent to the trappings of power. 'His office is a simple small room, with "President" printed in black on the frosted window,' Gunther noted, likening it to 'the kind of room which a modest executive official of a very modest business might use. No particular decoration; no covey of secretaries; no swank.'[80] Harold Nicolson thought the Taoiseach's office 'ill-designed, with cold, high windows' and 'a clock that strikes the quarter-hours with a loud noise'. However, even the Irish government had adopted modern technology. 'On his desk he has a telephone box which buzzes occasionally and to which he talks in Gaelic.'[81] One of the few decorations was a facsimile copy of the American Declaration of Independence, which de Valera described to the British socialist Aneurin Bevan as 'my political bible'.[82]

In the dark years of the war, the British found Irish neutrality incomprehensible, and negative perceptions of de Valera easily reasserted themselves. Churchill, whose ideas on dominion status had evidently not fully caught up with the evolution of the commonwealth, was convinced that legally Ireland was 'at war but skulking'.[83] De Valera justified neutrality to Menzies, by explaining that his country was 'virtually defenceless', an objection that the Australian leader thought might be overcome by the supply of anti-aircraft guns. 'He would step across to the window, and gaze out, and say, 'My beautiful Dublin could be destroyed.''[84] The Anglophile American statesman, Wendell Willkie, 'did not conceal his contempt' when de Valera told him that he feared that if he allowed the British base facilities in Ireland, Dublin would be bombed.[85] Cardinal Hinsley, leader of the English Catholics, dismissed the argument as hypocrisy, pointing to the fact that de Valera had ignored German threats of retaliation when he had sent the Dublin fire brigades into the Belfast blitz. De Valera dismissed that argument. 'When an Irish city's on fire,' he told Grattan O'Leary, 'no matter in what part of Ireland, it's our duty to help put it out.' If the German ambassador chose to complain, 'I'll kick him out of my office.'[86]

While Churchill privately denounced de Valera as 'that wicked man',[87] he jovially advised Archbishop Spellman of New York that a dressing-down that he planned to administer to de Valera would 'give the poor man a fit'. Spellman grimly replied that 'if Almighty God should wish that De Valera should lose his life on hearing the truth, I shall say many masses for his soul.'[88] Grattan O'Leary found himself cast in the role of emissary from an angry Cardinal Hinsley, demanding an explanation for the suppression of one of his sermons in Catholic Ireland.[89] For once, princes of the Church found themselves in agreement with Russian communists. Ivan Maisky, Stalin's ambassador in London, dismissed de Valera as 'very narrow' and 'rather stupid'.[90]

In reality, there was another side to Irish neutrality and de Valera's dilemma. For all his later denunciation of an Irish government determined 'to frolic' with Axis diplomats,[91] even Churchill recognised in 1940 that 'the implacable, malignant minority can make so much trouble that de Valera dare not do anything to offend them.'[92] When de Valera argued that it was in Britain's interests to have a neutral neighbour rather than a weak ally, Malcolm MacDonald felt that there was 'quite a lot of sense in what he said.'[93] In Dublin in 1942 Professor Daniel Binchy of UCD counselled Harold Nicolson that 'a visiting Englishman is apt to be taken in by blarney and to imagine that the feelings of this country towards us are really friendly.' Neutrality was seen as a positive assertion, something that few had believed would be possible at the outbreak of war, an achievement which many 'attributed to the genius of de Valera, who has thereby gained enormous prestige'. Others regarded neutrality as an example of divine providence, so that it had 'taken on an almost religious flavour ... something which Ireland is not ashamed of, but tremendously proud'.[94] De Valera himself assured Menzies that his fellow citizens had a 'passion for neutrality', an emotion that the Australian prime minister had failed to detect among those of Irish descent in his own country.[95] The arguments were complex but none the less neutrality added a new layer of negative incomprehension to outsiders' perceptions of Eamon de Valera.

In his memoirs, Robert Menzies was disingenuous about his motives for visiting Dublin in April 1941. In many respects, the Menzies visit was a pastiche of the Smuts mission two decades earlier. The Australian prime minister was on an extended visit to Britain, which with poetic justice weakened his hold on Canberra politics and brought about his own downfall at the end of the year. In London, however, Menzies connived with Churchill's critics, and may even have seen himself as an alternative consensus prime minister. At one level, a visit to Dublin would generate photo-opportunities likely to please Irish-Australia. At another, it might just enable Menzies to pull off a coup for the allied cause by talking de Valera out of his neutral stance.[96]

Menzies flew to Belfast, where he encountered the suspicion that Churchill was 'going to sell us out to the south', and travelled onto Dublin by train. De Valera met him at the station. 'He was a striking figure, tall and spare and ascetic.' Wearing a dark overcoat and broad-brimmed hat, 'he looked positively saturnine'. In the talks that followed, Menzies found de Valera 'vastly interesting', 'a scholar, and in a quiet way, passionately sincere'. There were 'blind spots occasioned by prejudice' and 'a failure to realise the facts of life' of a world at war, but 'he grew on me'. Given the failure of his machinations in London, and his post-war identification with Churchill as a fellow elder-statesman of the commonwealth, it suited Menzies to portray himself as naïve tourist. He was allocated a senior Irish civil servant to show him around Dublin, a man who could scarcely disguise his irritation with a colonial monarchist who innocently enquired if he might visit Sackville Street. In similar vein, he portrayed an exchange with de Valera over his own discussions in Belfast. When the Taoiseach spoke 'pleasantly' of the Stormont premier, J. M. Andrews, Menzies asked 'whether he saw him frequently', and was astonished to be told that the two had never met. Menzies subsequently argued that a senior minister should be sent on a mission to Dublin, a step which Churchill resisted.[97] In fact, Churchill had already despatched Malcolm MacDonald to Dublin for secret and fruitless talks in June 1940.[98] When the United States entered the war in December 1941, another cabinet minister was despatched to de Valera. Lord Cranborne reported 'a long, friendly, but fruitless talk', mainly about partition.[99] Personal diplomacy might modify negative preconceptions of the Irish leader, but it was not going to change Irish policy.

Harold Nicolson was a writer and shrewd diarist, who moved in the inmost circles of power and had briefly held minor government office under Churchill. As with so many visitors, his preconceptions were shattered when he met de Valera in March 1942. He had expected 'a thin sallow man' with 'lank black Spanish hair'. De Valera was neither thin nor sallow, although there was an unhealthy puffiness about his smooth face, while his hair was 'soft and almost brown'. In place of the 'huge round black spectacles' of photographs, there were 'benevolent cold eyes behind steel-framed glasses'. It was not de Valera's 'soft Irish accent' that intrigued Nicolson but his 'admirable smile … lighting up the eyes and face very quickly, like an electric light bulb that doesn't fit and flashes on and off'. Nicolson saw happiness and sincerity in de Valera's smile. 'He is a very simple man, like all great men … Deep spiritual certainty underneath it all, giving his features a mark of repose.' The two men talked about the war, with de Valera, fully aware that his remarks would be reported back, speaking sympathetically of the challenges facing Churchill. He criticised the British press for hostility to Ireland. Nicolson deflected the complaint by saying that since his recent appointment as a governor of the BBC, he had become equally convinced that every newspaper devoted columns of unfair criticism to the organisation. 'He is amused by this, and the faint flash of his smile lights up his porridge-coloured face.'[100]

As the tide of war turned in favour of the Allies, Ireland and its mysterious leader could once again be left alone. Britain's post-war Labour government had problems enough, and did not turn its attention seriously to Ireland until 1949, when it was necessary to respond to the final secession from the commonwealth, carried out by a coalition of de Valera's opponents who had unexpectedly ousted him from power in 1948.[101] As a result, there remained one notable figure who had not succumbed to de Valera's charm. Churchill's victory broadcast of 13 May 1945 had contained an 'envenomed attack'[102] on de Valera's policy of neutrality, so much so that when the two men first encountered each other at a Council of Europe meeting four years later, de Valera took care to avoid a formal introduction to avoid the risk of being snubbed.[103] Yet one of Churchill's more intriguing characteristics was a desire to reach out to former enemies, as he had shown in South Africa after 1906 and with less benign consequences in his eager endorsement of the Free State in 1922. By fortunate coincidence, the two veterans returned to office in 1951, neither in good health and each mellowed by the ravages of time. The British prime minister was touched by de Valera's message of sympathy on the death of George VI in February 1952, even if the gesture was perhaps of no more significance than the notorious offer of condolence to the German ambassador on the death of Hitler. Churchill's response, of 'sincere goodwill' to Ireland through all its many difficulties, can be read as a reply to the appeal that de Valera had made for British generosity in the battle of the broadcasts in 1945. The two men finally met over lunch at 10 Downing Street in September 1953. De Valera noted that his host 'went out of his way to be courteous'. In private talks, de Valera as always raised the issue of partition, and then suggested the return to Ireland of the body of Sir Roger Casement. Churchill seemed sympathetic, although Whitehall second thoughts ensured that Casement's remains stayed in Pentonville for another decade.[104] 'A very agreeable occasion,' was Churchill's verdict. 'I like the man.'[105]

'I liked de Valera,' Lloyd George had commented after alternately cajoling and threatening him in Downing Street thirty years earlier.[106] No doubt outsiders who met de Valera were bound to some extent to be favourably impressed, simply on discovering that he lacked the horns and forked tail of British mythology. Yet, it is clear that the positive impressions of Eamon de Valera the man went far beyond modest surprise at his mere humanity. The question arises: could the positive elements of de Valera's personality have been mobilised more effectively on behalf of Ireland's interests in dealing with Ireland's neighbours?

Two of the most controversial aspects of de Valera's behaviour between 1916 and 1921 remain his eighteen-month absence in the United States during 1919–20, and his refusal to head the delegation sent to London that signed the Treaty in December 1921.[107] It would be a contradiction in terms to condemn de Valera for having declined to make mollifying the British his first priority. Yet, paradoxically, with the British throughout the Troubles searching for a Parnell whom they might convert into a Smuts, de Valera might have found his enemies bolstering his position against his rivals. Haldane's testimony suggests that by 1921 enlightened opinion in Britain was moving towards direct negotiation with the leader of Irish republicanism. De Valera's decision to decamp to the United States cast understandable doubt on the extent of his control over the movement. It was especially unlucky that the British chose as their miracle-working persuader in June 1921 the one man whose own political image could be discredited by de Valera's refusal to accept his assigned role, Jan Smuts. None the less, by the middle of the year, the British government had swung back to regarding de Valera as the leader of southern Ireland. Had he taken part in the negotiations leading to the Treaty, he might have dispelled some British misunderstandings about his naïvety, and would probably have been able to enforce more effective and obvious control over his delegates.

As a might-have-been, the strategy of dealing more frequently and openly with the British is open to one obvious riposte: what, beyond his intriguing smile, would de Valera have had to offer? A persuasive interpretation of his later career sees his emphasis upon partition as a cover for a general retreat after 1923 from the substantive case against the Treaty, whose provisions he either tamed or accepted as the years went by.[108] The problem with this interpretation is that while British observers found de Valera's obsession with the border tedious and impenetrable, they never doubted the sincerity with which he harped upon the issue. It can be argued that Smuts, if somewhat brutal, was correct in contending that Ulster had ceased to be a practical obstacle by the summer of 1921. Yet while we can see how Griffith would embrace a compromise agreement with the British for reasons of principle and Collins would support him on tactical grounds, it is hard to imagine a more flexible de Valera under any circumstances.

It is just possible that de Valera might have exploited his charm to conduct a more subtle campaign against partition from the 1930s, not head-on but by concentrating on the practical grievances of the northern nationalist minority. While British politicians of all parties were formally committed to preserving the link with Northern Ireland, it would be easy to over-estimate the closeness of relationships between Westminster and Stormont, as Menzies discovered in Belfast in 1941.[109] The civil rights movement of the mid-1960s suggested that Northern Ireland could be destabilised far more effectively by Catholics trying to get into the northern state than had ever been the case with their campaigns to get out of it. However, to hold the British responsible for any aspect of northern administration would have been, for de Valera, too close to recognising the legitimacy of their position. In any case, the war ensured that Northern Ireland had a political credit balance on which it drew for two somnolent decades, while the principled stand of neutrality ruled out even such small favours as the return of Casement's bones.[110]

Fundamentally, then, we come face to face with de Valera, not the ogre that many imagined, nor the amiable companion that a surprised few discovered, but as that republican symbol that he conceived himself to be. 'Some said of de Valera that he had the well springs of greatness,' wrote Grattan O'Leary. 'No one meeting him and looking into his eyes as I did could doubt that statement.' O'Leary never forgot de Valera's 'hawk like face', even though they met only once.[111] Yet, de Valera himself discounted the personal factor in diplomacy. In 1938, he was a guest at Malcolm MacDonald's country home. While his host busied himself with traditional diplomatic courtesies, even to removing Northern Irish whiskey from his drinks tray, de Valera chilled the American ambassador by dismissing personal factors altogether: 'the individual who projected the cause was merely an instrument'.[112] It was probably for this reason that Malcolm MacDonald concluded that de Valera's 'greatness as a leader' was 'confined to certain limits'.[113] One of those limits may have been that he kept too close a rein on his own humanity. Eamon de Valera towers over twentieth-century Ireland, and it is right that scholars should study him as something more than a passing figure in a historical cartoon strip. Yet in the last resort there is little reason to think that Irish history would have been notably different if de Valera's personality had been as prominently engaged as his principles.

Women in de Valera's Ireland 1932–48: a reappraisal

Caitriona Clear

It has got to the stage where only five words are needed for a shorthand history of women in twentieth century Ireland before the changes set in motion by the 1960s. The three words 'de Valera's Ireland' are used to convey an oppressive, stagnant, uncomfortable social environment for women. No elaboration is necessary, except perhaps to throw in the two words 'comely maidens' (a reference to Eamon de Valera's St Patrick's Day speech of 1943) to imply prescription and hypocrisy in about equal measure. More detailed commentators will go on to refer to article 41.2 in the 1937 constitution; to the marriage bar against women public servants and national school teachers; and the bans on divorce and contraception. Arensberg and Kimball will be mentioned, to depict a strictly segregated and inferior space for rural women; a thirty-year leap might be made to the corroborating anthropological testimony of John Messenger or Nancy Scheper-Hughes; the fiction of, perhaps, John B. Keane or William Trevor, for colour; and there it is, de Valera's Ireland. It is less a wonder that women were queuing up to leave the country, than that any of them stayed.[1] It is possible to come away from reading some of the sociologists, historians and commentators on the period with the impression that Irish women were completely powerless and silenced in these years, and that change, if it took place at all, was for the worse.[2]

Legal scholar Yvonne Scannell and historian Mary Clancy, however, by placing discussions of women in de Valera's Ireland firmly in the context of the time, give us a more nuanced perspective,[3] and my own research mainly on women's household work and on the public definitions and lived experience of that work, has caused me to question what is now the very strong consensus that women in Ireland in the 1930s and 1940s had very hard lives because of the dominant 'ideology of domesticity' (as it is sometimes called) and the oppressive patriarchy of everyday life.[4] Neither Scannell, Clancy nor myself deny the quite serious attacks on women's citizenship and women's work in Ireland in these years; and the strong anti-feminist tendency in government and among some of those who gave public lectures, published articles in journals and issued pastoral letters. However, there was a citizenship to be attacked, there were jobs from which it was considered necessary to exclude women, and there was a feminism to be against. Nor is there any suggestion, in this article, that Irish women's lives were easy, in the first sixteen-year unbroken period of de Valera's premiership. Many Irish people suffered desperate privation in these years, and women in charge of houses and women who were mothers in particular, often underwent considerable physical discomfort and ill-health, in the course of a daily round of a kind of hard work unimaginable today. It will be argued that in some key areas, however, women's lives changed slowly but surely for the better in these years, and that it is difficult, if not impossible, to generalise about 'women' and 'domesticity' when talking about this period.

PUBLIC PERCEPTIONS AND PUBLIC LIFE

In some writings by and about women in Ireland in the 1930s and 1940s there is a strong sense of space and light. An article by feminist and republican Dorothy Macardle in one of the first issues of the *Irish Press* describes the female occupational tables in the census as 'a story of infinite romance and adventure'.[5] The same air of progress and excitement is found in the Irish-produced magazine *Woman's Life*, from 1936, where every issue, for the first few years, carried, as well as the staples of women's magazines (health, beauty, romantic fiction), an interview with a working woman: a packer in Brown and Polson's factory, a secretary working in a trade union, a commercial traveller, two 'Tiller girls', a radiographer, a hotel receptionist, a street-seller, a nurse, a wife-and-mother who found it hard to believe that the modern girl is not interested in men.[6] This magazine, which had a countrywide middle/lower-middle/upper-working-class circulation, judging by the addresses of competition entrants and other correspondence, also carried regular news items about women in public life. The confidence with which Maura Laverty blends traditional and modern perspectives on women in her autobiographical writings, fiction and cookery writing is also typical of this optimism.[7]

Many Catholics who commented directly on modern women believed that it was good and desirable for women to participate in public life so long as they were upholding Catholic principles and not neglecting their domestic duties. Alice Curtayne, in a lecture entitled 'The Renaissance of Woman' in 1933 (published a year later with an imprimatur by the Bishop of Ferns), attempted to give Catholicism the credit for women's equal citizenship, and although she questioned some of the achievements of feminism it was obvious that she welcomed women having a public role.[8]

Not all Lenten pastorals were concerned with reinforcing patriarchal authority. Dr Dignan of Clonfert, in his Lenten pastoral letter in 1934, urged mothers and fathers to ensure that daughters got as good an education as sons, commenting that a good education was more important than a dowry.[9] The *Catholic Bulletin* in the 1930s approved of the French movement towards women's franchise, and of the improvements in French women's legal position within marriage that came about in the late 1930s.[10] The *Irish Monthly* published many articles in the 1930s and 1940s on the debate about women in public life.[11] Articles supporting equal pay for equal work, and women in the workplace, appear in the late 1940s and early 1950s in Catholic periodicals such as *Christus Rex* and the *Irish Messenger*.[12] The *Messenger*, it is true, spent much of the 1920s and 1930s lamenting women's desertion of the home ('a place to keep clothes in and for sleeping') and carrying stories about girls who left farms and withered away in towns and cities until they returned home or went to the bad, but by the early 1950s it was quoting papal encyclicals to the effect that women needed paid work and it confined itself to exhorting females to brighten up their homes, no differently from any women's magazine.[13]

Christus Rex, the *Catholic Bulletin* and the *Irish Monthly* were not wide-circulation publications it is true (the *Messenger*, on the other hand, was), but neither were many of the writings which are usually taken as examples of the public attitudes of the period. How many women were aware of article 41.2 in the 1937 constitution?[14] It is simply not true to claim as one historian does, that 'by 1937 women's political, economic and reproductive rights had been so seriously curtailed that women were explicitly barred from claiming for themselves a public identity'.[15]

Leaving aside, for the moment, the ban on contraception, as far as public identity was concerned, women politicians were quite vocal in their support of women's issues, and women's organisations flourished in these two decades.[16] The Joint Committee of Women's Societies and Social Workers, an amalgam of women's organisations of all denominations that were oriented towards social or philanthropic work, comprised 28,000 members in 1940. It was not afraid to call itself 'feminist', nor was the Catholic Federation of Secondary School Unions (past-pupil), which had a few thousand members. Older, smaller organisations like the National Council of Women in Ireland kept a watchdog role and could count on the support of the larger organisations on issues to do with protection of young girls, protection of the rights of women workers, and a public voice for women in the house. The Irish Countrywomen's Association had some 2,000 members in 1940 and kept growing. While it did not call itself 'feminist', it stated clearly that one of its aims was to prepare women for public life, and it was loudly lobbying for better working conditions for women on farms as early as 1938.[17] The Irish Housewives Association, set up in Dublin in 1942 on a wave of awareness of the poor living conditions of urban women in particular, drew attention to poor housing, health, quality of foodstuffs (especially milk) and child-care provisions. It was a direct successor of the Irish Women's Suffrage and Local Government Association and self-consciously, proudly femin-ist.[18] Government commissions in these years invariably had two or three female members – women like Lucy Franks of the ICA, Maire MacGeehin, Brigid Stafford of the Department of Labour, Louie Bennett – who com-mented on issues relating to women, and were not slow to issue reser-vations and minority reports when they disagreed with the main report.[19] These women could of course be called 'token women', but it is signifi-cant that even token women were seen to be necessary.

There were substantial infringements on women's rights in the years 1932–48; no attempt is being made to gloss over these injustices. But these injustices did not come about as a result of a prevailing ideology of domesticity, however much de Valera might have given the impression that they did. The marriage bar against women national teachers was introduced in a cynical attempt to make jobs available for young, single women and men.[20] The same is true of the marriage bar against women in the public service. Had these bars been introduced because of a co-herent and consistent commitment to domesticity, married women would surely have been statutorily barred from industry and non-public ser-vice employment also, which they were not. The ban on women doing certain kinds of industrial work in the mid-1930s was a pragmatic at-tempt to prevent new industries from hiring female labour (by definition cheap) in preference to paying breadwinner wages to men, rather than an explicit attempt to limit women to the home, though this might have been a by-product of such a policy.[21] Furthermore, women's organisations did not come out strongly against the marriage bar; perhaps in these hard times there was popular resentment, from women and men, at two-income households – Alice Kessler-Harris tells us that in the USA in the Depression years, wives of unemployed men and single unemployed women were often among the loudest clamouring for married women to give up their jobs.[22]

Hostility to married women workers was a cause of tension among the rank and file and the leadership of the Irish Women Workers' Union in the early 1930s.[23] The Conditions of Employment Act 1935–6 aroused concerted opposition from organised women but also from represent-atives of social-work organisations, who argued that women needed this work to survive. There was always a philanthropic element in feminist activism, in Ireland no more so than anywhere else; concern for working-class women was voiced by middle-class women, who either did not want or did not dare to take up the cudgels against issues like the marriage bar which affected them in particular.[24] It is likely that Eamon de Valera intended article 41.2 in the constitution as retrospective justification of the marriage bar against women in the public service, and the Conditions of Employment Act; the women's organisations that objected to the constitution feared that the implications of article 41.2 in particular would be wide-ranging and oppressive.

However, de Valera did not succeed in omitting 'without distinction of sex' in article 16 and according to Clancy and Scannell, this was a significant achievement for the women objectors.[25] And, indeed, article 41.2 was never used to discriminate further against women in the workplace in this period (e.g., no statutory marriage bar was introduced against women in industry or non-public service employment); to curb their mobility (no restrictions were introduced on female emigration); or to curtail their citizenship (taking the vote from already enfranchised women was by no means unheard of in the Europe of the 1930s).[26] Article 41.2 was mentioned in 1953 by the Department of Education as one justification for the continuation of the marriage bar, but the bar was beginning to be dismantled at this stage, and was eventually done away with by the end of that decade.[27] We have to see the fact that article 41.2 was not used against women in the ways suggested above, as a significant if invisible victory for women's activism in Ireland.

It is inaccurate – to say the least – to depict de Valera's Ireland as a graveyard of women's rights. It was an intensive care unit, maybe, but dedicated attention ensured that the patient survived. The very fact that women's rights were constantly being debated, defined and defended indicates that they were very much alive.

WHOSE DOMESTIC SPHERE?

The women's organisations when they defended women's rights and women's work did not always get it right. One of the areas they, in common with nearly all public figures in the period, got completely wrong was that of domestic service. In 1940 there was a cartoon in *Dublin Opinion* that showed the father of a family, his wife and three children grouped behind, offering a domestic servant a silver service to thank her for the completion of six months' service with them. Such jokes would become more common as time went on, as *Dublin Opinion* loved to mock the pretensions and preoccupations of the upper-middle-class to which its editor belonged.[28]

One of the biggest changes in Irish women's lives in this period was their rejection of domestic service as an occupation, particularly after 1940. As early as 1936, a Fr McCarthy in rural Cork was complaining that girls were rejecting 'good situations' and going to England.[29] By 1950 advertisements for domestics take on a note of desperation, such as the following extract from the *Irish Independent* in 1950: 'Young girl wanted to train as Mother's Help: good wages and outings; card stamped, uniform supplied, treated as one of family, help given, present girl four years.'[30] The very fact that such 'advantages' are specified indicates that they were not standard.

Complaints about the 'servant problem' surfaced. 'I am a Model Mistress but where are the Model Maids?' said an anonymous journalist in 1947, complaining of ignorance, laziness and surliness in her rapid-turnover of household help.[31] The Irish Housewives Association, the veteran feminist Louie Bennett, the Commission on Youth Unemployment (1951) and the Commission on Emigration (1956) all proposed reform – that domestic service be developed as 'a vocation and a social service' (Bennett's phrase) with proper hours, pay scales, training, and time off; that what was needed was government regulation and better mistress-servant relationships (the IHA); and the Commission on Emigration proposing that 'middle-class families' be subsidised to employ servants.[32] Ruaidhri Roberts pointed out in a reservation to the report that if any families were to be subsidised in this way these should be hard-pressed working-class mothers.[33]

The speed with which females deserted domestic service in the 1940s is an indication of their loathing of it. The rationing, privation and even physical danger, of wartime and post-war Britain was preferable to domestic service in Ireland. Those well-meaning reformers who suggested calling domestic servants 'houseworkers' and giving them status, good pay rates, a recognisable uniform and good time off,[34] had gone into denial on this subject. Women just did not want to work long hours 'on call' in other peoples' houses anymore. So if we are talking about women being more confined to the 'domestic sphere' in de Valera's Ireland, we have to be very specific about what women and whose domestic sphere we are talking about. It is conceivable that the inability to hire paid help caused some middle-class women to curtail their activities outside the house – paid work or voluntary work or even political campaigning. If these women were being confined more to their domestic sphere as a result, other women were foregoing the domestic sphere as a site of unpopular work, in favour of other kinds of work which gave them more independence, and, perhaps, greater opportunity to acquire a domestic sphere under their own authority eventually.

THE CHANGING FARM FAMILY

Contested authority over the workspace that was the house/home was also a factor in women's leaving of the land in these years. The sharp decline in the number of females assisting relatives on farms, evident in the census figures, happened mainly between 1936 and 1951, though some decline was already underway since 1926 and Joanna Bourke's research would indicate that the leaving of the land by females in the twentieth century was the culmination of a process which began with the agricultural modernisation of the 1890s.[35] The destination of most of these assisting relatives was either England or education (depending on the size of the farm); more girls were being kept on at secondary school from the mid-1940s, particularly girls from farms.[36] These would then get jobs in the civil service or other white-collar work, or shop service.

Looking at census figures and at emigration statistics early on in my research, I was tempted to believe that the departure of sisters, sisters-in-law, daughters and other relatives, must have been a tragedy for the women in rural Ireland left behind, bereft of help and company. However, personal testimony and other sources like the Limerick Rural Survey, Commission on Emigration, and writings in, for example, the *Irish Countrywoman*, rapidly disabused me of that notion.[37] There seems to have been fierce resistance on the part of the woman of the house to the presence of another woman in the house, particularly among those who married from the mid-1940s. A mother-in-law was bad enough, but a sister-in-law (or even one's own sister) was not to be tolerated: the nuclear or at least only vertically extended farm family became the desired norm and the uninheriting daughter or sister (or son/brother) had, in most cases, to go in search of paid work, in Britain or in towns and cities.

Can female emigration or migration, be seen as an improvement for the individual woman? Again, it depends on what women we are talking about. What seems to have been a growing insistence of women (in general) on marital privacy, has to be seen as one of the reasons extra women were not wanted on the farm – and very often it was the 'extra woman's' own adherence to an ideal of a higher standard of living, her aspirations to a well-paid job and financial independence, and perhaps eventually, a companionate 'private' marriage for herself, which gave her the final push out. At least, this is what all the evidence from the period suggests.

SAFER MOTHERHOOD

It was not just that the single females were choosing – or being forced to choose – paid work and eventually, companionate marriage or fulfilled singlehood above assisting subsistence, but that there was less need for single girls and women in the household economy (urban and rural) as time went on. The gradual decline in maternal mortality and general improvement in women's health was one reason for this. One of the forgotten casualties of maternal mortality was the oldest daughter or youngest sister/sister-in-law of the woman who died, often had to give up any career or marital plans she might have had, to rear her siblings/nieces and nephews. An examination of the ages of single females 'engaged in home duties' over these years shows a marked decline in those who were in their teens or early twenties.

Article 41.2 conflated the terms 'woman' and 'mother' which might lead one to conclude that single women had a very low status in these years but again, we must beware of taking constitutional recommend- ations as reflections of reality, and there is an argument for seeing these two decades as ones of dawning freedom and improved status for single women. Late marriage age meant that many women who eventually mar- ried would spend between a third and a half of their lives single.

When all the risks of older childbearing are taken into account it might seem at first surprising that in this era of later marriage the numbers of women dying in childbirth fell significantly. In 1932, 256 women died in childbirth; in 1948, 104.[38] Death in childbirth was an agonising death for the woman and a tragedy for husband and children. If the fact that all these changes, agonies, sacrifices, miseries and disruptions became con- siderably less probable for married and single women during the years 1932–48 cannot be seen as an improvement in women's lives, then it is hard to know what can. Up to the mid-1930s, between a quarter and a third of women who died in childbirth died of puerperal sepsis, or puer- peral fever, as it was also called. This was a fatal infection which could set in hours or days after a perfectly normal delivery. Medical historian Irvine Loudon remarks that it dogged the footsteps of the cleanest and most careful birth attendants.[39]

The year 1936 saw a revolution (in the parts of the world touched by western medicine) in the treatment of puerperal sepsis, with the intro- duction of sulphanomide drugs, and the numbers began to fall quite dra- matically. That was the first improvement. The third was the introduc- tion of a comprehensive, free countrywide maternity scheme in 1953.[40] However there was also a second improvement – a fall, particularly in 'other maternal mortality ' from about 1942 (see Appendix 1). The aver- age maternal deaths per year between 1933–41 were 209; between 1942– 51, 140. Most deaths in childbirth other than those from puerperal sepsis, happened as a result of toxaemia, or from haemorrhage (see Appendix 2).[41] Toxaemia is associated with either poor nutrition and/or stress. Haemorrhage is much more likely to be fatal in a woman who is under- nourished or deficient in iron, and a survey carried out by two Dublin obstetricians, Drs Fearon and Dockeray, in 1939, of a number of pregnant wives of unemployed men, found that all were anaemic and the major- ity did not get enough protein.[42]

What happened in the early 1940s to bring down maternal mortal- ity? A simple comparison of the maternal mortality figures for 1936 with those of 1950 shows that an almost identical proportion of maternal deaths at either date took place in hospital, so greater hospitalisation was not the reason for this decline in maternal mortality.[43] Hospitals, apart from specialised maternity hospitals – the three in Dublin, the Erinville in Cork, Lourdes in Drogheda, Bedford Row in Limerick – were not necessarily equipped for midwifery in any case, often having simply a ward of the hospital devoted to maternity cases, good nursing care but not necessarily enough midwives or doctors skilled in midwifery.[44] In the 1940s many people still harboured what was, given these conditions, quite a reasonable fear of hospitals, from Mary Healy in Kilkenny to the Dublin artisans' wives interviewed by Alexander Humphreys in the late 1940s.[45]

Even though sulphanomide drugs had been developed to combat puerperal sepsis, women very often did not have access to these drugs, the problem of wartime shortages of the drug being compounded with the fact that many women still gave birth without midwives, or doctors. There was a shortage of midwives in Ireland in the early 1940s, as many were attracted to better pay and conditions in Britain by newspaper advertisements.[46] From 1933 it was illegal for untrained persons to assist at childbirth, but a handywoman or relative was often the only attendant available right into the 1940s.[47]

Something else must have been happening to reduce maternal mortality. Certainly, more women were attending ante-natal clinics from one year to the next, where such facilities existed,[48] but they were not universal – this implies growing awareness of the need for some kind of care. As late as 1956, however, 28% of the women who delivered in Holles Street hospital in Dublin had received no ante-natal care whatsoever.[49] So the perceptible, if small, decline in maternal mortality in the 1940s must be due to factors other than those to do with midwifery facilities. An improvement in nutrition, offering women greater protection from maternal death, would seem to be the only possible reason, however unlikely this might seem in the desperate Emergency years. The free pint of milk for pregnant women introduced by the government during the Emergency might have had some effect on mothers' health,[50] and two other important sources of financial aid would have been remittances from Britain, and the introduction of children's allowances in 1944. Children's allowances were conceived of as a subsidy to breadwinner incomes, and payable to the head of the household, usually, except in the case of a widow, the father.[51] However, the father could sign for the mother to collect this payment, and this seems to have been what happened in many cases.[52]

In any case, this extra income seems to have had an almost immediate effect on women's health and nutrition. Money sent home from England, from about 1940, is remembered by people as far apart as John Healy in Mayo and Frank McCourt in Limerick city as having brought about a big change in the spending power of the small farming/working-classes. Emigration of some family members would also have eased pressure on slender resources at home.[53] The improvement in mothers' health was not dramatic and according to the National Nutrition Survey carried out in the 1940s and published in the early 1950s, the more children in a family, the poorer a mother's nutrition.[54] Still, the maternal mortality rate went from 4.98 in 1932 to 1.88 in 1948; a decline which, according to Loudon, compares well with other countries. If poverty and want are the major maternal killers,[55] a significant step was already being taken towards the reduction of maternal mortality before 1953.

I haven't discussed the ban on contraception in 1935 because this was not an issue taken on by women's organisations in these years, and this discussion is focused on the relationship between the public issues and what was actually happening. 'Reproductive rights' as defined today were an unknown concept in the western world in general of the 1930s and 1940s, when the flip side of the reproductive freedom of the rich and powerful was often the coercive sterilisation of the poor, powerless and 'racially unfit' – and not just in fascist countries.[56] Support for birth control or 'voluntary motherhood' in Europe in the 1930s, 1940s and 1950s was sometimes clouded by association with eugenicism.[57] One of the addenda to the Emigration Report which dissented from the main report's encouragement of large families, did so on chillingly eugenic grounds.[58]

However, the main report and Dr Cornelius Lucey's Minority Report, also chillingly dismissed the discomforts, dangers and chronic bad health (well-documented at this stage) risked by 'grande multiparas' – women with large numbers of children – without even discussing them.[59] Cormac Ó Gráda has uncovered some Irish correspondence to Marie Stopes, which prompts many questions about women's own attitudes to the issue of pregnancy prevention.[60] I did not, in the personal testimony I sought, find any sense of grievance at constant pregnancy but plenty of complaints about conditions surrounding childbirth and childrearing. Mary Healy, an ex-domestic servant married to a county council worker who had six children in the 1940s, states: 'I never considered the rearing of my family a burden' but confesses she found it a great financial strain.[61] This is not to say that others shared her opinion. This entire area needs its own very sensitive and thorough historian. We must never forget that many married women in Ireland in the 1930s and 1940s did not have any choice about pregnancy, that this lack of choice sometimes cost them their lives or their health.

In conclusion, I would argue that 'de Valera's Ireland' was a period when Irish women's lives changed significantly, often for the better, especially at the lower income levels. Women's work and authority in the domestic sphere or spheres was so diverse and changed so significantly in these years that it is difficult to speak generally about 'women' and the 'domestic sphere'. We could be talking about farm women (on big, little or small farms, on good or bad land) and if farm women, the woman of the house or the assisting relative; domestic servants or domestic servants' employers, urban middle, lower-middle or working-class women and if working-class, women living in dwellings with or without an indoor water supply, women in towns whose husbands were in England, women on small farms whose husbands were in England, single women going out to work or staying at home, married women staying at home or going out to work. The improvements in housing in this period also, arguably, lightened women's burden of work: an average of 12,000 local authority houses a year were built 1932–42.[62] Whatever the social disadvantages of the new housing estates it cannot be denied that a single standard of housing was being slowly established in this period, and tenements/slums increasingly seen as shameful. The implications for women's household work were enormous and nobody who spoke or wrote to me about it, was in any way nostalgic for the old ways.[63]

The problem with Eamon de Valera's vision of women in Ireland was that he envisaged a single recognisable 'domestic sphere' and idealised it in an opportunistic way to justify having introduced some gender-specific labour legislation. The fact that he had to justify is itself important. One could argue that he did go some way toward realising the promise implicit in article 41.2 when he introduced Children's Allowances but these were officially paid to fathers of families/breadwinners and explicitly intended to bolster the father's position, as the correspondence and debate on whether to pay the mothers or the fathers shows.[64] The fact that they were collected by mothers, for the most part, and understood by ordinary people as payments to mothers, shows perhaps how out of touch Eamon de Valera was with the Ireland inhabited by most women and men.

Given that women's lives were so different, can we talk about 'women in de Valera's Ireland' at all? We have to, because de Valera and some other public figures who tried to limit women's participation in paid work and public life set this agenda for us. One of the most serious results of their failure to discriminate between different kinds of women is the danger that historians and others looking at the past will take their ignorance as a matter of fact, and assess women in the past as a monolithic group, ignoring their differing, often conflicting, interests.

Better sureshot than scattergun:
Eamon de Valera, Seán Ó Faoláin and arts policy

Brian P. Kennedy

In early 1987, I interviewed Seán Ó Faoláin, a sprightly man in his eighty-seventh year, who walked without the aid of a stick, was well groomed, wore thick-lensed glasses, and expressed strongly-held opinions, offered to me freely and with a good sense of humour. Ó Faoláin told me that 'the artist is a rare bird. There are only about two or three in every generation.' He believed that 'little amounts of money do not create great art. Even big amounts of money do not create great art. The artist is there or he is not there.'[1] This sounds very like the so-called 'bubble up theory' of Charles J. Haughey outlined in the only lengthy interview ever conducted with him on the subject of arts policy.[2] Although Haughey defended the independence of the Irish Arts Council, he stated: 'I don't think you should be too concerned about structures and infrastructures. Art is very much its own thing. It bubbles up unexpectedly here and there ... I don't think you should policy-ise it'.[3]

The development of arts policy in Ireland, as in many countries, has seen a continuing tension between those who believe in fostering conditions for growth in the arts through specific initiatives, like Seán Ó Faoláin and Charles J. Haughey, and those who wish to plan, foster and promote it through co-ordinated government intervention. Clearly the establishment of a Ministry of Arts, Culture and the Gaeltacht in 1992 reflects a different, more centralised and pro-active approach to arts policy. Seán Ó Faoláin's policy as Director of the Arts Council from 1956 to 1959 can be described as 'better sureshot than scattergun'. It was better to target expenditure on particular initiatives than to attempt, with very limited resources, to spread money thinly on a wide range of arts activities.

The Arts Council, or to use its statutory title, An Chomhairle Ealaíon, was established by the Arts Act, 1951, and was, after the Arts Council of Great Britain, only the second such organisation in the world. It is, in effect, a type of quango, a quasi-autonomous non-governmental organisation, and operates the arms-length principle which is supposed to keep it free from political interference. According to the Arts Act, 1951, the arts are 'painting, sculpture, architecture, music, drama, literature, design in industry and the fine arts and applied arts generally'. The first director of An Chomhairle Ealaíon was Patrick J. Little and he worked tirelessly to promote arts activity throughout Ireland. He believed in a type of community arts policy of art for the people and by the people: 'The appeal should be as wide as possible for the benefit of the community as a whole', and he considered that: 'Rural Ireland holds the heart of Ireland and it will not do to confine the Council's activities to urban centres'.[4] The Arts Council's purpose was, in Little's view, 'to stir the spirit of independent artistic functions'.[5]

Some people were cynical about these sentiments coming from a politician. The poet and author Patrick Kavanagh wrote, tongue in cheek, that there had traditionally been 'Four Pillars of Wisdom' in Ireland – 'the Christian Brothers, Croke Park, Radio Iran and the Queen's Theatre'. 'Wearing the cultural smile which withers all life within range of its venom', politicians were now attempting to impart further wisdom:

> Government ministers, not being content to confine their confused discussions to economics and high finance, have recently been adding to their repertoire to gabble matters concerning Irish art and letters. Phrases like 'Irish culture' and 'Irish cultural relations' are beginning to compete with the worn-out and tired references to 'our glorious martyrs'. Men who in a well ordered society would be weeding a field of potatoes or cutting turf in a bog are now making loud pronouncements on art.[6]

There was a degree of truth in the contention that some politicians had questionable motives when using the theme of the arts for speech material. Little was an idealist whose motives were not in doubt. His tendency to philosophise gave him a reputation as a political lightweight. He seemed too sincere for hard-nosed politics. The public relations work involved in launching the Arts Council suited his temperament. He was rarely out of the news during his years as director, opening exhibitions, promoting festivals, pleading for the restoration of historic buildings and lauding the work of amateur arts groups.[7] He was wildly ambitious and the Department of the Taoiseach felt it necessary to keep a close eye on the Arts Council's activities. Dr Nicholas Nolan, assistant secretary in the department, telephoned the Council's office at least once each week to receive a progress report.[8] He was concerned especially that the Council should be known by its legal title 'An Chomhairle Ealaíon'. This created a practical problem because 'a great many people did not know where to look for the telephone number in the Phone Directory'.[9] People looked for it under 'Arts Council' and found nothing. Dr Nolan gave permission for the additional entry to be made in the telephone book: 'Arts Council – see Comhairle Ealaíon'. This type of bureaucratic ingenuity was typical of the tight control maintained by the Taoiseach's Department. The Arts Council had been foisted on the department whose officials, by their actions, indicated a distrust of the new institution.

By the end of 1952, the Arts Council had spent about £10,000 and the emphasis had been on funding for drama and music groups in accordance with Little's policy. The Taoiseach and his department were not impressed. In their opinion, the Arts Council's main task was the promotion of the visual arts and industrial design. It was decided to call representatives of the Council to a meeting with the Taoiseach on 15 January 1953. An agreed report was prepared in which Eamon de Valera outlined the policies he thought the Council should pursue.[10] From de Valera's point of view, the meeting provided an opportunity to use his influence although he 'stressed the fact that he had no desire to interfere with the discretion of the Council in the exercise of their functions'. His wishes were expressed politely: 'It would be a pity,' he remarked, 'if the Council were to depart from the original intention with regard to their functions.' He thought that music was perhaps a matter for Radio Éireann and the Department of Education. Drama was, in his opinion, much less in need of encouragement than the visual arts and design in industry.

The Taoiseach advised the adoption of two important guidelines. He suggested 'that the Council should exercise special care in regard to any branch of art for which an existing state organisation was catering' (that is, grants should not be given from two state bodies to one organisation). The second guideline in the agreed report read: 'The Taoiseach said that the restoration of the Irish language was not, in itself, a function of the Council, and money was being spent in other directions by the State for this purpose.' The Arts Council followed the Taoiseach's advice literally and refused all future applications for funding of arts activities by Irish language groups.

It may seem surprising that it was Eamon de Valera who established the key guidelines for the Arts Council in its early years. This was due to P. J. Little's direct influence because he was de Valera's trusted advisor on cultural matters. Little represented Waterford County in Dáil Éireann from 1927 to 1954. He was de Valera's parliamentary secretary from 1933 to 1939 before being appointed Minster for Posts and Telegraphs from 1939 to 1948.

Edward MacLysaght thought that de Valera 'almost alone of leading public men in Ireland at the time, was not only sympathetic but positively helpful in promoting cultural endeavours'.[11] In contrast, Mervyn Wall, while acknowledging that de Valera had 'many virtues', has said:

The regrettable thing was that he hadn't the slightest understanding of, or interest in, the arts. He didn't think them important. I remember a public statement of his in which he said that he couldn't see any reason for playing the work of foreign composers in Ireland, as we already had our own beautiful Irish music. When he was in his fifties, he visited the Abbey Theatre to see a play about Saint Francis of Assisi, remarking rather innocently that he had never been in the Abbey Theatre before, a truly remarkable admission.[12]

De Valera's admission was not so remarkable – Cosgrave had admitted in 1924 that he had never been to the Abbey. But how can these two opposing views of de Valera be reconciled?

De Valera certainly viewed the fine arts as a luxury which the country could not afford. In 1928 he said that the country:

had to make the sort of choice that might be open, for instance, to a servant in a big mansion. If the servant was displeased with the kicks of the young master and wanted to have his freedom, he had to make up his mind whether or not he was going to have that freedom and give up the luxuries of a certain kind which were not available to him by being in that mansion … If he goes into the cottage, he has to make up his mind to put up with the frugal fare of that cottage. As far as I am concerned, if I had that choice to make, I would make it willingly. I would say, 'We are prepared to get out of the mansion, to live our lives in our own way, and to live in that frugal manner.'[13]

It is only fair to state that de Valera did not envisage that Irish families should forever be confined to frugal lives in little cottages. In 1932, he told the Dáil: 'If there are hair-shirts at all, it will be hair-shirts all round. Ultimately I hope the day will come when the hair-shirt will give way to the silk shirt all round.'[14]

It is obvious that de Valera would have included the fine arts among 'the luxuries of a certain kind' which had been part of life in the mansion of Anglo-Ireland. The fine arts had been the preserve of the landed gentry for centuries. Orchestral concerts, dance galas and opera were the fashionable recreations of the wealthy ruling class. Fine paintings were seen only on the walls of rooms in the 'big houses'. Therefore, it was believed that the fine arts were not part of native Irish tradition. De Valera knew that it was politically viable to support what were perceived to be native art forms, political dynamite to fund 'non-national' art. The government had to proceed cautiously. It would be some time before the Irish people would regard the fine arts as legitimate recipients of government funds.

De Valera believed in an Irish culture comprising native sports, music, dancing, storytelling, folklore and literature. He would take time to assist cultural endeavour if it was in spirit with his religious and nationalist beliefs. In the task of nation-building, de Valera saw it as essential to promote activities which were rooted in the traditions of the majority of the Irish people. This attitude led to praise from those, like MacLysaght, who emphasised the need for an Irish culture. For others, like Wall, such an introverted attitude was equated with philistinism.

De Valera put political before artistic considerations as Dr George Furlong (Director of the National Gallery of Ireland, 1935–50) found out to his dismay:

> De Valera never came to visit the National Gallery. The only time he requested advice from me was in connection with his Christmas card which was sent to foreign Heads of State. In 1936 I proposed that a new design should be used instead of the stock designs like the Rock of Cashel. I suggested a 'Greetings from Ireland' card with the heraldic shields of the four provinces. Dev's initial reaction was favourable. He thought it looked well but after some discussion he asked me what was the origin of the heraldic designs. I told him they were probably of Norman origin. He immediately cooled on the idea and a stock design was used again that year. I was surprised when the next year, he called me to see him. He asked me did I remember the design I had proposed with the heraldic shields. He thought it would be very appropriate for 1937. The new constitution had laid claim to the four green fields.[15]

In a speech to open Radio Éireann's Athlone station in 1933, de Valera offered a *précis* of the achievements of Irish culture.[16] The speech was no doubt prepared for de Valera but it offered a public declaration of what was considered by officialdom to be significant in Irish cultural history. De Valera praised, first and foremost, the Irish language which was 'one of the oldest and, from the point of view of the philologist, one of the most interesting in Europe.' Next, he referred to 'the tradition of Irish learning' which had been preserved by the monastic and bardic schools; the contributions of Irish ecclesiastics in Louvain, Rome, Salamanca, Paris and elsewhere, the schools of poetry and the hedge schools in the eighteenth century. Despite the Penal Laws, Irish poetry, language and song had flourished. They had provided the roots of modern Irish culture.

De Valera paid a half-tribute to Anglo-Irish literature which 'though far less characteristic of the nation than that produced in the Irish language includes much that is of lasting worth.' He singled out Dean Swift, 'perhaps the greatest satirist in the English language', Edmund Burke 'probably the greatest writer on politics', William Carleton 'a novelist of the first rank', Oliver Goldsmith 'a poet of rare merit', Henry Grattan 'one of the most eloquent orators of his time' and Theobald Wolfe Tone who 'left us one of the most delightful autobiographies in literature'. He noted: 'Several recent or still living Irish novelists and poets have produced work which is likely to stand the test of time.' It is significant that de Valera did not venture to name any of these writers.

Turning to drama, de Valera said: 'The Irish theatre movement has given us the finest school of acting of the present day and some plays of high quality.' He continued, 'Ireland's music is of singular beauty … It is characterised by perfection of form and variety of melodic content … Equal in rhythmic variety are our dance tunes – spirited and energetic, in keeping with the temperament of our people.'

The speech then progressed to even more sweeping generalities about Ireland's mission in the world:

> The Irish genius has always stressed spiritual and intellectual rather than material values. That is the characteristic that fits the Irish people in a special manner for the task, now a vital one, of helping to save western civilisation. The great material progress of recent times, coming in a world where false philosophies already reigned, has distorted men's sense of proportion; the material has usurped the sovereignty that is the right of the spiritual.

De Valera concluded:

> You sometimes hear Ireland charged with a narrow and intolerant nationalism, but Ireland today has no dearer hope than this: that, true to her own holiest traditions, she may humbly serve the truth and help by truth to save the world.

Translated into practical politics, de Valera's remarkable idealism meant that the arts were to be encouraged when they observed what he termed 'holiest traditions'. It was quite proper that they should be censored when they failed to live up to this ideal. As for state involvement in the arts, de Valera believed that: 'It is much better to proceed quietly and to try to get results by stimulating the endeavour of private individuals and organisations'.[17] He was a 'bubble-up theorist', and was anxious to encourage the cultural life of the nation but reluctant to involve or add to the machinery of the state. He generally supported the arts initiatives of his colleagues in government but he preferred when their suggestions made no call on public funds. In conclusion, it can be stated that de Valera considered the arts to be desirable but he had little personal interest in them.

P. J. Little's Fianna Fáil background meant that in December 1956, when the first Arts Council's five year term was complete, the Taoiseach, John A. Costello, did not intend to reappoint him and set about finding a successor. Costello first turned to his own arts advisor, Thomas Bodkin, who had written a highly critical report on the arts in Ireland, at Costello's request, in 1949. Bodkin declined the offer and informed Costello that: 'the reason is simple … Paddy Little and his colleagues have quite obviously made the Arts Council a body which no one takes seriously.' Little had made the Council 'mainly a conduit for subsidising minor and purely local activities, many of which could scarcely be called artistic in the most liberal use of the word'. He concluded: 'Were I a dictator I should have no hesitation in sacking the lot.'[18] Costello was disappointed but set about finding a replacement who was actively involved in the arts. His son, Declan, and his son-in-law, Alexis Fitzgerald, put forward Seán Ó Faoláin's name.[19] John A. Costello did not know Ó Faoláin,[20] but Bodkin agreed that the writer would make an excellent candidate for the position. The Catholic Archbishop of Dublin, John Charles McQuaid, thought otherwise. Ó Faoláin's reputation was that of a rebel, an anti-establishment figure who had often disagreed publicly with the archbishop. Bodkin pleaded Ó Faoláin's case to McQuaid:

> I knew he had gone off the tracks from a religious point of view but I had been informed within the last year that he was safely back in the fold and I knew that he stayed with the Oratorians in Birmingham who thought well of him while he was working on his recent book about Newman … If he were appointed I believe that he would feel put upon his mettle to justify that trust and to make some worthwhile concern of the Arts Council which has failed so lamentably to be of use since its inception. If he is not appointed at this stage there is a danger that he might be tempted to run amok and do damage by spreading the belief that his appointment has been practically made but frustrated at the last minute by some extra-governmental influence.[21]

The Taoiseach also wrote to the archbishop:

> I considered the present nominee because of the feeling that artists and writers have got no support in Ireland from an Irish government. I think the present opportunity is a good one and while I cannot expect your grace's blessing, I feel sure I will have your prayers.

Dr McQuaid was determined however, and paid a visit to Government Buildings where he spent over an hour with the Taoiseach and Professor Bodkin, 'trying', he noted, 'to prevent Ó Faoláin's nomination by persuading Bodkin to take the job.[22] Bodkin refused and the archbishop told Costello: 'I can only hope the nominee will not let you down.'[23] Dr McQuaid explained to Bodkin in a letter:

> You will allow me to say how sorry I am that we cannot have a genuine expert, on whose direction and life experience we could very confidently rely. We shall stumble on, in the semi-gloom of minds that have never been disciplined from youth and that have not matured in the tranquillity of assured knowledge. At best, you will advise, and I hope, strongly.[24]

Costello appointed Ó Faoláin as Director of the Arts Council on 21 December 1956, having chosen to ignore the archbishop's foreboding which proved to be entirely unfounded. It was anticipated that, compared to

Little's gentlemanly style of directorship, Ó Faoláin's approach would be sharper and more unorthodox. His term of office was five years and remuneration was £1,000 per annum. The post was part-time and he was to 'devote to the office so much of his time as may be necessary adequately to discharge his functions and duties as director'.[25] This suited Ó Faoláin, who wished to maintain his lecturing commitments in America as well as his career as a writer. He had been appointed director of a distinguished Council whose members were Sir Alfred Chester Beatty, Dr Thomas McGreevy, John Maher, Niall Montgomery, Very Rev. Donal O'Sullivan, SJ, The Earl of Rosse, Muriel Gahan, Sir Basil Goulding, Dr Richard Hayes and Dr G. A. Hayes McCoy.

The day after Ó Faoláin's appointment, the *Irish Times* offered the following assessment of the first Arts Council's achievement:

> It would be very difficult to say just what the Arts Council has done – what positive contribution it has made to the cultivation of artistic taste in Ireland – during the first five years of its life … If it has not built theatres, or enriched civic museums and shown itself a beneficent patron – how could it, with the microscopic sum at its disposal? It has done much in a quiet way to inculcate an acquaintance with the liberal arts, especially in the provinces, where it is most needed.[26]

There would be widespread regret, the editorial continued, at the retirement of Paddy Little who had 'shown himself a pleasant and discreet director, and a welcome speaker at dozens of public functions concerned with the Council and its activities.'

Seán Ó Faoláin, warming to his new appointment, wrote a letter to the *Irish Times* to say that it was not at all difficult to say what the Arts Council had done.[27] If people looked through the Council's annual reports, they 'would be astonished by the amount of practical encouragement given to the arts in the past five years'. In Ó Faoláin's opinion, it was:

> an open question whether the Arts Council, far from not doing enough, may not have attempted too much with so small a budget. To bestow patronage on everybody actively concerned in painting, music, drama (amateur and professional), sculpture, literature, design in industry, and the fine arts and applied arts generally, could absorb anything up to £1,000,000 per annum; and we have only £20,000 …. Perhaps it might be wiser for us to concentrate on things of the first rank, in order to establish standards of excellence. I mention it only because it is a question of future policy.

It was courageous that the new director should raise such an important question in a newspaper before it had been discussed by the Council. With a few exceptions, the membership of the second Council was the same as its predecessor. Ó Faoláin's suggested policy ran counter to the established strategy of operating 'on a nation-wide basis by spending small sums in scattered parts of the country.'[28] He explained his views in a letter to Bodkin:

> Clearly the Council has dissipated a good deal of its energy on activities which, however laudable when taken in isolation … become questionable when considered as part of an over-all policy. If the policy has been that of a very long-term cumulative effect, intended to be achieved by more-or-less minor isolated and sporadic bursts of activity all over the country, I do not believe in it at all … My misgiving is that I virtually inherit the Council which for five years developed this policy. I should have asked the Taoiseach for a wholly new Council. As it is I shall have to be very tactful or else very ruthless. I shall try the first.

Ó Faoláin then made the remarkable admission:

> I am (odd thing for me to say in my present situation) not at all sympathetic to the principle of state support for artists, except on the really grand scale, e.g., Czarist patronage of the ballet, or the establishment of the Comédie Française, or the foundation of Galleries, or conservatoires of Music, or even Academies of Letters, or Science – in short only where the ordinary energies of commerce and enterprise and public spirit cannot apply.[29]

It was bizarre that the director of the Arts Council was at best lukewarm about the existence of a state agency to assist the arts. Ó Faoláin was correct in anticipating resistance to his views by Council members. The Earl of Rosse suggested:

> To a large extent I think that we should continue to be guided by local demand for our support, to encourage local initiative and enterprise subject of course to the essential provision that we are satisfied as to the standards in each case. For one thing it seems to me right in principle to foster individual efforts throughout the country, rather than to give directions from above; and for another we are bound by the smallness of our grant to keep our own expenditure to a minimum.[30]

Dependence on local demand was far too haphazard a policy for Ó Faoláin to accept. He wanted the Council to plan its future development and to cease being purely reactive. After considerable debate, a compromise standing order was agreed at the Council meeting of 6 March 1957. It read: 'Future policy, while not failing to encourage local enterprise, would insist on high standards'.[31]

Ó Faoláin was frequently amazed by the dearth of official support for the arts. In July 1957, for example, he was so irritated by the failure of the Department of Education to adequately finance the National Museum and the National Gallery that he sought a meeting with the minister, his fellow Corkman, Jack Lynch. The meeting took place on 8 August 1957 and Ó Faoláin gave the Council's view that sales counters should be established in the Museum and Gallery to sell publications, small-scale replicas and postcards, and that 'any profits accruing therefrom shall revert to the Gallery and Museum for further developments of a like nature.'[32] He expressed 'in the strongest possible way, dismay at the lamentable paucity of publications at present on sale in the National Museum'. He drew attention 'even more forcibly still' to the situation at the National Gallery where a director and a registrar administered the Gallery with no other help.

The miserable response of the public to certain Arts Council initiatives was also something Ó Faoláin had to accept. In 1958, the Council decided to sponsor a scheme for the design of a Christmas card, the winning design to be used by the Council at Christmas that year. The competition was advertised widely but only twenty-five applicants submitted designs and none was considered of sufficient merit for use by the Council.[33] A useful initiative that met with modest success was the 50/50 purchase of pictures scheme. The Council agreed in January 1958 that it would fund half the cost of any one painting purchased in any one year by a local authority, provided that the Council approved of the painting, and that it was exhibited in a public place.[34] The response was slow but the scheme encouraged local authorities to set aside even minimal funding for the purchase of original works of art. Ó Faoláin's combative nature was given full vent in May 1959 when the Arts Council took the decision to recommend none of the paintings in the annual Royal Hibernian Academy exhibition for inclusion in the 50/50 purchase scheme. The RHA was incensed by what seemed a slur on the quality of their members' work and a lively debate began in the letters column of the *Irish Times*,[35] and in the Dáil chamber during question time on 9 June 1959. The artist Seán Keating took particular issue with Ó Faoláin's defence of the Council's decision.

Just as during P. J. Little's directorship, Ó Faoláin entered into a tussle with Dr Nicholas Nolan about the use of the English title 'The Arts Council' as against 'An Chomhairle Ealaíon'. This sort of argument seems petty perhaps, but it was a sensitive issue at the time. In March 1958, the Council launched a Package Design Scheme to try to improve the quality of industrial packaging. In the competition advertisements, the Council's English title was printed in larger letters than the statutory Irish title and Dr Nolan was quick to spot the transgression. Ó Faoláin was irritated and argued the case with Dr Nolan but the civil servant insisted correctly but pedantically that 'there is no statutory provision for an English translation of that title.'[36]

There can be no doubt that Ó Faoláin's view of what constituted the arts was a more rarified one than that of P. J. Little. Ó Faoláin, for instance, sought to exclude traditional Irish dancing and folk dancing from the Arts Council's remit and a delightful piece of English law was cited in favour of this opinion. The judgement of 27 July 1955 in the British Court of Appeal stated, relative to folk dancing:

> Folk dancing was not one of the fine arts: since the fine arts, although construed more widely than formerly and including music and perhaps poetry, eloquence and ballet dancing, did not include recreational dancing such as ballroom dancing, and folk dancing as practised was dancing for the enjoyment of those practising it as opposed to a form of artistic expression giving aesthetic satisfaction to those perceiving it.[37]

In a Canute-like stance in December 1957 Ó Faoláin wrote to the Department of the Taoiseach on behalf of the Arts Council deploring the proposal to establish commercial television in Ireland and 'respectfully begged the Taoiseach to reconsider the matter.[38] By 1957, it was estimated that there were already 25,000 television sets in the Republic of Ireland.[39] The reasons given by Ó Faoláin against the introduction of commercial television in Ireland are worth citing in full:

> 1. Commercial television cannot be considered to be Irish television as long as a great many if not the great majority of its programmes are – as they are morally certain to be – for reasons of cost, imported programmes initially manufactured for and governed by the tastes and standards of audiences outside Ireland.

> 2. It is to be borne in mind in this connection that for reasons of self-concern, commercial interests tend unscrupulously to relate the cultural level of the majority of programmes to the tastes and standards of the most undeveloped mass-audiences.

> 3. It follows that in commercial television not only does self-interest, of its nature, over-ride cultural values for the sake of appealing to mass-audiences but, in doing so, produces a proportionate and progressive vulgarisation of public taste as a whole.

> 4. That the establishment of commercial television here, far from diminishing the influence of television from elsewhere – not to speak of eliminating it – will on the contrary by increasing the habit of televiewing among the public make this influence more and more widespread.

> 5. That any really effective control of the objectionable features inherent in commercial or commercial sound-broadcasting has been proved by experience to be impracticable.

In view of the foregoing the Arts Council believes that no system of commercial television should receive the sanction and practical support of an Irish government.

Given such a negative attitude, the Council should not have been too surprised when it was not asked to join the Television Commission established by the government on 10 April 1958. The Council felt itself snubbed and sent the Commission its resolution against commercial television, and finally had the resolution published in all the national newspapers on 29 June 1959.

In a further emphasis on the policy of 'high standards', Ó Faoláin directed the Council away from sponsorship of amateur dramatic activity. There were over 850 drama groups in Ireland,[40] and he judged that the Council's grant was needed for other purposes. The Council advised the Amateur Drama Council of Ireland that, in future, it would advance amateur dramatic activity by sponsoring courses for producers rather than performances by local groups. Ó Faoláin felt that professional dramatic activity was capable of operating without the Arts Council's support. This was debatable. Although the Dublin Theatre Festival was launched successfully in 1957 without an Arts Council grant, brave ventures like the Pike Theatre, Dublin's best-known little theatre of the 1950s, fought a hand-to-mouth existence before final extinction for want of a subsidy.

Ó Faoláin's priority was to provide Irish people with opportunities to see, read and hear the work of renowned artists, poets, writers and musicians. Concerts by the Vienna Philharmonic Orchestra, the London Symphony Orchestra, and Yehudi Menuhin, were sponsored by the Arts Council. In the winter of 1958/9 selected art experts and writers were invited to participate in a lecture series titled 'The Artist and his Milieu'. The initial guest list of speakers drawn up largely by Seán Ó Faoláin included Albert Camus, Mies van der Rohe, Tennessee Williams and Salvador Dali. The lecturers who finally came were distinguished but not quite such major names – Rene Huyghe, Pierre Emmanuel, Felix de Nobel, John L. Sweeney, Angus Wilson and Gabriel Marcel – and they addressed audiences at the Royal Hibernian Hotel, Dublin, and the Imperial Hotel, Cork. The lecture series became something of a social event but its usefulness was questionable because some of the speakers had either poor English or none at all.[41] Ó Faoláin should not have expected Irish audiences to understand French. The exercise therefore created a sense of exclusivity, the opposite of that stimulated by Little's more indiscriminate policy.

Ó Faoláin's challenge to civil servants in order to win greater independence for the Arts Council continued concerning the appointment of a successor to the Council's secretary, Dr Liam O'Sullivan, who decided reluctantly in April 1957 to leave the Council to take up the higher paid post of Keeper of the Art and Industrial division in the National Museum. Although the Council was statutorily empowered to select a new secretary, Dr O'Sullivan explained to Ó Faoláin that de Valera, who had recently replaced Costello as Taoiseach, had his own views on the matter. Dr O'Sullivan wrote:

> At Dr Nolan's request I had an interview with him last evening in the Department of the Taoiseach about the position of secretary. He said to me that the Taoiseach would be glad if the Council would consider favourably the appointment of the present director of the government Information Bureau, as the next secretary. His position had become redundant there.[42]

Ó Faoláin was indignant and made his feelings known to Dr Nolan. After three difficult weeks, the Taoiseach and his department finally relented. Dr Nolan excused the Taoiseach's indiscretion by suggesting that it was thought that the Council 'in recruiting a secretary, might be looking for a public relations officer.' The director was 'now free to look around' for a suitable secretary.[43] Ó Faoláin had someone in mind. He sent a telegram to Mervyn Wall, author and broadcaster, who was on holidays in Roundstone, County Galway: 'Would you be willing, if invited, to accept this post?'[44] Wall travelled back to Dublin for an interview with Ó Faoláin, and two other Council members, John Maher and Dr Hayes. He was the only candidate invited to apply for the post and, predictably, the Council 'had no hesitation in recommending him.'[45] He took up his new position on 1 July 1957.

Ó Faoláin's Council followed up this little victory by rejecting representations from the Taoiseach, the Minister for Education and several other politicians, on behalf of a young musician who had applied for an Arts Council grant to help her to take up a place at the Royal College of Music, London. The Taoiseach felt that the case appeared to be 'worthy of further consideration by An Chomhairle Ealaíon'.[46] The Council decided to stand firm and reiterated its refusal to accept applications by individuals for grant aid. Ó Faoláin supported this policy and was determined to quash political pressure in order to guarantee the Council's independence.

In the autumn of 1958, the Department of the Taoiseach asked the Arts Council to reduce the grant which had been awarded to the Wexford Festival because the tourist board, Bord Fáilte, was also funding it. Having spurned political interference, Ó Faoláin decided it was time to seriously challenge Dr Nolan. He wrote:

> It would help in this matter if you would be so good as to explain to them in what manner their decision to grant the original sum to the Wexford

Festival runs contrary to the Arts Act, 1951, as it may conceivably occur to some members of the Council that the Arts Council is entitled to spend the grant made to the Council 'for such purposes connected with their functions as in their discretion they think fit.'[47]

Dr Nolan was not to be easily outdone. He reminded Ó Faoláin that the Council's decision to fund the Wexford Festival 'was expressly qualified by the Council as being "subject to the approval of the Taoiseach".'[48] Ó Faoláin refused to be made the victim of his own words. He replied to Nolan:

The point at issue was not whether the Taoiseach's approval should be sought in the matter. The issue was the Taoiseach's power in the light of the Arts Act, 1951, to determine how much the Council should offer to the Wexford Festival.[49]

Dr Nolan was forced to agree that while it was for the Taoiseach to decide the amount of the Arts Council's annual grant-in-aid, the Council did not require the Taoiseach's approval to spend it.[50] He advised that in future the Council should seek the Taoiseach's approval only in relation to proposals involving the employment and conditions of Council staff which, under the Arts Act, required it. Having clarified the position, Dr Nolan sensibly relaxed the level of supervision of the Council's activities and allowed it to get on with its business.

The Council realised that Ó Faoláin's hard-nosed style paid dividends and authorised him 'to pursue a policy of protesting privately or publicly against unsightly public buildings, erections, hoardings or street furniture.'[51] Ó Faoláin was concerned particularly about roadside advertising hoardings which were transforming Irish roads into American-style 'billboard alleys'. Ogden Nash wrote a pertinent little poem on this theme: 'I think that I shall never see/a billboard lovely as a tree/Indeed, unless the billboards fall/I'll never see the trees at all'.

Ó Faoláin applied his campaign to three separate industries – petrol and oil, beer and spirits, and tobacco.[52] He began with the petrol and oil companies and asked that, for aesthetic, scenic and tourist reasons, they should refrain from erecting advertisements on roadside hoardings. Representatives of all the companies involved were invited to a meeting and, to Ó Faoláin's surprise, they agreed to his proposal. He was less successful with beer and spirits companies who argued that if they did not erect advertisements on the hoardings, their competitors would do so. The tobacco companies advised Ó Faoláin to secure the collective agreement of advertising agencies to withdraw the hoardings.

The campaign was welcomed enthusiastically by journalists who praised the Arts Council for its valuable lead on an important issue.[53] Ad-

Eamon de Valera and Sinead Flanagan on their wedding day in 1910.

Commemoration of the foundation of Rockwell College, 27 December 1925.

The 1932 Disarmament Conference at Geneva. L–R: Eamon de Valera, Senator J. Connolly, Senator Connor Maguire.

© *Examiner Publications (Cork) Ltd*

Eucharistic Congress, 23 June 1932. President Eamon de Valera accompanied by his secretary, P. Walsh and Seán T. O'Kelly, arriving at the Pro-Cathedral.

© *Examiner Publications (Cork) Ltd*

Eamon de Valera arriving in Dun Laoghaire in 1932 following talks with the British government; behind is Frank Aiken, Minister for Defence.

© *Examiner Publications (Cork) Ltd*

President Eamon de Valera opening the Teachers' Summer Course at UCC in 1936.

© *Examiner Publications (Cork) Ltd*

Eamon de Valera visiting Fords and Dunlops, 9 September 1936.

Eamon de Valera in Cobh for the return of the naval facilities from British forces in 1938. Also in the picture are: Lt Viscon, Colonel Brennan, Hugo Flynn, Dr Jim Ryan, Frank Aiken, Kevin Boland, Eoin Ryan, Oscar Traynor, P. J. Ruthledge, Seamus Fitzgerald.

Eamon de Valera and Irish High Commissioner, John Dulanty, at 10 Downing St in London, for talks with Neville Chamberlain, January 1938.

© Examiner Publications (Cork) Ltd

Eamon de Valera replies to Winston Churchill's VE speech, Radio Éireann studios, Dublin, May 1945.

© Examiner Publications (Cork) Ltd

Eamon de Valera opens new Fianna Fáil premises at Grand Parade, Cork, 30 May 1952.
© *Examiner Publications (Cork) Ltd*

Tom Tiernan and President Eamon de Valera at Lansdowne Road, Ireland v Scotland, 25 February 1958.

Eamon de Valera attending the funeral of Tom Hales in Bandon, 2 May 1966.

Eamon de Valera and Charles de Gaulle, June 1969.

The funeral of President Eamon de Valera in 1975 in Dublin.

vertising agencies were anything but happy. One of them, Messrs David Allen & Sons, Ltd, threatened to sue the Council on the grounds that the campaign was 'outside the functions of the Arts Council as prescribed in the Arts Act, 1951.'[54] Ó Faoláin sought legal advice which confirmed his view that the Council's action was in line with its statutory functions and was not directed at the business of Messrs Allen & Sons, Ltd, but at preserving 'the natural beauties of the countryside because of the salutary effect on public taste'.[55] The advertising agency decided not to pursue the matter. Although the campaign gained useful publicity for the Arts Council, it did not work. The oil companies honoured their agreement until it became obvious that different advertisers had replaced them and no hoardings had been taken down.[56] The Department of Local Government began to plan new legislation which would include restrictions on hoardings at tourist sites.

There was a clear need for legislation to preserve buildings of architectural significance. The Council played its part in highlighting the issue by entering into a public controversy with the Office of Public Works in protest at the proposed demolition of Georgian houses at nos 2 & 3 Kildare Place, Dublin. Despite the Council's objection, the OPW demolished the buildings.[57] The Council at its meeting on 25 June 1957 approved a draft letter for issue to the press which criticised the OPW strongly. Having considered the wisdom of entering into conflict with another exchequer-financed agency, Ó Faoláin asked the Council not to issue the letter.[58] The Council could not afford to be so openly aggressive when it was pleading for more funds.

It would have been odd if Seán Ó Faoláin and Mervyn Wall had done nothing for the cause of writers, poets and publishers. The Council sponsored an International Book Design Exhibition held at the Technical Institute, Bolton Street, Dublin, in November 1957.[59] Financial support was given to periodicals of literary and cultural merit such as *Irish Writing*, *Studies* and *The Dublin Magazine*. Mervyn Wall proposed that memorial tablets should be placed on buildings throughout the country to commemorate notable artists and writers who had resided in or been associated with them. Ó Faoláin's view was that it was not the Council's job to put up signs saying 'So and so lived here' but only to erect signs which had sculptural or artistic importance in themselves. The Council agreed in principle to the idea of supporting such memorial tablets but it was later decided that it would be more appropriate for Bord Fáilte to implement it.[60] This was done successfully during the 1950s.

It would be incorrect, despite all the activities recorded here, to interpret that Seán Ó Faoláin was an executive director. Mervyn Wall had full responsibility for managing the Arts Council office. Ó Faoláin, in fact, rarely visited it as recorded by Wall:

Dr Ó Faoláin did not ordinarily attend at the Council's offices at all. He was in daily telephonic communication and arranged that he would visit the premises for a half-an-hour on two occasions each week. This was his practice, and he did not use during his tenure of office either a room or even a desk.[61]

Ó Faoláin lectured in the United States for two months in the spring each year and tried to keep in touch with Council business by corresponding with Wall. In April 1958 this arrangement caused a serious problem because the annual accounts could not be passed without the director's signature. Ó Faoláin apologised to Wall: 'I'm sorry about this ... For me the directorship has to be a part-time job, as I made clear to the former Taoiseach and it is in these 2 months that I mainly make the annual income of the O F.s.'[62]

Ó Faoláin was never able to convince himself that the Arts Council's existence was sustainable with minimal funding. In November 1958, two years after his appointment as director, he began to consider resigning from the post. He wrote to Thomas Bodkin:

I have become gravely discouraged by the Arts Council's work. In sum I am obliged to pose to myself and to the Council the blunt question: Can the Arts Act be considered a fully workable Act within the intentions of the Legislature and at a constant level of achievement in accordance with the standards of the Council members, while being permanently endowed with a sum inadequate to implement its terms of reference? By my standards it cannot. [The sum was £20,000 each year during his directorship]. The Council can only do (some) useful work (a) by ignoring large parts of their terms of reference, and (b) by lowering their own personal standards.

This is going to be understood by NOBODY outside the Council and not by everybody in it ... The result is inevitable. So if you hear of my wish to withdraw from an unequal battle do not be surprised.[63]

Bodkin sympathised with Ó Faoláin's predicament. He replied:

The great trouble is, of course, that nobody in Ireland, with the exception of John Costello, and very few others, is prepared to pay more than lip service to the cause of the Arts; a cultivated class in the full sense of the term, has ceased to exist in our country, and the present methods of education are not likely to encourage the growth of one to serve us in the near future. It was made clear to me years ago that the civil servants and the vested interests do not want to touch Art, fine or applied. Yet I would urge you strongly to try and hold on to the directorship of the Council. There is no one but yourself who can fill the position with any credit or utility at the moment.[64]

Ó Faoláin decided that he no longer wanted the position. He let it be known that he intended to resign as director with effect from 1 July 1959. He wished to take up the post of resident Fellow and Lecturer at Princeton University, New Jersey.[65] In the month of his resignation, the Arts Council moved from 45 St Stephen's Green to more spacious premises at 70 Merrion Square, a fine Georgian residence which had been the home of the writer, Joseph Sheridan Le Fanu (1814–73).[66] An exhibition room was opened on 27 October 1959 with a display of modern and antique English silver.[67] The change of premises was an important move and signalled the arrival of the Arts Council as an established institution. It now had a respectable address close to government buildings where it still resides today, and had secured considerable independence thanks to the courage of Seán Ó Faoláin.

Reading and writing

John McGahern

I came to write through reading. It is such an obvious path that I hesitate
to state it, but so much confusion now surrounds the artistic act that the
simple and the obvious may be in need of statement. I think reading and
writing are as close as they are separate. In my case, I came to read through
pure luck.

There were few books in our house, and reading for pleasure was
not approved of. It was thought to be dangerous, like pure laughter. In
the emerging class in the Ireland of the 1940s, when an insecure sectarian
state was being guided by a philistine Church, the stolidity of a long
empty grave face was thought to be the height of decorum and profund-
ity. 'The devil always finds work for idle hands' was one of the warning
catch phrases.

Time was filled by necessary work, always exaggerated: sleep, Gaelic football, prayer, gossip, religious observance, the giving of advice –
ponderously delivered, and received in stupor – civil war politics, and
the eternal business that Proust describes as 'Moral Idleness'. This was
confined mostly to the new emerging classes – civil servants, policemen,
doctors, teachers, tillage inspectors. The ordinary farming people went
about their sensible pagan lives as they had done for centuries, seeing all
this as one of the many veneers they had to pretend to wear, like all the
others they had worn since the time of the druids.

During this time I was given the free run of the Moroney's library.
They were Protestants. Old Willie Moroney lived with his son, Andy, in
their two-storeyed stone house, which was surrounded by a huge orchard and handsome stone outhouses. Willie must have been well into
his eighties then, and Andy was about forty. Their natures were so stress-
free that it is no wonder they were both to live into their nineties. Old
Willie, the beekeeper, with his great beard and fondness for St Ambrose
and Plato, 'the Athenian bee, the good and the wise ... because his words
glowed with the sweetness of honey', is wonderfully brought to life in
David Thompson's *Woodbrook*.

Willie had not gone upstairs since his wife's death, nor had he washed, and he lived in royal untidiness in what had once been the dining-room, directly across the stone hallway from the library, that dear hallway with its barometer and antlered coat rack, and the huge silent clock. The front door, with its small brass plate shaped into the stone for the doorbell, was never opened. All access to the house was by the back door, up steps from the farmyard, and through the littered kitchen to the hallway and stairs and front rooms.

David Thompson describes the Moroneys as landless, which is untrue, for they owned a hundred and seventy acres of the sweetest land on the lower plains of Boyle, itself some of the best limestone land in all of Ireland. The farm was beautifully enclosed by roads which ran from the high demesne wall of Rockingham to the broken walls of Oakport. The Moroneys should have been wealthy. They had to have money to build that stone house in the first place, to build and slate the stone houses that enclosed the farmyard, to acquire the hundreds of books that lined the walls of the library. David Thompson, though, is right in spirit, for Willie and Andy had all the appearance of being landless.

Most of Andy's time was taken up with the study of astronomy. Willie lived for his bees. He kept the hives at the foot of the great orchard. They both gathered apples, stored them on wooden shelves in the first of the stone houses of the farmyard, and they sold them by the bucketful, and seemed glad enough for the half-crowns they received. As a boy, I was sent to buy apples, somehow fell into conversation with Willie about books, and was given the run of the library. There was Scott, Dickens, Meredith and Shakespeare, books by Zane Grey and Jeffrey Farnol, and many, many books about the Rocky Mountains. Some person in that nineteenth-century house must have been fascinated by the Rocky Mountains. I didn't differentiate, I read for nothing but pleasure, the way a boy nowadays might watch endless television dramas.

Every week or fortnight, for years, I'd return with five or six books in my oilcloth shopping bag and take five or six away. Nobody gave me direction or advice. There was a tall slender ladder for getting to books on the high shelves. Often, in the incredibly cluttered kitchen, old Willie would ask me about the books over tea and bread. I think it was more out of the need for company than any real curiosity.

I remember one such morning vividly. We were discussing a book I had returned, drinking tea with bread and jam. All I remember about that particular book was that it was large and flat and contained coloured illustrations, of plants and flowers probably, and these would have interested Willie because of the bees. The morning was one of those still true mornings in summer before the heat comes, the door open on the yard. Earlier that morning he must have gone through his hives – the long grey beard was stained with food and drink and covered his shirt front – and while he was talking some jam fell into the beard and set off an immediate buzzing. Without interrupting the flow of his talk, he shambled to the door, extracted the two or three errant bees caught in the beard, and flung them into the air of the yard.

I continued coming to the house for books after the old beekeeper's death, but there was no longer any talk of books. Andy developed an interest in the land, but, I fear, it was as impractical as astronomy. Because of my constant presence about the house, I was drawn into some of those ventures, but their telling has no place here.

I have often wondered why no curb was put on my reading at home. I can only put it down to a prejudice in favour of the gentle, eccentric Moroneys, and Protestants in general. At the time, Protestants were pitied because they were bound for hell in the next world, and they were considered to be abstemious, honest, and morally more correct than the general run of our fellow Catholics. The prejudice may well have extended to their library. The books may have been thought to be as harmless as their gentle owners. For whatever reason, the books were rarely questioned, and as long as they didn't take from work or prayer I was allowed to read without hindrance.

There are no days more full in childhood than those days that were not lived at all, the days lost in a favourite book. I remember waking out of one such book in the middle of the large living-room in the barracks, to find myself surrounded. My sisters had unlaced and removed one of my shoes and placed a straw hat on my head. Only when they began to move the wooden chair on which I sat away from the window did I wake out of the book – to their great merriment.

Nowadays, only when I am writing am I able to find again that complete absorption when all sense of time is lost, maybe once in a year or two. It is a strange and complete kind of happiness, of looking up from the pages, thinking it is still nine or ten in the morning, to discover that it is past lunchtime; and there is no longer anyone who will test the quality of the absence by unlacing and removing a shoe.

Sometimes I have wondered if it would have made any difference if my reading had been guided or structured, but there is no telling such things in an only life. Pleasure is by no means an infallible, critical guide, W. H. Auden wrote; but it is the least fallible. That library and those two gentle men were, to me, a pure blessing.

A time comes when the way we read has to change drastically or stop, though it may well continue as an indolence or pastime or drug. This change is linked with our growing consciousness, consciousness that we will not live forever and that all human life is essentially in the same fix. We have to discard all the tenets that we have been told until we have succeeded in thinking them out for ourselves. We find that we are no longer reading books for the story and that all stories are more or less the same story; and we begin to come on certain books that act like mirrors. What they reflect is something dangerously close to our own life and the society in which we live.

A new, painful excitement enters the way we read. We search out these books, and these books only, the books that act as mirrors. The quality of the writing becomes more important than the quality of the material out of which the pattern or story is shaped. We find that we can no longer read certain books that once we could not put down; other books that previously were tedious take on a completely new excitement and meaning: even the Rocky Mountains has to become an everywhere, like Mansfield Park, if it is to retain our old affection.

That change happened to me in the Dublin of the 1950s. Again, I think I was lucky. There were many good secondhand bookshops in which one could root about for hours. One book barrow in particular, on a corner of Henry Street, was amazing. Most of the books found there then would now be described as modern classics. How the extraordinary Mr Kelly acquired them we never asked. Those were times when books were discussed in dance halls as well as in bars. It was easy then to get a desk in the National Library. The staff were kind and even would bring rare books on request. There were inexpensive seats at the back of the Gate Theatre, and there were many pocket theatres, often in Georgian basements. Out in Dun Laoghaire there was the Gas Company Theatre where we had to walk through the silent showroom of gas cookers to get to see Pirandellor or Chekhov or Lorca or Tennesee Williams.

The city was full of cinemas. I remember seeing *Julius Caesar* with Gielgud and Brando playing to full houses in the Metropole. At weekends, cinema tickets were sold on the blackmarket. One such blackmarketeer, a pretty girl I knew, showed me a fistful of unsold tickets one wet Sunday night shortly before eight o'clock and said, 'If I don't get rid of some of these soon – and at bloody cost at that – I'll have to let down me drawers before the night is out'. And there was the tiny Astor on the quays where I first saw *Casque d'Dor*, *Rules of the Game* and *Children of Paradise*.

Much has been written about the collusion of Church and State to bring about an Irish society that was insular, repressive and sectarian. This is partly true, but because of the long emphasis on the local and the individual in a society that never found any true cohesion, it was only superficially successful.

I think that women fared worst of all within this paternalistic mishmash, but to men with intellectual interests it had at the time, I believe, some advantage. Granted, we were young and had very little to lose, but the system was so blatantly foolish in so many of its manifestations that it could only provoke the defence of laughter, though never, then, in public. What developed was a Freemasonry of the intellect with a vigorous underground life of its own that paid scant regard to Church or State. Even an obscene book, we would argue, could not be immoral if it was truly written. Most of the books that were banned, like most books published, were not worth reading, and those that were worth reading could be easily found and quickly passed around. There is no taste so sharp as that of forbidden fruit.

This climate also served to cut out a lot of the pious humbug that often afflicts the arts. Literature was not considered 'good'. There was no easy profit. People who need to read, who need to think and see, will always find a way around a foolish system, and difficulty will only make that instinct stronger, as it serves in another sphere to increase desire. In no way can this clownish system be recommended wholeheartedly, but it was the way it was and we were young and socially unambitious and we managed.

The more we read of other literatures, and the more they were discussed, the more clearly it emerged that not only was Yeats a very great poet but that almost single-handedly he had, amazingly, laid down a whole framework in which the indigenous literature could establish traditions and grow. His proud words 'The knowledge of reality is a secret knowledge; it is a kind of death', was for us, socially as well as metaphorically, true.

The two living writers who meant most to us were Samuel Beckett and Patrick Kavanagh. They belonged to no establishment, and some of their best work was appearing in the little magazines that could be found at the Eblana Bookshop on Grafton Street. Beckett was in Paris. The large, hatted figure of Kavanagh was an inescapable sight around Grafton Street, his hands often clasped behind his back, muttering hoarsely to himself as he passed. Both, through their work, were living, exciting presences in the city. I wish I could open a magazine now with the same excitement with which I once opened *Nimbus*: 'Ignore Power's schismatic sect,/Lovers alone lovers protect'. (The same poet could also rhyme catharsis with arses, but even his wild swing was like no other).

When I began to write, and it was in those Dublin years, it was without any thought of publication. In many ways, it was an extension of reading as well as a kind of play. Words had been physical presences for me for a long time before, each word with its own weight, colour, shape, relationship, extending out into a world without end. Change any word in a single sentence and immediately all the other words demand to be rearranged. By writing and rewriting sentences, by moving their words endlessly around, I found that scenes or pictures and echoes and shapes began to emerge that reflected obscurely a world that had found its first expression and recognition through reading. I don't know how long that first excitement lasted – for a few years, I think – before it changed to work, though that first sense of play never quite goes away and in all the most important ways a writer remains a beginner throughout his working life. Now I find I will resort to almost any subterfuge to escape the blank page, but there seems to be always some scene or rhythm that lodges in the mind and will not go away until it is written down. Often when it is written it turns out that there was never anything real behind the rhythm or scene, and it disappears in the writing; other times those scenes or rhythms start to grow, and you find yourself once again working every day, sometimes over a period of several years, to discover and bring to life a world through words as if it were the first and (this is ever a devout prayer) last time. It is true that there can be times of intense happiness throughout the work, when all the words seem, magically, to find their true place, and several hours turn into a single moment; but these occurrences are so rare that they are, I suspect, like mirages in desert fables to encourage and torment the half-deluded traveller.

Like gold in the ground – or the alchemist's mind – it is probably wise not to speak about the pursuit at all. Technique can certainly be learned, and only a fool would try to do without it, but technique for its own sake grows heartless. Unless technique can take us to that clear mirror that is called style, the reflection of personality in language, everything having been removed from it that is not itself, then the most perfect technique is as worthless as mere egotism. Once work reaches that clearness the writer's task is ended. His or her words will not live again until and unless they find their true reader.

Public holidays, commemoration and identity in Ireland, north and south, 1920–60

Brian Walker

Public holidays and commemorations of important anniversaries often reflect the values, secular or religious, of a society. Christmas Day and Easter Monday, for example, have special Christian significance in many countries of the world. May Day is also reserved as a holiday in honour of workers in a number of countries. Some public holidays, however, are specific to particular countries, such as Bastille Day on 14 July in France and Independence Day on 4 July in the United States of America, and often refer to events of significance in the history of these countries. Indeed, most countries mark by way of annual commemoration the anniversaries of important episodes, events or people in their history. On Remembrance Day in Great Britain, for instance, people recall all those British and allied servicemen who died in the two world wars. Whether celebrating the early or recent history of a society, these occasions often help to engender a sense of common purpose and identity, even though there may be differences of opinion about the exact significance of the events being celebrated. In Ireland, however, while Christmas Day and Easter Monday have been celebrated by the vast bulk of the population, this has not been the case with some of the other principal public holidays and acts of annual commemoration.

This chapter looks at how four public holidays or annual commemorative events have been marked in some form or other in both political states in Ireland during the period, 1920–60. The special dates on which these subjects are recalled are as follows: 17 March, when St Patrick, Ireland's patron saint, is commemorated; Easter Sunday, when the Easter Rising in Dublin in 1916 is commemorated; 12 July, when the Battle of the Boyne is celebrated; 11 November, or a Sunday nearest to that date, when people remember those who died in two world wars. Two of these dates mark historical episodes or personalities of antiquity, while the other two commemorate more historical events. We will explore what these commemorations tell us about people's identity and sense of history over this period. Particular attention will be paid to the way in which the respective governments viewed the four commemorations, to the way in which the commemorations were claimed by various groups and to how dominant groups within each state viewed minority groups and opinions. The period dealt with covers the four decades from the creation of Northern Ireland and the Irish state, later the Irish Republic, in the early 1920s until 1960.

In the new Northern Ireland of the early 1920s, the 12 July celebrations which marked the anniversary of the Battle of the Boyne were already an important annual event. Since the 1880s the Orange Order had enjoyed widespread support and these July parades were well attended. The particular importance, however, of this date in the calendar of the new state had not yet been established in the early 1920s. There is evidence that Sir James Craig and the government sought to place some distance between themselves and the Orange movement. In July 1922, Craig was asked in the Northern Ireland parliament to use his influence to have 12 July made a general holiday. He rejected this call and stated: 'In view of the large number of existing statutory holidays, and the fact that the 12th of July has for many years been observed as such, there does not appear to be any necessity to take the action suggested.' Three years later when the matter was raised again in parliament, the Minister of Home Affairs, R. D. Bates, agreed that the date should become a special holiday.[1] In October 1924 ,the cabinet had decided that there was no objection to the proposal but any such measure was postponed until the following year. In August 1925 the cabinet discussed whether the Westminster parliament should be asked to make 12 July a permanent bank holiday or whether this should be done annually by proclamation, and decided to opt for the latter course of action.[2] By the late 1920s, 12 July had become a statutory as well as a general holiday.

There is other evidence that Craig and his fellow ministers tried to downplay links between themselves and the Orange Order in this early period. Craig and most of his cabinet were Orangemen but at this time they took a minor role in the annual July proceedings. On 12 July 1922 Craig spoke at the Belfast demonstrations and described enthusiastically how he and his wife had attended the July celebrations every year since their marriage.[3] In the following year, there was no report of Craig attending the July celebrations and few other ministers spoke from Orange platforms. In July 1923, however, Craig issued a message intended especially for Orange 'brethren' in the USA and Canada, but which was also read at local parades: 'It is our earnest desire to live in peace and amity with the Free State, and to encourage in every way a better understanding between all classes and creeds.'[4] In 1924, there was again no report of

Craig's appearance at the 12 July celebrations. In 1925, he sent apologies from England for his non-attendance and explained his absence as due to the recent death of his brother, although, in fact, his brother had died nearly two weeks before the 12 July anniversary.[5] In 1926, the press noted Craig's apologies for his non-attendance but gave no explanation.[6] During these years few of his prominent colleagues spoke on 12 July platforms. Finally, however, in 1927 Craig made a major speech on 12 July at the demonstration in Belfast and from this time on he and other leading ministers attended and spoke regularly on these occasions.[7]

This picture of limited involvement by the unionist leadership in 12 July proceedings in the early 1920s fits in with other evidence that the government was trying to avoid becoming completely identified with only the Protestant section of the population. Among examples of this are the attempt by Lord Londonderry to establish non-denominational school education and the appointment of a Catholic, Sir Denis Henry (formerly unionist MP for Londonderry South), to the post of Lord Chief Justice of Northern Ireland.[8] These gestures of moderation, however, did not continue, partly because of a lack of nationalist and Catholic co-operation and partly because of ultra-Protestant opposition and concern about unionist unity in the face of political threats from Labour and other groups. When Craig returned to an Orange platform in 1927 it was to take the opportunity to warn against the danger of division in unionist ranks and to justify the government's plan to abolish proportional representation in elections to the Northern Ireland parliament: it is generally accepted that this move was not designed as an attack on nationalists but was an attempt to curtail unionist splinter groups.[9]

From 1927 onwards members of the government used these 12 July parades to espouse their political stance and promote unionist unity. By the early 1930s Craig made a point of attending the 12 July proceedings every year in a different county of Northern Ireland. Clearly, the government was availing of these occasions to their advantage, but matters were not always under their control. Because of the fear of sectarian violence the authorities tried to stop the 12 July demonstrations in Belfast in 1935 but had to back down due to strong Orange opposition. The celebrations that year were in fact followed by nine days of serious rioting in Belfast.[10]

At the July parades during the 1930s, speeches by politicians, clergymen and members ranged over various religious and political subjects. Loyalty to the crown and empire was reaffirmed regularly. In 1933 Craig declared: 'British we are and British we remain'.[11] Protestant principles were upheld and Catholicism was denounced. In 1932 Craig stated: 'Ours is a Protestant government and I am an Orangeman'.[12] Political affairs in the south were often mentioned and the fate of southern Protestants was frequently referred to. Links with the empire were stressed. In 1939 Craig declared that: 'the British empire, and all it stands for, is the sun and air of our existence'.[13] The importance of the 12 July commemorations and the Orange Order for unionists was stressed in a report in the *Northern Whig* on 13 July 1933:

> Throughout people recognised the need for keeping at full pitch the unity and strength of the Order. It has proved in the past the nucleus around which unionism of the province gathered when danger of submission in a nationalist and Roman Catholic dominated Ireland threatened.

The outbreak of war resulted in the curtailment of parades between 1940 and 1942. These restrictions, voluntary in 1940 and mandatory in 1941 and 1942, covered not only the main 12 July processions but also parades before 12 July, including the annual march to a church service at Drumcree, County Armagh, on the Sunday before 12 July.[14] Thereafter the annual 12 July parades resumed, although in a limited form, for the rest of the war.

During the 1940s and 1950s the government and the unionist party remained strongly identified with the 12 July proceedings and the Orange movement. Speeches by Lord Brookeborough during the 1950s referred to IRA attacks and also the greater economic benefits which the north enjoyed compared to the south.[15] Not until the late 1950s and early 1960s did questions begin to emerge from both Orange and unionist circles to challenge the link between the two organisations. On 13 July, 1960 an editorial in the *Belfast Newsletter* referred to the new thinking on these matters and put it down to a more stable political climate in Northern Ireland and better north/south relations. In Brookeborough's last years as prime minister some Orange leaders urged that the religious aspects of the twelfth should be increased at the expense of the political and by the early 1960s fewer prominent politicians were involved in the 12 July proceedings.[16] At the same time, some politicians urged that unionism should not be restricted to Protestants. In July 1960, R. S. Dixon MP, declared that 'civil and religious liberty must be for all sections of the community', while in July 1961, W. M. May MP, stated that 'we must do our best to impress on our Roman Catholic citizens that this order stands for toleration'.[17] Historical ghosts resonated at the Orange demonstration at Bangor, County Down in 1960! A report in the press recounted:

> One of the most unexpected people to turn up at the Bangor demonstration was Michael Collins. When his name was announced over the loudspeakers there was consternation on the faces of the platform party and gathering. But smiles were soon in evidence when it was explained that Michael was a little boy who had got lost.[18]

The first Armistice Day on 11 November 1919, commemorated the end of the First World War, and was widely marked in many parts of Northern Ireland by both nationalists and unionists. Services were held in churches of all denominations. The *Irish Times* described the situation in Belfast on 11 November 1919:

> The Armistice silence was observed in an impressive manner in Belfast. All the tramcars were stopped, and in the large industrial concerns, such as the shipyards and the spinning factories, the workers stopped for two minutes and stood by their machines.'[19]

From the early 1920s, the event was commemorated not only with a two-minute silence and church services, but also with parades to new war memorials. There is evidence that in the early days there were efforts to keep the event open to all sections of the community. At the unveiling of the Enniskillen war memorial in 1922, for example, Protestant and Catholic war orphans laid wreaths.[20] At a ceremony in Ballymena on 11 November 1924, Major General Sir Oliver Nugent who had commanded the 36th (Ulster) division at the Somme, declared that 'the service given by the Ulstermen in the war was not confined to one creed or one denomination; it was given by Ulstermen of all denominations and all classes'.[21] The ceremony for the unveiling of the Portadown war memorial in 1924 involved the Catholic parish priest along with the other clergy, and wreaths were laid by representatives of the Orange Order and the Ancient Order of Hibernians.[22] On 12 November 1924, the *Irish News* reported commemorations in both Northern Ireland and the Irish Free State with the headline 'Brotherhood of bereavement – north and south pause to salute the dead'.

In spite of these comments and inclusive incidents, however, the Armistice Day commemorations became largely linked with unionism. To some extent this arose because of a reluctance in certain Catholic and nationalist quarters to acknowledge the Catholic role in the war. For example, Cardinal Patrick O'Donnell, Catholic Archbishop of Armagh, refused to attend the unveiling of the County Armagh war memorial in 1926.[23] More importantly, many unionists came to see Armistice Day as an occasion for the affirmation of their own sense of Ulster or British identity. As Professor Keith Jeffery has commented: 'For them the blood sacrifice of the Somme was equal and opposite to that of Easter 1916.'[24] At the unveiling of Coleraine war memorial in 1922 Sir James Craig declared that 'those who passed away have left behind a great message to all of them to stand firm, and to give away none of Ulster's soil.'[25] Only Protestant clergy attended the unveiling of the cenotaph at the Belfast City Hall in 1929 and there were no official representatives from the 16th (Irish) Division in which Belfast Catholics had tended to serve.[26]

The government played no direct role in organising events on Armistice Day and speeches were rarely made on the occasion, but the large parades and well-attended services on the day, with army and police involved, were seen by many not only as an expression of grief but also as a mark of the British link among the unionist community. It would be wrong, however, to write off entirely Catholic and nationalist involvement in the Armistice Day commemorations. Catholic ex-servicemen continued to mark the occasion in some places. In Newry, in the 1930s, on Armistice Day ex-servicemen held a parade before making their way to their respective Catholic and Protestant churches for memorial services.[27] During the 1930s Armistice Day wreaths were laid in Belfast for the men for the 16th (Irish) Division and in Derry for the 'Irish Catholic officers and men who fell in the Great War', while at Portadown a wreath was laid for the Connacht Rangers, in which Portadown Catholics had served.[28]

After the Second World War, Armistice Day was replaced by Remembrance Day and held on the Sunday closest to 11 November. Names of those who had served or died in the war were added to existing memorials. Parades and services continued as they had done on Armistice Day, and they remained largely the concern of the Protestant and unionist community. While the government had no formal involvement in these events it was quite common for the prime minister or a cabinet minister to take the salute of ex-servicemen on these occasions. There is little evidence of involvement of Catholic clergy in public ceremonies at cenotaphs or at council services. At the same time we should note that in some places, such as Dungannon, Newry and Sion Mills, parades of Catholic and Protestant ex-servicemen continued to take place as they had done in the 1930s.[29]

The degree of polarisation between the two communities over this commemoration is revealed starkly in a comparison of coverage of these events in Belfast nationalist and unionist papers in the mid-1950s. In 1955 and 1956 the unionist papers, the *Belfast Newsletter* and the *Northern Whig* gave extensive coverage to Remembrance Day in various places in Northern Ireland as well as in London, while the nationalist paper, the *Irish News*, ignored the occasion and carried not a single report on any event connected with the commemoration.[30]

By the early 1900s, St Patrick's Day on 17 March was widely celebrated throughout Ireland, north and south. In 1903 an act of the Westminster parliament made St Patrick's Day a bank holiday, a measure supported by unionist and nationalist MPs. After 1921, St Patrick's Day was still observed in Northern Ireland but on a lower key than in the south where it took on special importance. During the 1920s and 1930s in Northern Ireland the shamrock continued to be worn widely and the day remained a bank holiday when banks, government and municipal offices and schools were closed, although most shops and factories seem to have been un-affected.[31] In Catholic churches St Patrick's Day was an important feast day which was well-attended. The Ancient Order of Hibernians continued to organise demonstrations on this date and nationalist politicians often used the occasion to make speeches. From 1925, the BBC in Northern Ireland commenced an annual series of special St Patrick's day broadcasts.[32]

The Patrician Year of 1932, which marked the anniversary of St Patrick's arrival in Ireland was marked by all the churches. At Saul, the site of St Patrick's first church, the Church of Ireland built a new church while the Catholic Church erected a statue of St Patrick on a nearby hill top. Each of the main denominations took advantage of the occasion to reaffirm its belief that St Patrick belonged exclusively to its tradition.[33] Sporting activities on St Patrick's Day, including the Ulster schools rugby cup, and special theatrical events, dances and dinners, were well attended in the 1920s and 1930s. On 18 March 1939 the *Belfast Newsletter* reported that 'in Belfast and all over the province Ulster folk said goodbye to St Patrick's Day with dances and other entertainments'. Special ceremonies of the trooping of the colour and presentation of the shamrock to Irish regiments remained a tradition (begun by Queen Victoria at the end of her reign). There was, however, no official involvement in or recognition of St Patrick's Day, apart from a number of dinners or dances on the day, organised by the Duke of Abercorn, as governor of Northern Ireland.[34] On the unionist and government side there was no attempt to hold parades or make speeches on 17 March. The speeches of southern politicians on the day denouncing partition or declaring Ireland's attachment to Rome were reported regularly in the northern press and sometimes criticised in editorials but there was no attempt by the government in this period to respond.

After the war, banks and government offices continued to close on St Patrick's Day, while the wearing of the shamrock remained popular and the tradition of presenting it to the Irish regiments abroad continued. Catholic churches still observed it as a special feast day and the Ancient Order of Hibernians organised parades and demonstrations as before. In the late 1940s and early 1950s the Northern Ireland prime minister, Lord Brookeborough, used the occasion of St Patrick's Day to issue public addresses to Ulster people abroad, while members of his cabinet spoke at dinners organised by Ulster associations in Great Britain.[35] By the mid 1950s, however, these attempts to match the political use made of St Patrick's Day by the southern government had mostly ceased. In the late 1950s a government information officer urged the cabinet that it might be wise to 'quietly forget' St Patrick's Day and abolish it as a bank holiday.[36] The suggestion was rejected, but it is clear from newspaper reports in the 1950s that for many people St Patrick's Day was 'business as usual'.

Many schools dropped it as a holiday and shops and businesses remained open.[37] Correspondents in the unionist press denounced the political overtones of the day in the south and elsewhere. One letter on 17 March 1961 stated that 'the day is now chiefly memorable to the average Ulsterman as the day on which repeated threats against his stand for constitutional liberty are pronounced in the Republic and on which Ulster's position is vilified throughout the English-speaking world.'[38]

Nonetheless, it should be noted that there were some in unionist and Protestant church circles who believed that more attention should be given to the event. From the mid-1950s the editorial in the *Belfast Telegraph* often urged that the day should be a full public holiday, a request backed by the Church of Ireland diocesan synod of Down and Dromore.[39] In 1961 a resolution of the Young Unionists' Conference deplored the apathy in Northern Ireland towards St Patrick's Day.[40] In the 1950s the Church of Ireland inaugurated an annual St Patrick's Day pilgrimage and special service at Downpatrick and Saul, which was well attended. Such events were still strongly limited by denominational barriers although small elements of change were occurring. In 1956 the nationalist members of Downpatrick council refused an invitation to participate in a joint wreath-laying ceremony at St Patrick's grave on the grounds that the Catholic Church 'had arranged adequate celebrations for the Feast and they could not add anything to them'. Eight years later, however, when the Archbishop of Canterbury was the special guest at the St Patrick's Day service at the Church of Ireland cathedral in Downpatrick, nationalist councillors turned up to greet the archbishop at the entrance to the cathedral, although they felt unable to enter the building.[41]

Commemoration at Eastertime of the 1916 Rising was low-key and without much public notice in Northern Ireland until 1928 when well-publicised ceremonies were held at republican plots in Milltown cemetery in Belfast and in the city cemetery in Derry. In the following year and throughout the 1930s, the government, using the Special Powers Act, prohibited these commemorations. In support of the ban the Minister of Home Affairs, R. D. Bates, stated that those involved were 'celebrating one of the most treacherous and bloody rebellions that ever took place in the history of the world' and claimed that there was IRA involvement in the commemorations.[42] The nationalist leader, Joe Devlin, challenged this view in parliament in 1932 and argued that the ban on the commemorations was a denial of people's right to free speech and referred to one such event in Newry as simply 'an annual commemoration for all those who died for Ireland'.[43]

Every Easter during the 1930s, commemorative meetings were announced and then declared illegal by the government, but there were often attempts to get round the ban.[44] In 1935, for example, about five hundred people gathered on Easter Monday some fifty yards beyond the cemetery gates at Milltown graveyard where they recited a decade of the rosary, while in Derry, republicans held their commemorations a week before Easter to get round the ban at Eastertime.[45] On a number of occasions in Derry and Armagh wreath-laying ceremonies were performed on Saturday night, hours before the ban came into operation on Easter Sunday.[46] Tension arose frequently over the flying of the tricolour and the wearing of the Easter lily. The most serious confrontation between the police and republican organisers came in 1942, when active IRA units became involved in the commemorations, leading to shooting in both Dungannon and Belfast, and the murder of a Catholic police constable in Belfast.[47]

By 1948, the government had decided not to impose a general ban on Easter commemorations of 1916. From this time on commemorative events were held in a number of centres by a range of organisations. In 1950, for example, the main event at Milltown cemetery in Belfast was organised by the National Graves Association.[48] This was followed by a separate service organised under the auspices of the Republican Socialist party, addressed by Harry Diamond MP, who referred to 'the shadow of a foreign occupation of a portion of their country'. Finally, there was another ceremony held by the 'Old Pre-Truce IRA'. In Newry a commemorative service was followed by a large parade, led by members of Newry Urban Council, and including members of the Catholic Boy Scouts, the Foresters and the Hibernians. There were also Easter commemorative events in County Armagh and County Tyrone and Derry city. Similar events occurred during the 1950s with few problems, although sometimes there was conflict between organisers and police over the flying of the tricolour, as for example in Lurgan in 1952 and 1953 when the Royal Ulster Constabulary confiscated flags and made arrests. In Newry in 1957, arrests were also made over the flying of the tricolour at the Easter commemorations, and in the following year a parade to commemorate 1916 was prohibited in the town, although the ban was ignored.[49]

In the new Irish Free State, St Patrick's Day quickly took on special significance. By 1922 it had been made a general holiday and from 1925, thanks to the Free State Licensing Act, all public houses were closed on that day. In Dublin, an annual army parade now replaced the processions organised by the Lord Lieutenant and Lord Mayor. Throughout the country there were parades, often involving army marches to church for mass. Dances, sporting activities, theatrical events and excursions were run on the day. The Irish language was specially promoted on the day, frequently with events organised by the Gaelic League. In 1926 the southern premier W. T. Cosgrave made the first official radio broadcast on St Patrick's Day. He called for mutual understanding and harmony and declared that:

> The destinies of the country, north and south, are now in the hands of Irishmen, and the responsibility for success or failure will rest with ourselves. If we are to succeed there must be a brotherly toleration of each other's ideas as to how our ambition may be realised, and a brotherly co-operation in every effort towards its realisation.[50]

In his St Patrick's Day's speech in 1930, Cosgrave declared that 'as we have been Irish and Roman, so it will remain', but he took care to preface his statement with the remarks that he was speaking for the majority of people in the state.[51] In 1931 in a St Patrick's Day broadcast to the Irish in America, and reported in the Irish press, Cosgrave again sought to make a reconciliatory gesture 'whatever be your creed in religion or politics, you are of the same blood – the healing process must go on'.[52]

With the accession to power of Eamon de Valera and Fianna Fáil in 1932, St Patrick's Day took on added significance. Links between Church and State were publicly stressed with the annual procession on St Patrick's Day of de Valera and his Executive Council, complete with a cavalry troop, to the Dublin pro-Cathedral for mass.[53] The Patrician Year of 1932, which included the Eucharistic Congress, gave an opportunity for large demonstrations, with considerable official involvement, emphasising connections between Ireland and Rome.[54] This religious aspect was taken up again by de Valera in his St Patrick's Day broadcast of 1935 in which he reminded people that Ireland had been a Christian and Catholic nation since St Patrick's time: 'She remains a Catholic nation,' he declared.[55] De Valera now used the St Patrick's Day broadcasts, which were transmitted to the USA and Australia, to launch vigorous attacks on the British government and partition. These speeches reached a peak in 1939, when, in Rome for St Patrick's Day, de Valera declared how he had made a pledge beside the grave of Hugh O'Neill that he would never rest until 'that land which the Almighty so clearly designed as one, shall belong undivided to the Irish people'. He urged his listeners to do likewise.[56] At the same time, however, the links between Catholicism and Irish identity as expressed on St Patrick's Day were not absolute. For example, the Protestant President of Ireland, Douglas Hyde, attended a St Patrick's Day service in the Church of Ireland cathedral of St Patrick's in Dublin in 1939.[57]

During the war, celebrations on St Patrick's Day were low-key although de Valera continued to make his annual broadcast. In 1943 he spoke of the restoration of the national territory and the national language as the greatest of the state's uncompleted tasks. He also talked of his dream of a land 'whose fields and villages would be joyous with the sounds of industry, the romping of sturdy children, the contests of athletic youths and the laughter of comely maidens'.[58] After the war St Patrick's Day became a major national holiday once again. In 1950 the military parade in Dublin was replaced by a trade and industries parade. In their St Patrick's Day speeches in the 1950s, heads of government, Eamon de Valera and John A. Costello, continued to use the event to make strong denunciations of partition. In his St Patrick's Day broadcast in 1950, Costello declared that 'our country is divided by foreign interference'.[59]

By the 1950s, government ministers and spokesmen, such as Seán MacEntee, were also making public speeches on the day at a range of venues in Britain and the USA, usually concentrating on attacking partition.[60] In 1955 a rare discordant note was struck by Bishop Cornelius Lucy of Cork when, in his St Patrick's Day address, he suggested that emigration was a greater evil than partition.[61] Irish leaders in their speeches continued to emphasise links between Ireland and Rome; by the mid-1950s, it was common for the President or Taoiseach to be in Rome on St Patrick's Day. The 1961 Patrician celebrations marked a high point in this religious aspect of the festival. It began with the arrival on 13 March of a papal legate, Cardinal MacIntyre, who in the words of the *Capuchin Annual* was 'welcomed with the protocol reception given only to a head of state'. This included a welcome at the airport from the Taoiseach and a full military guard.[62]

Annual commemoration of the Dublin Rising of 1916 proved a very contentious issue in the new Irish state, reflecting some of the political divisions which had emerged over the Anglo-Irish Treaty and also personal concerns about any such event.[63] During the commemorations in 1922, a number of prominent politicians from both the pro-Treaty and anti-Treaty sides addressed large crowds in various places, but the event was not marked publicly the following year, owing to the Civil War. On Easter Monday 1924, the government organised a ceremony at Arbour Hill (burial place of the executed rebels) for a specially invited list of guests, including politicians, soldiers and relatives of the deceased.[64] Few relatives of the deceased turned up, however, and in this and following years the event was marred by disputes about who should be invited. Also in 1924 republicans organised a march through Dublin to Glasnevin cemetery for the laying of wreaths on the republican plot. Subsequently, large parades to Glasnevin were organised and attended each Easter by republican groups, including Sinn Féin and (after 1927) Fianna Fáil. The Cumann na nGaedheal government did not participate in these marches, although there was some official remembrance of the Easter Rising in 1926 and after, in the form of broadcasts on the subject on the new Radio Éireann.

When de Valera came to power in 1932, the situation did not change greatly. In Dublin, there were two parades, the first organised by the semi-official National Commemoration Committee and attended by de Valera and members of Fianna Fáil, which marched to Arbour Hill, and the second run by other republican groups, including the IRA, which marched to Glasnevin.[65] The Fianna Fáil government changed the guest list to the Arbour Hill ceremony but also ran into difficulties with relatives of the deceased about who should be present.[66] In 1935, there was a large Irish army parade on Easter Sunday to the General Post Office where a statue of Cúchulain was unveiled and speeches were made by government ministers. This statue, supposedly symbolic of the Rising, had in fact been sculpted between 1910 and 1911 and purchased much later for this purpose.[67] The twentieth anniversary of the Rising saw some additional measures of commemoration, in particular radio programmes during Easter week on Radio Éireann. The event continued to be commemorated in Dublin principally by the two rival marches to Arbour Hill and Glasnevin. Outside Dublin the Rising was commemorated at Eastertime by competing republican groups. For example, in Cork the Old IRA Men's Association marched each Easter to several monuments and graves of their dead comrades.[68]

On the twenty-fifth anniversary of the Easter Rising in 1941, major celebrations were held in Dublin. On Easter Sunday a military parade, described as the largest ever held in Dublin, took place.[69] There were speeches at the GPO from President Douglas Hyde and members of the government. De Valera also made a broadcast from the GPO calling for improvements in the armed forces and for vigilance in preserving Ireland's independence. For the remainder of the Emergency public celebrations were severely limited. After 1945, rival parades recommenced in Dublin, with no special government involvement, apart from the appearance of Fianna Fáil ministers at Arbour Hill. In 1949, no doubt for symbolic reasons, the official inauguration of the Irish Republic occurred at one minute past midnight on Easter Monday. Only from 1954 did a military parade at the GPO in Dublin at Easter first become an annual event. It was part of the An Tóstal celebrations of that year but was continued in following years.[70] The fortieth anniversary of the Rising was celebrated extensively in 1956. President Seán T. O'Kelly, the Taoiseach, John A. Costello and other government ministers were on the saluting platform at the GPO; there were many radio programmes on the Easter Rising; and various groups in different parts of the country held parades.[71] After this, the commemorations returned to the practice of a military parade in Dublin and other marches in Dublin and elsewhere organised by various groups.

During the First World War an estimated two hundred thousand people from Ireland, a majority from the twenty-six counties which became the Irish Free State, served in the British armed forces. On the first Armistice Day, on 11 November 1919, in line with a papal decree, mass was held at all Catholic churches in Ireland to mark the occasion.[72] A two minute silence at eleven o'clock was observed widely. Subsequently, with the War of Independence and the setting up of the new Irish Free State, commemoration of this event became very controversial. As Jane Leonard has commented: 'division rather than dignity surrounded the commemoration of the war in Ireland'.[73] The civil unrest of the early 1920s restricted public expressions of commemoration. From 1923 onwards, however, Armistice Day was marked not just by a two-minute silence but also by parades and assemblies of ex-servicemen and their friends and families which were held in Dublin and in other parts of Ireland. Such events were organised by several ex-servicemen's organisations until they were eventually brought together under the British Legion in 1925. War memorials were erected in many places and the poppy was sold widely.[74]

Official attitudes were ambivalent but generally tolerant in the 1920s. Conscious of nationalist and republican susceptibilities, members of the Free State government looked askance at ideas to build a large war memorial in central Dublin, and insisted that it be erected at the outskirts at Islandbridge.[75] At the same time, conscious of the many Irish people who had died during the First World War, including members of their own families, the government sent representatives to the wreath-laying ceremonies in Dublin and London. The message on the wreath laid by Colonel Maurice Moore, the Irish government representative, at the temporary cenotaph cross in College Green in Dublin on 11 November read: 'This wreath is placed here by the Free State government to commemorate all the brave men who fell on the field of battle.'[76] In 1923, W. T. Cosgrave and some cabinet colleagues attended an Armistice Day mass in Cork.[77]

Early Armistice day commemorations in Dublin met with a certain amount of opposition, expressed in actions such as the snatching of poppies. From the mid-1920s, however, the intensity of this opposition grew, with various republican groups organising anti-Armistice Day rallies to protest against 'the flagrant display of British imperialism disguised as Armistice celebrations' and with physical attacks being made on some of the parades.[78] In 1926, this led to the main ceremony being moved from the centre of Dublin to Phoenix Park. De Valera spoke at one of the anti-Armistice Day rallies in 1930, and the formation of a Fianna Fáil government in 1932 led to a further downgrading of the commemorations. Official representatives were withdrawn from the main wreath-laying ceremony in Dublin from November 1932, although the Irish government continued to be represented at the Cenotaph in London until 1936. Permits for the sale of poppies, previously allowed for several days in the week before 11 November, were now reduced to one day only.[79] Those taking part in the annual parade to Phoenix Park in Dublin were prohibited from carrying Union Jacks or British Legion flags which featured a Union Jack. Work on the National War Memorial Park at Islandbridge was completed and handed over to the government in early 1937, but the official opening was put off a number of times by de Valera, until the outbreak of the Second World War led to its indefinite postponement. The official opening of the park occurred only in 1988 and without the direct involvement of the Fianna Fáil government, although at a later ceremony in 1994, Bertie Ahern, then Minister of Finance, declared the work on the memorial to be finished.[80]

Armistice ceremonies were held at Phoenix Park in 1939 and at Islandbridge in 1940, although without parades.[81] Thereafter public demonstrations in Dublin relating to this event were banned until after the war. Indeed the government maintained its ban in November 1945, after the end of the war, because it did not want to see any public demonstration of Irish involvement in the allied war effort. In fact, an estimated fifty thousand men and women went from the twenty counties of Ireland, along with many other Irish people already living in Great Britain, to serve in British armed forces during the war.[82] The Irish government, however, continued to ignore this matter. As elsewhere Armistice Day was replaced by Remembrance Sunday, on the Sunday closest to 11 November, and the event was marked by a parade of ex-servicemen in Dublin from Smithfield Market along North Quays to Islandbridge and by discrete wreath-laying ceremonies in other centres.[83] These parades and other commemorative events continued during the 1950s, but for many of those involved, as declining numbers attending Remembrance Day and veterans' memories showed, there was a clear sense that they had become marginalised and excluded from the new Irish identity and sense of history that had now become dominant.[84]

Before 1921, Orange parades had occurred regularly in the three Ulster counties of Donegal, Cavan and Monaghan, which went on to become part of the Irish Free State. These parades were restricted in the early 1920s because of disturbances and violence during the Civil War but recommenced in 1923. At the main Orange parade at Clones in County Monaghan in 1923 an Orange spokesman declared that:

> They did not desire to be placed under their present regime, but they paid tribute to whom tribute was due. They were not going to rebel, because it would be useless and would not be right. In face of great difficulties and trials the Free State government had done a great deal, but they had a great deal more to do …[85]

In 1925 it was reckoned that 10,000 people attended an Orange demonstration in July at Newbliss in County Monaghan.[86] At a large 12 July demonstration at Rockcorry, County Monaghan, in 1930, resolutions were passed which declared allegiance to King George V as head of the commonwealth, support for Orange principles, rejoicing in the good relations in County Monaghan and protest against compulsory use of the Irish language.[87] In the 1920s Orange parades were not so common in Donegal, because members from the county, especially the eastern part, often attended 12 July parades in Derry or other northern locations. South Donegal Orangemen held July demonstrations at Rossnowlagh and Darney.[88] In spite of incidents at Orange events in Cavan town in 1930 and in Newtowngore in County Leitrim in 1931, 12 July Orange demonstrations passed off reasonably peacefully in 1931 in Cootehill, County Cavan, and in Monaghan town.[89] The year 1931, however, proved to be the last time that Orange parades took place in counties Cavan and Monaghan.

A month after these 12 July celebrations in 1931, a large body of republicans, including IRA units, occupied Cootehill on the eve of a planned demonstration on 12 August by members of the Royal Black Institution from counties Cavan and Monaghan.[90] The railway line through the town was blown up and there were reports of armed men on the streets. The authorities reacted strongly and troops and extra police were dispatched to Cootehill to restore law and order. Although the Black demonstration did not take place the government gave assurances to local Orange and Black leaders that their parades would be protected.[91] In 1932, however, the Grand County Lodges of Cavan, Donegal and Monaghan cancelled all demonstrations in their counties. The minutes of the County Monaghan Grand Lodge show that in June 1932 members received information that 'arms were being distributed by the same party who had caused all the trouble at Cootehill with the object of interfering with our July demonstration'.[92] The Grand Lodge decided to cancel both this demonstration and also all parades to church services.

In future years Monaghan lodges did have limited marches to church services, but in spite of the fact that members throughout the 1930s wanted to resume their 12 July demonstrations, this never happened because of fear of the consequences.[93] Orange activities in counties Cavan and Monaghan were now restricted to church services and private meetings, and lodges attended the 12 July parades in Northern Ireland. In County Donegal, however, July Orange parades resumed in the 1930s at Rossnowlagh in the south of the county.[94] After the Second World War many of the lodges from Cavan and Monaghan attended the Rossnowlagh demonstration. By the 1950s the date of this parade had been moved to the Saturday prior to 12 July, so allowing Orange members from Northern Ireland to attend the event and southern members to take part in 12 July parades across the border.

The four decades between 1921 and 1961 saw the founding and con-
solidation of two new political states in Ireland. While both Northern Ireland and the Irish Free State, later the Irish Republic, marked all four of
the national holidays or days of commemoration examined here, the difference in the manner and extent of the celebrations tells us much about
how each state and its citizens viewed its own identity and sense of history. Undoubtedly for many involved, the subject of commemoration or
celebration, such as Armistice Day or St Patrick's Day, had a personal
and heartfelt meaning. At the same time, these occasions often took on a
special significance, and were related to issues of identity and politics as
they affected the broader community. Important changes occurred in how
such special days were marked. Sometimes these changes were influenced by the desire of leaders to respond to pressures and divisions within
their own group, while other times they were a response by a leader and
a group to the actions and statements of their opponents. De Valera's
opposition to Armistice Day may have been caused partly by a concern
to keep republicans on his side and partly as a reaction to attempts by
some in the 1920s to turn 'the 11th November into the 12th July'.[95] Craig's
new links with Orangeism and a Protestant identity may have been the
result partly of a concern to keep unionist unity, and partly as a response
by southern politicians who 'boasted of a Catholic state'.[96]

Pre-1920, St Patrick's Day and Armistice Day enjoyed widespread
support. Between 1920 and 1960, however, these occasions were increasingly dominated and endorsed by some sections of the community and
rejected by others. St Patrick's Day was used by nationalists/republicans
to help to boost an exclusive nationalist and Catholic view of Irish identity. Partly because of this, and partly because of a concern by some unionists to emphasise British links, many Protestants came to disregard St
Patrick's Day. Armistice Day was used by unionists to strengthen an exclusive unionist and Protestant view of British identity. As a result, and
thanks also to an effort by some nationalists to ignore or reject this part
of their recent history, Catholics and nationalists came to ignore Armistice day. In Northern Ireland the anniversary of the Battle of the Boyne
became institutionalised as an important historical event. In the Irish
Free State the anniversary of the Easter Rising was an important historical date, although different groups sought to claim it. In the case of Boyne
commemorations in the south and Easter commemorations in the north,
both majority communities showed little tolerance for the historical views
of their minorities.

During this period of the early years of both states, political relations
between north and south and between the different communities were
dominated by religious divisions and conflict over constitutional issues.
Some of the developments which we have seen here, however, helped to

polarise these relations even further. Both St Patrick's Day and Armistice Day had the potential to remind people of a shared history, of common interests and suffering. Instead they were used to emphasise differences and to develop more exclusive versions of identity and history. 12 July and Easter Sunday represented events special to the histories of Northern Ireland and the Irish Free State, respectively, but neither society showed any understanding of the history of the other nor allowed much opportunity for minorities to mark these events. It has been argued that the passion and confrontation aroused by the large number of commemorations in the 1960s was one of the factors which helped to destabilise political society in Northern Ireland and to lead to the outbreak of the Troubles.[97] The widely held conflicting views of identity and history, fostered in part by these commemorations of the previous forty years, helped to create the atmosphere of distrust and misunderstanding which made these 1960s commemorations so divisive and harmful for politics.

De Valera's other Ireland

Gearóid Ó Crualaoich

This paper will be concerned more with culture than with history but I hope that it can be taken as a contribution to certain common issues of a theoretical nature that have loomed large in recent years in respect of both historiography, the writing of history and ethnography, the writing and representation of culture. I want to suggest that the emphasis given in the cultural ideology of de Valera's Ireland to folk tradition, as an expression of Irish identity, served in effect to mask and to mute the actual cultural history of Ireland in the four middle decades of the century, and that another Ireland of those years has gone largely unrecorded. That other Ireland is the Ireland whose cultural expression was the popular culture of the city streets and the factories, the popular culture of town life in the urbanising countryside, the popular culture arising from the modernising aspects of village and rural life, as in the effect, for example, of rural electrification that culminated – in popular cultural terms – with the establishment of an Irish television station in 1961 when so many ordinary Dublin and east coast homes were already festooned with reception masts reaching for the popular media culture of the British stations.

De Valera's inaugural address to the new Irish television audience in 1961 reinforces, in a way, his radio message to the Irish people on St Patrick's Day 1943 regarding the nature of Irish cultural identity and the noble traditional heritage that nourished and sustained it.[1] Folklore was, still, in the official cultural perspective of de Valera's Ireland, one very important element, perhaps the chief one in that identity and that heritage, and was a main ground for the ideological bias that disregarded contemporary and urban popular culture in the official reckoning and promotion of cultural self-perception and in its official representation. This ideological bias had its historical roots in an era much earlier than that of de Valera's Ireland but was still sufficiently current, in the de Valera years, to result in the kind of ethnographic and historical denial of actual popular cultural creativity that matches the imaginative myopia underlying the denial and suppression of literary creativity that the Censorship of Publications legislation of 1929 implied.

As regards the quality of official Irish cultural thinking then, as much was already being said in 1940 by Seán Ó Faoláin who wrote, in the first issue of *The Bell*, that the magazine would stand for 'Life before any abstraction, in whatever magnificent words it may clothe itself'.[2] In the pages of his magazine, he promoted an intellectual pluralism and a cultural internationalism that was the antithesis of the prevailing ideology regarding Irish culture and Irish cultural identity. The folk tradition aspect of that view of Irish culture which *The Bell* opposed and, specifically, of Irish popular culture is also to be found, well in the aftermath of the de Valera years, in the closing words of an article published in 1979 and written two years earlier in commemoration of the founding a half-century before of the Folklore of Ireland Society in 1927. The title of this article is 'The Irish Folklore Commission: Achievement and Legacy' and its author, Bo Almqvist, Professor of Irish Folklore at UCD was successor in that position to Séamas Ó Duilearga, the father figure of folklore study in Ireland in the de Valera years. Bo Almqvist closed his article with this exhortation to the Irish people:

> A mhuintir na hÉireann!
> Do not neglect one of the greatest treasures you possess! I beseech you for your own sake, for the sake of your men and women, for the sake of past generations – all the humble but truly great men and women who cherished their national heritage and passed it on in trust to us – for the sake of understanding, identity and unity in this country in these troubled times, for the sake of joy and beauty in generations to come, for the sake of truth and love of learning, for the sake of everything you hold dear, noble and holy, do not let us down in our work![3]

This passage strikingly illustrates an essentialist and essentially romantic antiquarian notion of Irish identity – at least as far as popular culture is concerned – and represents the thinking, in regard to folklore and traditional culture as the expression of Irishness, that was endorsed by Irish governments of the de Valera years to the extent of their continual support of an official Irish Folklore Commission under the direction of Séamas Ó Duilearga. Ó Duilearga had been a student of, and later assistant to, Douglas Hyde at UCD. Douglas Hyde's role was paramount in promoting in Ireland the philosophy of the Romantic Antiquarian movement that underlay the nineteenth century nationalism of many of the European nations striving to build their identity in terms of native language and folk tradition.

Roy Foster has noted that Hyde's 1892 address to the National Literary Society 'On the Necessity for De-Anglicising Ireland', delivered in the same year as his *Love Songs of Connacht* anthology of folk poetry was published, 'rapidly achieved legendary status' being 'credited with inspiring the foundation of the Gaelic League a year later' and becoming 'a canonical text of Irish cultural nationalism'.[4] In a review of Hyde's *Love Songs of Connacht* by W. B. Yeats, we have the expression by Yeats too of a perceived need, as Foster puts it, 'to derive inspiration from a basic energy, by knowing one's roots' that is, I submit, on a par with the message Bo Almqvist still had for the Irish people as recently as the late 1970s. In his 1893 review Yeats had written:

> As for me, I close the book with much sadness. These poor peasants lived in a beautiful if somewhat inhospitable world, where little had changed since Adam delved and Eve span. Everything was so old that it was steeped in the heart, and every powerful emotion found at once noble types and symbols for its expression. But we – we live in a world of whirling change, where nothing becomes old and sacred and our powerful emotions ... express themselves in vulgar types and symbols. The soul then had but to stretch out its arms to fill them with beauty, but now all manner of heterogeneous ugliness has beset us.[5]

In the face of this modern metropolitan world, Irish cultural nationalism, of the sort Hyde and Yeats espoused and that de Valera was to attempt to practise – deriving, historically, from the philosophy of J. G. von Herder in eighteenth century Germany and flowing through the writings of Thomas Davis and the Young Irelanders – sought, in the later nineteenth and earlier twentieth centuries, to locate folk traditions at the heart of national identity. I believe that such a conviction regarding the essential nature of national identity still operated as an important element in the decision of de Valera to choose Douglas Hyde as an appropriate person to be inaugurated as first President of the Irish Republic in 1938.

At the level of party politics it is suggested that Hyde was not de Valera's first choice for President, but that the risk of having a party politician such as Seán T. O'Kelly rejected by the people in the aftermath of his narrow constitution referendum victory, caused de Valera to opt for someone who, in J. J. Lee's words could safely satisfy 'sundry national self-images' while still guaranteeing a Fianna Fáil presidency.[6] The factors motivating any such potential choice are surely complex and calculated – perhaps especially so in the case of Mr de Valera – but I believe that one significant element in the choice of Douglas Hyde to fill the presidential office was that, in de Valera's perspective and that of other Irish Irelanders – within Fianna Fáil and outside it – Hyde's career and public image had given public witness to a deep allegiance to the Irish-Ireland ideal. In office as first citizen and symbolic representative of the

Irish nation, Douglas Hyde would give effect to the cultural equivalent of the political policy of Sinn Féinism and the economic policy of protectionism which we can also associate with de Valera's Ireland. Such political use of Hyde as a kind of cultural icon by de Valera suggests something of a renewal in the de Valera years of the ideals of the early Gaelic League era regarding the cultural expression of national identity. In fact the more imaginative, ecumenical, and potentially unifying aspects of the kind of cultural revolution that Hyde and the early Gaelic League had intended and pioneered had not survived the lurch to physical-force nationalism. Instead a narrower, more conservative and, indeed, somewhat anti-modern tendency marked the cultural nationalism of the years between 1916 and the end of the de Valera years of power.

Mr de Valera himself would, in due course, also fill the presidential office in a manner similarly appropriate to the perception of Irish national identity as residing chiefly in matters of a conservatively defined cultural tradition. By then, however, the appeal-power of even the attenuated version of a romantic antiquarian definition of Irish cultural identity had waned. The centrality of ancient tradition in official cultural ideology was yielding ground to the influence and implications of the fresh economic and social thinking of the Lemass era. This focused on the less exclusively insular concerns of an Irish government less preoccupied with matters of basic political stability, economic survival or external threat in a time of war.

With hindsight, we can see that the implication of the cultural ideology that prevailed in de Valera's Ireland was to privilege the memory of traditional cultural forms that were expressive of the world-view and lifestyle of former rural, relatively unsophisticated, largely under-educated and perhaps only partly-literate segments of the Irish population. This memory culture of the non-elite and non-urban tradition formed, of course, the central concern of the activities of the Irish Folklore Commission that had been established in 1935 with de Valera's approval. The sense of an essential heritage of cultural riches in danger of being lost forever in the displacement and destruction of tradition by the forces of modernity was well caught in the motto of the Folklore of Ireland Society's Journal, *Béaloideas*, every number of which since 1927 has carried the Gospel quotation: *Colligite quae superaverunt fragmenta ne pereant*, a sacred injunction to preserve precious survivals now in danger of discard.

In Germany, we know that the implications of a similar later nineteenth and early twentieth century preoccupation in national cultural ideology, with the symbolic recovery and repossession of the past, had a more directly political and sinister outcome than was the case in Ireland. A recent study by Uli Linke of the focus of research in the history of German folklore scholarship has proposed a direct relationship between culture theory and the exercise of political power by the state, that is relevant to a consideration of the privileging of folk tradition in the cultural ideology of de Valera's Ireland. Linke's article raises issues in regard to the potentially negative side of an exclusive privileging of what Linke terms 'peasant lore' and 'commonplace culture' in showing how such a preoccupation in German folkloristics facilitated the emergence of social and political policies of a racist and totalitarian nature. In an introductory paragraph Linke writes:

> I begin, with a brief discussion of the fetishism of peasant lore, and of commonplace culture in the nineteenth and early twentieth centuries. During this era of European nation-building, the romanticised life-world of peasants served as a template for the political identity of an emerging German state. Contemporary folklorists equated peasant traditions with the unchanging customs of the past: peasant lore was presented as a pristine and authentic repertoire for building a common German culture. From this discussion of 'regressive modernisation' – the political journey into the future by detour through the past – I extract a nationalistic concept of culture in which a theory of power is absent: the workings of power are ignored or perhaps even silenced. I suggest that early German folklorists, as active participants in cultural politics, were not motivated to uncover or elucidate the hidden dimensions of power they so skilfully manipulated. This non-treatment of power is even more pronounced in the context of Nazi folklore scholarship: by concealing the strategies of power, the study of folk culture becomes a means for legitimating Hitler's imperialist policies and racial concerns for 'purity of blood' and reproduction.[7]

Linke goes on to show how, in Germany, the initial romantic perception of the value of common cultural tradition (akin to the Davis position in the Irish case) gave rise to expressions of distress that 'large segments of the German population had abandoned their native heritage in favour of foreign models of refinement' (akin to the Hyde de-Anglicisation position). In the twentieth century in both Germany and Ireland, we know that cultural nationalism took on radically political and militaristic form. Here in Ireland, Hyde had claimed that his message was essentially apolitical, holding that 'an agenda of cultural revival should be as attractive to unionists as to nationalists since it was above politics'.[8] Hyde relinquished his leadership of the Gaelic League in 1915 when he was unable to stop it from embracing an openly partisan political stance on the question of national self-determination by military means and returned to political office (albeit one allegedly above politics) only in 1938 to personify (at de Valera's wish) that partly self-determined nation as its President.

The significance of folklore studies in the newly established Irish Free State and in the later Republic was, meanwhile, endorsed by official government support and accorded the symbolic importance which I have argued that de Valera's choice of Douglas Hyde as President contained. Its influence on social and political affairs, however, was largely confined to its diverting of official and scholarly attention away from the lived popular culture of Irish people in the 1930s and 1940s in favour of a concern for the preservation of the record of past cultural forms. Things had, as we know, taken a grimmer turn in Germany where what matches the official Irish lack of interest in urbanised popular culture is a virulent aversion to cosmopolitanism that saw cities as the locus of decadence. Linke cites two quotations that vividly illustrate this. The first, dated 1935, is from an anthropological journal entitled *Volk und Rasse*:

> Dangers threaten the population when it migrates to the cities. It withers away in a few generations, because it lacks the vital bond with the earth. The German nation must be rooted in the soil if it wants to remain alive.[9]

In the previous year, 1934, the director of the Working Group for German Folklore had asserted:

> German folklore is the study of the racial and traditional world of the German people which is purest and most alive in those communities which have experienced the most eternal contact with blood and soil.[10]

Here in Ireland the anti-urban, anti-cosmopolitan bias of earlier twentieth century folklore studies amounted in effect to little more than neglect of the popular culture of the contemporary urbanising world – as evidenced in the exclusion of city schools from the Commission's 1937/8 Schools' Folklore Collection project (whereby the pupils of all primary schools in the state – barring the cities – were set to work to write down the folklore and traditions remembered by their elders). When, in 1938, de Valera greeted Douglas Hyde's accession to the presidency as that of a 'rightful prince' and hailed it as closing, in his (de Valera's) perspective, a symbolic breach that had existed since 'the undoing of our nation at Kinsale'.[11] His words remained at the level of rhetoric and cultural ideology fuelling, not social and political hatred, but rather the antiquarian and traditional construction put officially on Irish cultural identity – surely one of the abstractions against which Seán Ó Faoláin set his sights in *The Bell*.

That continuing antiquarian/traditional construction of what constituted Irish folklore or popular culture was effected by folklorists and cultural nationalists on the basis of traditional materials gathered more from the memories, than from the living, behaviour of informants and culture bearers, who were themselves of course living in a society and a culture deeply transformed by the technology and social organisation of the contemporary modern world.

Today, historians and ethnologists alike would question whether the concepts of an exclusive 'folklore' and an exclusive 'folk tradition' can be historically or ethnographically meaningful – given the artificial nature of the distinctions they imply in social reality and cultural experience. Is there any meaningful way in which 'folklore' can be separated off from the totality of a society's or an individual's production of and participation in cultural knowledge and cultural forms – material, social or symbolic? The fullest, most recent, Irish discussion relevant to this question is that of the historian, Seán Connolly, who attempts to outline and analyse the history of the idea of popular culture as addressed in historical writing about Ireland in the eighteenth and nineteenth centuries.[12]

At least two separate issues arise from Connolly's treatment of the historiography of Irish pre-twentieth century popular culture, that are relevant to a consideration of the neglect of the actual popular culture of de Valera's Ireland by folklorist and historian alike. The first of these has to do with the very idea of a popular culture that is in some way detached or detachable from the overall picture of cultural activity in the case of any society. Citing examples from the culture of the eighteenth and nineteenth centuries in Ireland – such matters as card-playing, dancing and hurling in the domain of recreation or beliefs and practices associated with the fairy faith in the domain of religion, Connolly is able to argue convincingly for a flow of cultural transmission, a sharing and a spreading out of cultural knowledge and patterns of behaviour within the social world that defies the setting of boundaries between folk and non-folk. The cultural reality of that world is, instead, best thought of in holistic terms as comprising an unbounded and unstructured flow of ideas, behaviours, institutions and material artefacts, that both shift and change in response to shifting and changing economic and political life in the framework of the general modernising tendency of the European world. In Connolly's view, any attempted rigid division of cultural reality into separate subaltern and elite cultural worlds is untenable, in a way that highlights a similar implausibility in the constructed, artificial nature of a distinctive Irish folklore world as this was officially understood in de Valera's Ireland.

Whether labelled as 'folklore' or 'popular culture' we should, in this reading, endeavour to regard the materials accumulated by the Folklore Commission as historic instances of cultural expression in particular historic contexts within the flow of a single universe of cultural discourse, without, of course, denying the very real ethnic, linguistic, economic and political diversity that existed in the social circumstances of people's lives. Viewed like this, the Folklore Commission materials retain their very considerable value as an ethnographic record. A different set of questions can, however, be brought to bear on them from the ones designed to elucidate exclusively their representative capacity in relation to some essential Irish tradition.

On this basis also, gaps in the ethnographic record can be better perceived, and the missing, or largely invisible, folklore and popular culture of the de Valera years themselves can be conceived of, as a target for research and elucidation by both historians and ethnologists working in partnership. Many topics quickly suggest themselves: music hall culture; the culture of the dance-hall and the whist-drive; the culture of popular urban Christianity; the culture of the new slum-clearance housing estates; the culture of the factory floor. Connolly himself draws attention to our relative ignorance regarding the culture of cinema in Ireland, given its enormous popularity from the 1920s. We need, he says, to know about the cultural response to this new cultural form of different regions of the country and of different groups of people. We need to know which particular film genres most appealed to Irish audiences and to what degree the characters and the motifs of commercial cinema were assimilated into the wider culture. He reminds us that the earlier eighteenth century Dublin playhouse was the site for a similar hybridisation of elite and popular, or metropolitan and local, or high and low culture in the context of a then socially-undifferentiated consumer demand for a commercially produced form of social recreation.

On the other hand, we can ourselves observe and experience at first hand the emergence and influence within our contemporary cultural world of similar, apparently novel, forms of group recreation such as comedy clubs, or of group religious practice, such as charismatic healing rituals. On examination, these may well turn out to be transformations of cultural forms already present at the local or folk or popular end of the cultural spectrum of de Valera's Ireland. Rendering the specifics of the actual popular culture of the de Valera years is thus a common task for history and ethnology that is essential to any analysis of the cultural history of Ireland in the twentieth century.

A second issue raised by Connolly also has direct bearing on the question of the relative invisibility of contemporary popular culture in de Valera's Ireland. This is the dominant focus, which, Connolly alleges, exists within Irish popular culture studies on the decline and disappearance of cultural forms, together with a prevailing sense of loss and dispossession in the face of great change. Connolly suggests two reasons why such a focus should exist; one having to do with the belief that the language shift from Irish to English inevitably constituted a decline in cultural creativity; the other with a belief that 'cultural subjugation', as he puts it, the muting and suppression of cultural expression, is also an inevitable consequence of the political subjugation that Ireland has experienced since the seventeenth century. Connolly argues instead for seeing creative cultural adjustment to changing circumstances and to new possibilities in place of the view that sees continual withering away of cultural expression and cultural identity. He draws attention to examples of evidence of a capacity on the part of Irish-speaking groups in the eighteenth century to deal ably with the expanding urban and commercial sector of society.

I might mention that I have myself discussed the County Clare poet, Brian Merriman, and his long poem 'The Midnight Court', as an example of this kind of hybridisation in cultural expression. It bridges native tradition and the social reality of the later eighteenth century north Munster world which was experiencing increasing literacy, increasing marketisation and monetarisation of the economy, and increased expansion in the operation of courts of law.[13] In that eighteenth century cultural world, with its mixture of tradition and commercialisation, Connolly contends that what he terms the 'triumph' of the metropolitan was inevitable, whatever the language spoken and whatever the political circumstances. The demonstration of the cultural mechanism of that metropolitan 'triumph' is what is relevant to our own concerns. The National Folklore Archive, built on the dedicated labours of the Folklore of Ireland Society and the Irish Folklore Commission, comprises a huge and hugely valuable primary resource for the study of that cultural mechanism, as it actually operated within the cultural and social reality to which the testimony of the Commission's contributors bears eloquent witness.

When we come to look at the popular culture of Ireland in the middle decades of the twentieth century we can see how a prevailing cultural ideology that saw cultural identity chiefly in terms of antiquarian tradition, served to divert attention away from the culturally creative nature of the adjustments to modernity that were expressing themselves in the world-view, the lifestyle and the material culture of the twentieth century urban and urbanising world, in which Irish people actually lived increasingly metropolitan-influenced lives. Hyde had spoken in his 1892 lecture of the Gaelic past at the bottom of the Irish heart 'that prevents us becoming citizens of the empire.'[14] De Valera in his turn spoke of the wish that lay in the heart of every Irish man and woman for a country not only free but truly Irish as well.[15] The ways in which the real men and women of de Valera's Ireland could be seen to be truly Irish were, to a significant degree, circumscribed by the ideological perspective that placed little or no value on cultural forms that deviated from a kind of folk norm in official thinking.

With later developments in folklore and popular culture studies, we are able to see today how official norms and representations of cultural identity are always destined to be static and crude and out-of-date when set against the ceaseless flow of cultural creativity and cultural transmission, the transmission of ideas, values, behaviours and objects that constitute the reality of a holistic cultural world out of which new cultural forms and new expressions of cultural identity are continually being created. As Connolly rightly insists in regard to the study of cultural matters by historians, it behoves us all as students of culture to try to avoid becoming prisoners of abstractions of our own making.

The terms 'folklore' and 'popular culture' must, therefore, be used in a way that is fully conscious of the unwarranted distortion of the reality of cultural history that their use has sometimes implied. Connolly would, in theory, countenance renouncing the possibility of talking about popular culture as an historical object or a historical system of cultural activity in its own right. He envisages, however, a continued interest by historians of culture in studying local, popular cultural manifestations.

Folklore studies and ethnology have, for their part too, undergone a veritable paradigm shift since the closing years of de Valera's Ireland, that has brought their thinking on the creation and transmission of culture to a position somewhat akin to that claimed by Connolly for historians. The model of culture process that is associated with the name of the anthropologist Ulf Hannerz,[16] is one that offers the possibility of studying the local and popular production and transmission of culture and cultural identity without either a) falling into the trap of resorting to unjustified and unsustainable abstractions; or b) having to forego entirely a vernacular focus. This is achieved by a continual framing of every subculture and of all local innovation within the increasingly globalised diffusion and interplay of cultural forces and forms.

Folklore and popular culture within this perspective are the cultural forms that give expression to local creativity and identity in divergent vernacular ways rather than in convergent cosmopolitan ones. Both these tendencies are, however, to be regarded as constantly at work together within the wash and flow of cultural production and transmission in the media and information age in which we live. A focus on the study of vernacular, local, popular aspects of culture and culture history within an overall frame encompassing cosmopolitan culture process, offers the prospect of being able to throw light on both the history and the cultural dynamic of the means whereby groups and individuals have, in Ireland as elsewhere, continually reconciled their traditional identities and world-views, with the demands and the opportunities of the prevailing economic and political circumstances, as these are created and transformed by developments in the wider world.

In mentioning, as a small example of this kind of focus, the UCC research project on the urban folklore and ethnology of Cork's northside – a project established by means of co-operation between the Department of Folklore of UCC and a number of Cork northside community organisations[17] – I want to draw attention to the considerable interest that is today being shown by communities in how best they can themselves represent (both to themselves and to others) their own traditions and their own cultural identity in the form of folklore and local history. This interest is not, of course, confined to urban communities only but, in general, it offers to folklorists and historians of culture alike, the prospect of being able to collaborate with each other and with local groups in order to collect an archive of primary evidence for the operation in de Valera's Ireland, outside of the official frame of antiquarian cultural ideology, of the actual cultural process that operated in Moore Street and in Mayo, in Donnycarney and in Donegal, in Gurranabraher and in Graigue na Managh.

That actual culture process produced – out of the reconciling of the local with the metropolitan, of the known with the new – a repertoire of cultural forms that were as valid an expression of Irish cultural identity in the de Valera years, as those officially endorsed by political and educational authority in the years from 1926 to 1973. A further important consideration that arises from the collaborative nature of the kind of vernacular cultural study that the Northside Project involves, is the reflexive, dialogical nature of both the fieldwork and the ethnographic description which it entails.[18] This raises issues of theory and methodology that were not directly addressed by students of culture in the de Valera years but they are of sufficient concern today, to the study of culture and cultural history, to merit being at least mentioned in the present context as matters that give further common cause to historians and folklorists / ethnologists alike in the pursuit of the culture and the cultural history of de Valera's other Ireland.

Cultural visions and the new state: embedding and embalming

Gearóid Ó Tuathaigh

In recent decades one of the more contentious ideological issues at the centre of critical debate in Irish cultural studies has been the appropriateness or adequacy of the discourse of colonialism/post-colonialism as a frame of analysis for the Irish cultural predicament – in its historical and contemporary settings. Discussion of the specific dynamics of the conflict in Northern Ireland is a central aspect of this ideological contention, and key sites of debate have been the Field Day cultural project (in particular, the *Field Day Anthology of Irish Writing* and its *Critical Conditions* series of essays) and the controversy surrounding 'historical revisionism' in certain writings on Irish history in recent decades. Perspectives drawn from a wide range of disciplines are represented in this debate (e.g., anthropology, sociology, political science, history, literary and cultural studies) but most of the main protagonists have been historians or cultural and literary theorists and critics. While the historians have tended to emphasise the particularity of meaning attaching to 'colony/colonial' in legal and constitutional commentaries on states and power relationships, cultural theorists have given more attention to discourse analysis, theories of representation and variations on Gramsci and cultural hegemony.[1] Yet there has been enough dialogue between the disciplines to produce some genuine intellectual engagement, and the terms of the debate have extended far beyond the specific areas I have just listed.[2]

An aspect of the debate which has received less attention than one might have expected it to receive is the major project of decolonisation which informed the ambitions of a section of the Irish nationalist leadership which came to power in the new independent Irish state in 1922. This project was explicitly identified as part of the obligation and the task of identity-formation in that new Irish state from its foundation. Variously described by its principal ideologues both before and after the foundation of the Irish national state as 'the formation of an independent Irish mind', the 'philosophy of Irish-Ireland' or 'the de-Anglicisation of Ireland', it had as its central objective the restoration as the main vernacular of the

Irish language – by then a minority language well-advanced on a long course of relentless decline, and increasingly contracting into relatively small pockets of territory where it still enjoyed a dominant position in the general process of social intercourse. This vulnerable minority language was to be restored in place of English, which by the early twentieth century enjoyed overwhelming dominance as the main vernacular of the vast majority of the people of every social rank throughout most of the island. The decolonising impulse, or cultural vision, which required for its completion such a massive linguistic revolution, would seem to merit some attention, at least to the extent that its sources and assumptions be identified and its encounter with the reality of political power involved in state-formation be reviewed. This essay is a contribution to such a review.[3] It seeks to examine the particular cultural visions present among the political leadership at the establishment of the independent Irish state and to ask what was done, or not done, to embed these visions within the policies and practices of the state up to the late 1950s, that is, during what is commonly regarded as the age of de Valera.

The relationship between a distinctive language or speech, and a sense of community or distinctive peoplehood, has been acknowledged throughout human history. In Ireland, the relationship between language, peoplehood and identity was already a source of comment during the medieval period, in the encounter between the long-settled Gaeil and the more recently settled Anglo-Normans. Language and, notoriously, religion were the key elements of cultural discrimination in the great convulsion of the sixteenth and seventeenth centuries, the outcome of which was the triumph and ascendancy of the English language, law and politico-administrative institutions throughout Ireland, and the corresponding defeat and dissolution of the whole institutional edifice of the Gaelic political and social order.[4] From that time forward, the matter of language, together with religion, has seldom been far from the centre of the debate on Irish culture, community and identity. And when, at the end of the eighteenth century, a further elaboration on concepts of identity and peoplehood congealed into the political ideology of nationalism, Ireland was not immune to the spread of the new ideology. An interest among a minority of the ruling elite (mainly Protestant and of planter descent) in the nature of Irish cultural particularity, allied to an encounter with early European romanticism, had already prompted the first in a series of 'Celtic Revivals' (Seamus Deane's phrase) in Ireland. These were inspired by a desire to 'know' (i.e., to divine and, in a certain sense, to appropriate) the genius and the roots of the imagination of the 'native' or indigenous Celtic people and culture in Ireland.[5]

Furthermore, among the disciples of the new political nationalism in

Ireland from the later eighteenth century there were a few thinkers, notably the young Thomas Davis, who were especially alert to the cultural implications of the constitutional-legal claims being made for an autonomous Irish 'state' on behalf an 'Irish nation', and who were aware of the general European criteria for recognising the claims of different groups to 'nationhood' (and to national states). In this valuation of claims to 'nationhood', a distinctive language was commonly acknowledged as a paramount criterion.[6]

However, it is from the last two decades of the nineteenth century that we come upon those ideas and programmes regarding cultural renewal, and language 'revival', that are commonly referred to as 'the philosophy of Irish-Ireland' or, in the case of some commentators, 'the Gaelic League idea'.[7] The timing of this stirring of ideas and cultural concern was not accidental, and neither was its focus. By the closing decade of the nineteenth century, as a result of the electoral success of Parnell's political movement for Irish 'Home Rule', some form of devolved self-government for Ireland seemed imminent.[8] At the same time, the census returns were clearly indicating that the death of the Irish language seemed now inevitable and hardly less imminent. It was at this juncture that what we may term a deliberate project of 'decolonisation' was formulated and adopted by a group of intellectuals and artists with, in time, significant support from a larger constituency of political activists who were to form the political leadership of the new Irish state eventually established in 1922.[9]

While a movement for the revival of nativist sports and athletics had already been founded in 1884, with an explicit declaration that it sought to reverse the tide of seemingly relentless adoption of English cultural and leisure pastimes in place of native Irish customs, the appropriate starting point for discussion of the project of decolonisation is probably Douglas Hyde's seminal lecture, 'The Necessity for De-Anglicising Ireland', delivered to the National Literary Society in November 1892. Hyde's personal encounter with the Irish language, and the manner in which it fired his imagination, is a familiar story, and need not be rehearsed here.[10] But, so far as his views on language and identity are concerned, it is worth noting that while he became committed to the 'extension of our [i.e., Irish] language among the people', it is clear that he was especially exercised to maintain and preserve Irish as a living language among the base-community of Irish-speakers whose vernacular it still was. By the late nineteenth century these were largely concentrated in areas in the western counties of the Atlantic coast. As he told a New York audience in 1891: 'What I wish to see is Irish established as a living language, for all time, among the million or half-million who still speak it along the west coast, and to ensure that the language will hold a favourable place in teaching institutions and government examinations. Unless we retain a bilingual population as large as we now have, Irish may be said to be dead, and with it nine-tenths of the glories of the past.'[11] When Hyde, with others, founded the Gaelic League two years later, the primary objective of the new movement was declared to be: 'The preservation of Irish as the national language of Ireland and the extension of its use as a spoken tongue.'[12]

While Hyde's principal concern may have been the maintenance (i.e., reproduction) of the existing Irish-speaking communities, the League's objective of preservation and extension was no more than the logic of Hyde's basic propositions regarding language and identity and the need for socio-cultural regeneration in late nineteenth century Ireland. Hyde claimed that the purpose of the Gaelic League and the language revival mission was 'to render the present a rational continuation of the past'. For Hyde, it would be a catastrophe of unimaginable proportions for any people (for both the individuals and the collectivity) were the continuity of its cultural tradition, articulated and given form principally through language, to be ruptured. Such a cultural tradition encompassed thoughts, feelings, perceptions, wisdom, a distinctive world-view based on a unique configuration of values. The case made for cultural continuity, through the medium of Irish, and, therefore, for language revival, rested on a set of assumptions and propositions that combined elements of general humanism with specific tenets of cultural nationalism.

Hyde's understanding of the relationship between language, thought and identity was unremarkable for his time. Whereas, in the beginning, thought and feeling may have given rise to language, the dynamics of language development and of cultural formation within human society had become more complex over time. Hyde quoted approvingly Jubainville's definition of language as 'the form of our thoughts during every instant of our existence'. As a language develops it encodes a complex system of understandings, meanings and values particular to its community of users – a distinctive world-view. As the Prussian philosopher and theologian, Friedrich Schleiermacher, had written some time earlier: 'every language constitutes a particular mode of thought, and what is thought in one language can never be repeated in the same way in another.'[13]

The abandonment of a language, therefore, to say nothing of its enforced abandonment, inevitably involved a disorientating rupture in cultural continuity at several levels; not only an alienation from landscape (placenames) and inherited historical narratives and communal myths, but also a deep psychological trauma, at an individual and communal level, caused by the loss of a rich inherited matrix of wisdom and knowledge – knowledge of self and of the world. This elemental trauma, it was believed, had been exacerbated by a number of features particular to the language change in Ireland: that it was the outcome of conquest, military and political, so that the abandonment of the native communal language in the face of the dominant new language of the conqueror (in law, commerce, politics, administration, etc.) became internalised as part of the shame of being conquered, of experiencing defeat, dispossession, humiliation and general impoverishment.[14] This general syndrome among a conquered people – the self-disparagement and shame, the contempt for the native culture felt by many of its carriers in the face of their need to come to terms with a seemingly invincible new culture sustained by a new ruling group – is well-documented in the literature on colonialism, from Memmi and Fanon to Said.

It was an outrage to Hyde and his fellow ideologues of the Gaelic League that this language abandonment had produced frightening inter-generational tension, incomprehension and emotional violence. The natural inter-generational transmission of love, wisdom, knowledge, sensibility and feeling was violently interrupted and sabotaged, through silence, reproach, repression and physical punishment, in the interests of a language-change enforced by the need to conform to an external structure of power and material opportunity. This, in essence, was the 'humanist' impulse advanced by Hyde on behalf of the language revival.

The specifically cultural nationalist aspects of Hyde's propositions are also of interest, though also unremarkable for his time. As Hyde saw it, by abandoning their own distinctive language, customs and traditions (for Hyde, a broad but conventional inventory of demonstrably nativist modes), and adopting uncritically the English language and cultural fashions (popular and elite) originating in England, while continuing at the same time to insist vehemently on their own distinctiveness as a people or nation, and, accordingly, their entitlement to an Irish national state, the Irish had succeeded in having the worst of all worlds:

> It has always been very curious to me how Irish sentiment sticks in this half-way house ... how it continues to clamour for recognition as a distinct nationality, and at the same time throws away with both hands what would make it so. If Irishmen only went a little further they would become good Englishmen in sentiment also.

In short, if thoroughly assimilated to English culture, they might at least be able to generate a truly creative life and to achieve something of consequence by their collective energy (in the economic or social sphere, for example), untroubled by contradictions in self-definition or disorientating cultural confusion. But this hadn't happened and, on the evidence of nationalist political rhetoric, seemed unlikely to happen. As Hyde saw it, general social debilitation had been caused by the simple fact that 'we have ceased to be Irish without becoming English. It is to this cause that I attribute more than to anything else our awful emigration and impoverishment.' Accordingly, if the Irish were determined not to be assimilated to the powerful English culture, and to insist on their distinctiveness as a people – and for Hyde all the evidence was that they were determined so to insist – then at least they owed it to themselves to try to give that claim to separate or distinct peoplehood some verifiable basis, some authentic and convincing evidence:

> It is just because there appears no earthly chance of their becoming good members of the empire that I urge that they should not remain in the anomalous position they are in, but since they absolutely refuse to become the one thing, that they become the other; cultivate what they rejected, and build up an Irish nation on Irish lines.

This was the basic formulation of the decolonising impulse. For Hyde and the Gaelic League activists the restoration of the Irish language as the national vernacular was the cornerstone of this project of national reconstruction; a healthy identity being a prerequisite for a reconstruction of the social and economic fabric and the collective energy and self-belief of the national community.[15]

Of course, the alternative badge of communal identity which might be widely recognised was religion. Religious identity was, for historical reasons, deeply and pervasively communal in Ireland. But religion was a divisive and exclusive instrument of cultural differentiation. While history had determined that 'the dispossessed people' in Ireland were in fact the Catholic people, no theorist of Irish nationalism advocated that Irishness be considered synonymous with, or a condition of Catholicism. This did not prevent Catholic leaders – clerical and lay – from regularly lapsing into such an identification of Catholic with 'Irish' and historically-oppressed 'native'.[16] This strong communal sense of religious identity, with its deep historical roots, would inevitably present a challenge to a project of decolonisation based upon language as the key marker of identity.

One further feature, or refinement, of Hyde's claim for the revival of Irish was that it was not simply a general plea for the cultural particularity encoded in language to be allowed to live and develop, but a specific set of claims for the kind of cultural differentiation which marked off the Irish from the English. This, it must be said, was fairly representative of the stereotyping common to cultural taxonomy in the later nineteenth century, benignly voiced by Renan, Arnold and others, with its more morbid versions formulated in racist discourse (Gobineau and Chamberlain, for example). In effect, the artistic and imaginative and spiritual Celts were contrasted with the solid and practical and materialist Teutons.[17] As with all stereotypes, it was not all pure invention, but, rather, exaggeration, distortion and omission. With Hyde, it involved a generous measure of hyperbole and more than a few grains of nonsense:

> The English race are admirable for their achievements ... their perseverance, their business faculties, their practical qualities ... wealth, power, and the teeming fruits of industry are theirs ... Well, the characteristics of this Irish race of ours are lightness, brightness, wit, fluency, and an artistic temperament. The characteristics of the Teutonic race are an intense business faculty, perseverance, and steadiness in details ... The more divergence of thought and genius, of natural aptitudes, the better, because, I tell you, there is an individuality in nationalities exactly as there is in persons – and to attempt to mould or crush everything into one particular type has invariably been fatal to the people that attempted it.

A version of this particular stereotyping also informed Yeats and his collaborators in the enterprise of establishing an authentic Irish national literature in Hiberno-English, and many Gaelic Leaguers gave the formula a more deeply religious hue.

In sum, 'the Irish revival', as a holistic project of decolonisation based on the restoration of the Irish language as the communal 'voice' of Ireland, was advocated on fairly orthodox grounds of cultural stereotyping as well as on the higher humanistic grounds of cultural continuity and 'wholeness' in language, thought and feeling.

Hyde's main collaborator in founding the Gaelic League, the noted historian and scholar, Eoin MacNéill, also emphasised the need for spiritual as well as social renewal in Ireland. Where MacNéill diverged from Hyde, perhaps, as Hutchinson's work has shown, was in MacNéill's emphasis on the way in which the glories of the Gaelic tradition and inheritance, still resonating in the living Irish vernacular, emerged from the uniquely rich cultural fusion of the Celtic genius with the light of Christianity; it was this encounter with the Christian vision which had fructified and given a unique focus to the Celtic spiritual and artistic genius in Ireland.[18] Again, the noted journalist and propagandist, D. P. Moran, produced a more schematic model than Hyde of cultural absorption (with the Gael as the matrix absorbing all later arrivals), and a more colourful and corrosive flagellation of the contradictions and paradoxes present in the Irish debate on cultural identity; but Moran's views, though influential, did not present any fundamental challenge to the main Gaelic League propositions.[19]

It is generally accepted that the political leadership of the popular front Sinn Féin, after 1917, and of the first generation to exercise political power in the Irish Free State, after 1922, included a substantial quota of men, and, to a lesser extent, women, who had been influenced, some deeply, by the Gaelic League idea and the cultural agenda of the revolution. Indeed, the political scientist Tom Garvin has suggested that 'the Gaelic League was in many ways the central institution in the development of the Irish revolutionary elite'.[20] This claim needs some qualification. The actual number of those in the new political establishment from the 1920s through to the 1950s who were fully or firmly committed to the project of cultural change (or, more crucially, perhaps, who had any clear idea of what such a project might mean in practice) was probably significantly lower than is commonly supposed, even if the ranks of the committed included some of the more notable political leaders. A larger question, however, is the extent to which the commitment to cultural, and specifically the language, change penetrated other elements of the ruling classes, the key elites of the new Irish state: the bankers, merchants and business class, the lawyers and doctors, financiers, bishops and wealthy farmers.[21] The new state was, from the outset, a conservative and substantially confessional bourgeois state. The established power elites of the pre-independence era remained largely undisturbed in the exercise of their economic and social dominance. How likely was it that such a power structure would be hospitable to a radical programme of linguistic and cultural change? Controversies over the place of Irish in the education system – notably in the new National University of Ireland – had already given evidence of sharp differences within the nationalist community.[22]

Nevertheless, in the first generation after independence the leaders of the main political parties in Ireland all gave obeisance to the notion that it was right and proper, indeed that it was a solemn obligation, for the government of an independent Irish state to enhance the status of the Irish language and to attend to its preservation and extension as a living 'national' language. There was a large measure of consensus among the political leaders that the Irish language was the principal and most irrefutable mark of that sense of nationality on whose behalf an Irish national state had been demanded and, whatever its shortcomings, established. Accordingly, Irish was accorded official status as the national language in the 1922 Free State constitution, and this was later repeated and indeed strengthened in de Valera's 1937 constitution.[23] Additionally, policy initiatives in the 1920s and 1930s, notably in the areas of education and recruitment to the public service, sought to extend competence and use of the language. With subsidised publications, progress in lexicography and standardisation of the language, a modest presence in the arts and broadcasting, and significant symbolic recognition for Irish (in the nomenclature of state offices, public companies, ritual use in solemn state occasions, etc.), it would be wrong to say that no progress was made. By the 1950s a substantial cohort of secondary bilinguals had emerged from the schools and Irish had achieved a degree of penetration and a presence in public domains in Ireland from which it had been excluded for many centuries.[24]

Yet, all this fell very short indeed of the radical cultural project of decolonisation proclaimed by the more advanced Gaelic Leaguers. The constitutional status of Irish was not elaborated or translated into statutory legal rights for Irish-speakers; the ritual symbolic use was minimalist and increasingly seen as tokenism; the degree of real penetration by Irish even within the state services and the apparatus of government (local and national) was very limited; and, above all, the actual base-communities or enclaves of Irish-speakers – the Gaeltacht communities – continued to contract at an alarming rate, due to the ravages of emigration and the continuing shift to English within the diminished communities, and there seemed to be no coherent state strategy for arresting this accelerating decline.[25]

In seeking explanations for this, however qualified, 'failure' of the cultural project of the Gaelic League and its political offspring, one may choose to begin from any one of a number of ideological positions. A primary site of explanation is the Irish state itself, its nature and the capacity for identity-endorsement instinct in its very existence as a national state. In terms of economic and social power structures, the Irish Free State was a conservative bourgeois state from its inception. The new political leaders made relatively few changes – and none of substance – in the centralised apparatus of government they inherited from the British. Nor were there many changes, apart from ritual matters of nomenclature and minor procedural and ceremonial matters, in the structures of law, government and public administration: the decision to opt for an unarmed police force was probably the most radical departure from the prevailing systems. The economic and fiscal policy of the new state was considerate of existing interests.[26]

The state was also deeply confessional, predictably so, perhaps, given the overwhelmingly large (over 90%) majority of observing Roman Catholics among its citizens.[27] Its civic culture was deeply imbued with a Catholic ethos. Indeed, the sheer size of the Catholic majority (as a result of the partition of the island and the exclusion of the north-east of the island, with its sizeable Protestant community, from the Free State), and the historic experience of Irish Catholics since the sixteenth century, meant that a strong communal identity based on religious loyalty was, so to speak, ready-made and available to the Irish Free State at its foundation. This Catholic communal identity was easily shared and culturally comfortable even for elements of the nationalist political leadership who were politically committed, at a cerebral level, to a more inclusive, reli-

giously pluralistic and republican version of 'Irishness' than that suggested by simple 'Catholic nationalist' sentiment. In fact, a language dimension to Irish identity which demanded nothing too burdensome,
nothing beyond a symbolic recognition of the ancestral language and a
care to ensure its presence in the ceremony and ritual of occasions of
state, was probably the ideal 'finishing' of identity for many Irish Catholics, utterly secure in the historical identity and the civic culture defined
and shaped by their religion.[28]

The growing assurance of the Irish state itself as a stable democratic
state in a very turbulent world in the two decades after 1922, and its in-
cremental march towards full political sovereignty by 1937 and a formal
declaration of its status as a Republic in 1949, meant that the Irish state
came to be taken for granted by its citizens, and Irishness (or 'identity')
became, as it were, a function of citizenship of the independent Irish state
– a comfort, let it be noted, not available to the Irish nationalists living in
Northern Ireland, for whom issues of identity remained inevitably much
more fraught with anxiety.

It would be wrong to suggest that some at least of the cadre of political leaders in the new state did not wish and work for a more substantial cultural change, and specifically for more substantial progress in respect of the 'preservation and extension' of the Irish language. Their own
understanding of the enormity and complexity of the task being undertaken may, in retrospect, seem seriously deficient. But the geocultural
location of Ireland, right in the middle of the Anglo-American highway
of communications and entertainment, increasingly the main artery of a
global technology grid of communications whose dominant language
was English, made the challenge of achieving any viable form of bilin-
gualism – to say nothing of a reverse language 'shift' – especially daunt-
ing in Ireland (Quebec invites comparison, but only on certain limited
grounds).

The disproportionately large majority of monoglot English-speakers
in Ireland at the turn of the century, and the reassuringly high status
achieved by the 'English of Ireland' in the forum of world literature (Yeats'
Nobel Prize came in 1923, Shaw's two years later, while Joyce's *Ulysses*
was first published in 1922), as well as its robustly creative energies in all
aspects of popular culture, further weighted the advantages in favour of
English being overwhelmingly the dominant vernacular and of its continuing to erode the fragile base of the Irish-speaking community. English was also the language of the vast majority of the Irish of the diaspora
and of the countries in which most of them settled; while for the leaders
of the Irish Catholic Church, English was the vital instrument of their dynamic global missionary effort from the middle of the nineteenth century forward.

It is not surprising perhaps, that, in the face of such overwhelmingly unbalanced prospects, some who were early enthusiasts for the cultural project based on the revival of Irish should, over time, have lost faith and hope in the project. Some also lost charity. In particular, a section of the intelligentsia, from relatively early in the life of the new state, began to articulate a dissident critique of the 'official culture' of the state: an official culture, substantially embodied in legislation as well as in a host of more symbolic ways, which they denounced as excessively confessional, conservative, censorious and philistine. The preponderant influence of conservative Catholic social teaching may have been the main target of this criticism. But it was significant that the language revival policy, especially the formulaic exhortations and heavily bureaucratic emphases which were seen as dominant features of state policy and its implementation, was increasingly seen by some intellectuals as merely another aspect of the sterile 'official culture', and denounced accordingly.[29]

It is only fair – indeed, it is necessary – to point out that the 'cultural vision' of decolonisation that centred on the language project was, for many of the revolutionary generation of Sinn Féin, linked to other social visions – notably, the social vision of a self-reliant, closely integrated Christian society, free of extremes of wealth and poverty, and bonded by a sense of reciprocal obligation up and down the social ladder.

This particular version of the Sinn Féin social vision is strongly present in Fianna Fáil's list of aims and objectives at its foundation, and again in its 1932 election manifesto.[30] Certainly, de Valera's own vision was set out repeatedly by him in a series of substantial statements – in the Dáil, in public speeches and in some of his radio broadcasts to the Irish abroad on St Patrick's Day. The most frequently quoted of these statements is, of course, the 1943 St Patrick's Day broadcast. But this was not an idiosyncratic view of the Ireland that some, at least, of the revolutionary generation of the Gaelic Leaguers dreamed of. As I have pointed out elsewhere, similar rhetoric can be found in statements by other contemporary leaders, for example, Richard Mulcahy.[31] The vision was expressed also in more sinewy political terms: for example, it is significant that in several of de Valera's pronouncements on economic ideas the source he quotes again and again is James Fintan Lalor (with an occasional nod towards Connolly, depending on the political requirements of the occasion). The ideal was a communal view of economic resources, rights and shared entitlements, but one that stopped short of socialism.

In fact, if this 1943 vision can be criticised (as it has been) on the grounds that it conjures up and valorises a somewhat static, hierarchical Jeffersonian society, with a strong rural ethos ('cosy homesteads', 'respect for the wisdom of old age', etc.), there are elements in it which seem to reflect deep longings within the wider community. These elements included the valorisation of rural life and the desire for industrialisation without urbanisation – a kind of limitless dispersal or decentralisation of economic opportunity. This particular strand of the early Sinn Féin ideology was to cast a long shadow on twentieth century Irish economic policy, with enduring political resistance in local communities to industrial or development 'growth-centres', as recommended by Buchanan and other planners, and with continuing demands being made by political and community leaders on development agencies for the widest possible 'dispersal' of industries or plants. Neither should we ignore the fact that the Irish nationalist valorisation of the healthy (in mind and body) stock of the countryside – living the life that God intended – was part of a wider current of opinion, sentiment and aspiration among political and cultural nationalists in many parts of Europe in the later nineteenth and throughout the early decades of the twentieth century.[32] This general sentiment – the identification of the land and rural society as a privileged habitat for 'authentic' living, close to nature and to God, bonded in feeling and in values – was bound to be especially strong in Ireland with its emotive history of land dispossession.

What matters, however, in the context of this essay, is the way in which this 'social' vision was also embedded in policy as well as in rhetoric in de Valera's Ireland. Thus, for example, the land distribution policy of the 1930s and, more critically, the tillage drive (through incentives in the 1930s, through compulsion in the war years), and the food self-sufficiency policy and reduction in the cattle herd, were all aspects of an agricultural policy consistent with, if not driven by, the vision of a well-stocked rural countryside of 'comfortable' small-holders. That these policies, and the vision that inspired them, reflected one important strain of contemporary Catholic social thought is well known.[33] In fact, the objectives of Muintir na Tíre, established in 1931, are, in language as well as in substance, very similar to de Valera's declared vision. Based on the Boerenbond Belge (founded 1890) Canon Hayes's organisation stated its aim as:

> to unite the rural communities of Ireland on the Leo XIII principle that there must exist friendly relations between master and man; that it is a mistake to assume that class is hostile to class, that well-to-do and working men are intended by nature to live in mutual conflict. This new rural organisation ... intends to unite in one body the rural workers of the country, not for the purpose of attacking any one section of the community but to give agricultural workers in Ireland their due and proper position in the life of the nation.[34]

The methods of Muintir na Tíre (fireside chats, domestic forum for discussion, 'rural weeks', publications) were also consistent with de Valera's version of the good life of a citizenry involved in responsible politics.

Yet, notwithstanding the valuable contribution of Muintír na Tíre to the quality of life in rural Ireland, it is significant that by the later 1930s the degree to which this 'social vision' was embedded in the policies and practices of the state was already being criticised as being inadequate. The facts, though they rarely speak for themselves, found a sufficient number of concerned community leaders to speak for them. The tillage acreage scarcely expanded in the 1930s, and the bruising tariff war with Britain in the 1930s inflicted damage which hurt, and provoked discontent among farmers well beyond the category of 'ranchers'. After the temporary tillage increase of the 'Emergency' years (1939–45), there was an early reversion to the by then well-established pattern of land-use, with the emphasis on pasture. The flight of the small-holders from the land continued, and the number of farm labourers – the class for whom de Valera might have been expected to show the surest instinct – was halved (from 160,000 to 80,000) in the twenty-five years after 1930.[35]

Bishops and others began to demand more purposeful intervention to halt the drift from the land: public pronouncements and their contributions to such government enquiries as the Commission on Vocational Organisation (1943) and the Commission on Emigration and other Population Problems (1948–54) gave the Catholic bishops scope for advocating a more thorough-going programme of social action based on the family.[36] But the signs of public concern at the failure to realise the promised land were apparent in other ways also. Politically, Clann na Talún arrived on the scene in the late 1930s, to challenge Fianna Fáil on its own terms – the survival and improvement of the condition of the rural small-holders – while in 1943 Macra na Feirme was founded, through which young farmers were to offer an impressive critique of the direction of state policy in agriculture and in rural development in general.[37]

It is in the light of this growing criticism and debate from the later 1930s on the 'social vision' of de Valera and Fianna Fáil, as it related to the creation of the contented, integrated Christian rural society (staying at home in frugal comfort), that we can best reflect on the manner and timing of the questioning of the 'cultural vision' of Irish-Ireland's project of decolonisation, and of the extent and effectiveness of its embedding in the life of the Irish state. Here, also, the coincidence of timing in the emergence of new and critical voices is quite striking.

Thus, for example, while sections of the teachers were understandably critical of aspects of the language policy (though mainly of 'means' and 'methods' rather than of 'ends') from the early years of the Free State, and while undoubtedly the commitment of many teachers to the language project must have been weakened by the constant preaching to them of their 'obligations' by ministers stone-walling on a long list of other pressing educational issues (teachers' salaries, school resources, etc.), it is again from the later 1930s that we come upon the evidence that indicates the emergence of growing doubts on the progress being made in realising the cultural vision of the Gaelic League within the Irish state.[38]

Among those who continued to believe in and to support the language revival and the broader cultural 'autonomy' project, anger, frustration and stoic resignation were to be found in heavy measure, if randomly distributed. The most radical response to the evidence of failure in maintaining or sustaining the Gaeltacht community came from groups of political and social activists within the Gaeltacht community itself, supported by a cadre of urban intellectuals. The distinguished Irish writer and political activist, Máirtín Ó Cadhain, was prominent and influential in this movement. Ó Cadhain came to adopt a recognisably Marxist position (with strong Gramscian elements) on the language question and the depopulation, through emigration, of the Gaeltacht. The cultural hegemony of English was the outcome of socio-economic interests inherent in the power structure; the breaking of this cultural hegemony, therefore, would require a revolutionary socialist assault on these power-structures and the interests they served. Or, as he put it: '*Sí athréimniú na Gaeilge athghabháil na hÉireann.*' ('The restoration of Irish means the repossession of the country.')[39]

Less radical language revivalists sought, at different times and in different ways, to advise, cajole, persuade, bully and shame the government of the day into showing more urgency and giving a higher political priority (and resources) to the language task than successive governments seemed prepared to do. The politicians were berated for infirmity of commitment, as reflected in their own behaviour and in the apparatus of the state over which they presided. The methods, policy directions and deployment of resources involved in state language policy were regularly and, at times searchingly, criticised. Revivalists with some more sophisticated and scholarly understanding of the socio-linguistic complexities of language change, and of the need for sustained and intelligent language planning at state level, suffered their own frustrations when regularly finding government ministers and their senior advisors deaf or indifferent to their advice.[40]

But there are dates and events which are suggestive of, at the least, new stirrings among the ranks of the converted and the committed. In 1935, An Comhchaidreamh, an organisation for Irish-speaking graduates of all the Irish universities, was founded.[41] In 1938 the Oireachtas, the major cultural festival of Irish-language artistic life, was revived after years in abeyance. A new Irish-language magazine of opinion and creative writing, *Comhar*, was launched by graduates in 1942 and a year later a new Irish-language newspaper made its appearance: *Inniu*, originally intended as a daily but eventually published for many decades as a weekly. A radical mood of impatience within the Irish-language movement saw new challenging branches established within the Gaelic League and a new departure, Glúin na Buaidhe (1942), while an Irish-language version of the Legion of Mary, called An Réalt, also attracted support from its foundation in 1942. For young Irish boys, the Christian Brothers established Ógra Éireann (1945), and, significantly, a new umbrella co-ordinating body for all the voluntary Irish-language organisations, Comdháil Náisiúnta na Gaeilge, was established with the support of de Valera's government in 1943. There were those who believed that this government support for co-ordination was a shrewd tactic to get the various strands of the Irish-language movement in the community together under one tent before the radicals became too subversive. And, in 1953, a young group of Irish-speaking graduates emerged from An Comhchaidreamh to found Gael Linn, which in the decades that followed was to prove most innovative (in terms of schemes and funding) in bringing the Irish language to the wider public through a range of activities and in particular through use of the emerging mass media of information and entertainment.[42]

It is arguable, of course, as with Muintir na Tíre and Macra na Feirme, that this flowering of new Irish-language organisations and groups should be taken as a healthy sign of the vitality and energy of the 'Gaeilgeoirí' as a community: with new specialist activities and initiatives betokening its growing diversification of interests and demands, in fact its growing sophistication and maturity. But, on the other hand, there can be no ignoring the more than ample grounds for concern among committed revivalists. By the early 1940s, the number of 'A' schools (those conducting all teaching and activities through Irish) had peaked; and the discontent and opposition of the teachers was getting to the government and even to the Minister for Education, Tomás Ó Deirg.[43] Above all, the relentless weakening of the core communities in the Gaeltacht, through emigration and the continued advance of English in all areas of life, was evident to all and, as experts agreed, was not likely to be easily reversed, even after the belated establishment of a special Department of the Gaeltacht in 1956.

The concerns of the Irish-language organisations were registered by Comhdáil Náisiúnta na Gaeilge which in 1947 submitted to the government a substantial reappraisal document on the state language strategy and the implementation of government policy. But the core of the cultural vision – the 'restoration' of Irish as the main vernacular – so inspirational to key groups of the revolutionary generation who established the Irish Free State, maintained a tenacious hold on the imagination and certainly on the rhetoric of several of the leaders, particularly de Valera, even when the 'facts' of Irish social and cultural development, and the shortcomings of the state's 'performance' in many areas, seemed to demand serious and candid revaluation.[44] This tenacity, understandably, could seem more like obduracy to those who were impatient for change or who sought a more robust response to failure than a mere further dose of exhortation. For certain writers and commentators, satire seemed the only response to a rhetoric which they found ritualistic and hypocritical: this was the response of Brian Ó Nualláin/Flann O'Brien/Myles na Gopaleen.[45] Máirtín Ó Cadhain, for his part, continued to flail and to shame the inadequacy of the state's language commitment and policies relentlessly, in print and on platform.[46]

Yet, it is remarkable how little fundamental re-thinking of the basic assumptions of the language revival project – the corner-stone of the project of cultural decolonisation – took place within the revival movement in the early decades of the state. The basic ideology of the Gaelic League continued to be articulated in much the same terms as those of the founders. The two most prominent figures addressing these philosophical questions in the twenty years after the foundation of the Irish Free State were Daniel Corkery, whose *Philosophy of the Gaelic League* was published in 1943, and Fr Donnchadh Ó Floinn of Maynooth College. Both were able men of impressive intellectual calibre; but neither added anything original or made any significant revision of the ideas and assumptions of Hyde, MacNéill and the founders of the Gaelic League.[47] Indeed, as late as 1964, a group of eminent scholars and leaders of the language revival movement, in the report of a special government commission established to review the 'progress' of the Irish revival project to date, stated the raison d'être of the revival in terms almost identical to the terms used by Hyde and MacNéill.[48]

But by the early 1960s, the landscape of Irish politics and indeed of every facet of Irish life was radically changing. The 1950s had all but buried the last remnants of the revolutionary rhetoric and optimism. Social and economic failure on a grand scale, leading to an emigration haemorrhage of almost 420,000 people in one decade, made the belief of the revolutionary generation in the creative possibilities of political sovereignty seem cruelly misplaced. The continuing viability of the society, no less than the state, was being questioned, in the face of such massive emigration and the resultant social and economic anaemia. The old political guard moved on and with them much of the old rhetoric. Economic protectionism, the nationalist route to self-sufficiency, was abandoned, and free trade for a competitive small open economy was announced as the road to salvation. That road was to lead, all going well, to membership of the European 'Common Market' (as the EU was then known).

The language of cultural protectionism became an embarrassment; the future prospects for the Irish language would lie in a bilingual pluralist Ireland, where the rich cultural and linguistic diversity of Europe would provide just the setting and the stimulus needed to enable the Irish to become confident of their identity in the larger European family, when they had found difficulty in the more claustrophobic Anglo-American grid. Optimists saw this final renunciation of the deeply 'protectionist' nationalism of de Valera as a welcome opening of the shutters and a breath of fresh air. Others were not so sure; there were some voices who analysed the failures of the Free State in standard neo-colonialist terms.[49]

Few, if any, of those in Ireland who participated in the debate in the early 1960s, facilitated by the arrival of television in Ireland, could have anticipated the seismic nature of the changes that would in the decades that followed utterly transform the terms of that debate. The pace of European economic integration and the issues which the creation of a single market raised for cultural diversity in Europe; more fundamentally, the collapse of communism in the Soviet Union and eastern Europe and the triumph of liberal capitalism; coinciding with the globalisation of trade and technology and the emergence of the phenomenon of global media consortia of the Murdoch type; all have changed the parameters of the discussion of culture, identity and democracy itself across the world. The explosion of long-festering conflict in Northern Ireland brought back to the centre of political debate in Ireland and in Britain issues of ethnicity, dignity, identity and rights, individual and communal, which had seemed exhausted or 'resolved' in the Irish state. Elsewhere in Europe these same issues were also re-emerging; with their own dynamic in the Iberian peninsula in the post-Franco era, and further east, in parts of eastern and south-eastern Europe, with a shuddering insistence and brutality. Indeed, far beyond the European world – in the Middle East, Asia, Africa and elsewhere – these same fundamental issues were mocking Fukyama's complacent announcement of the end of serious ideological conflict. The Irish condition and debate at the end of the twentieth century remained, as it had been a century before, during the last spasm of European imperialist expansion, a recognisably representative detail of a larger canvas.

For those concerned with the complex and multiple realities of identity-formation and culture in the many post-colonial states established during the past half-century, and indeed for those concerned with the historical experience of colonialism and neo-colonialism at any place or time, there may be some lessons in the Irish experience. In particular, it may be useful to draw attention to one central fact of the Irish experience which may have wider relevance. When the cultural deposit of the colonial experience has been protracted, pervasive and deeply penetrative, as was the case with the long period of English cultural hegemony in Ireland; and when, whatever the pain, the trauma or the hurt involved, key modalities of that culture have become widely appropriated by the people at large (as was the case with the English language in Ireland), the task of identity-formation in a post-colonial situation must then take account of the total historical experience of 'the people' who are to be liberated and empowered.

For the Irish people of Hyde's day, 'the past' to which they were heirs was not only the Gaelic past, with all its rich matrix of meaning, but also the more recent past in which English had taken up residence in the Irish mind. There were many ways of responding creatively to this historical legacy – as the very different strategies of Yeats and of Joyce were to demonstrate. But what was not a viable strategy was an ahistorical or counter-historical impulse for erasing or expunging the settled deposit of a long historical experience. In the circumstances of twentieth century Ireland, the project for the 'restoration' of the Irish language was never likely to succeed in terms of the simple 'replacement' of English by Irish; not only because of the enormous power of English as a dominant world language (a function of British and later American world power, not least in global communications, in information and entertainment), nor because the Irish diaspora was itself a crucial element in the dispersal and world dominance of English. It was, rather, that English had already become so embedded in the social and cultural fabric of the majority of the people that any sustained attempt at replacement would itself have involved rupture and a new form of cultural coercion. The only terms in which 'restoration' could hope to gather support and popular endorsement in an open democratic society was by its being offered as an invitation to a privileged register of Irishness, likely to enrich the full experience of living a creative and confident life at ease in time and place with one's cultural habitat. The prospect of a viable bilingual society in twentieth century Ireland required, as a prerequisite to enlightened and effective state language policy, an acceptance of the long cohabitation of the Irish mind by the two languages, and the determination, intellectual rigour, courage and constancy of purpose to ensure that while both were fully acknowledged as having the right of permanent settlement, the duty of an independent Irish state was to ensure that in their cohabitation the weaker, unique to its Irish habitat, was not smothered by the stronger, thriving in many climes across the globe.

A well-disposed critic, Breandán S. Mac Aodha, writing in 1972 had this to say of the Gaelic League: '… the greatest indictment one may make against the League … is that it did not succeed in effectively moulding the state which it more than any other body had helped to bring into being'.[50] In the context of this verdict, when we come to consider the experiment in decolonisation proposed by the Irish-Ireland movement and by some of its idealists who came to positions of political power within the independent Irish state, and before we rush to fix the political leaders of de Valera's Ireland with our condescension or our condemnation, we may be well-advised to ask a few questions as to how the intellectuals (including academics) in Ireland discharged their responsibilities during these decades.

Eamon de Valera: the price of his achievement

Garret FitzGerald

With O'Connell and Parnell, de Valera was one of three Irish political leaders of the nineteenth and twentieth centuries who had not alone the capacity and the ability to play a major political role over an extended period
of time, but also the opportunity to do so. There are others who, if they had
lived and had had the opportunity to exercise their remarkable talents in
the political sphere under conditions of peace, might have rivalled or even
outshone some or all of these three – most notably Michael Collins in this
century. But those whom the gods love die young, and the nature of Ireland's almost always tragic, but at times heroic, history has been such
that many men of exceptional talent have died or, more frequently, been
killed before they reached the age of 35, no more than a third of the way
through their potential working life.

All three of the men I have mentioned – O'Connell, Parnell and de
Valera – excited controversy and division amongst Irish nationalists at
some point in their lives. O'Connell especially, perhaps, towards the end
of life, when he and the new generation of Young Irelanders found themselves at odds, and Parnell also at the end of his career and life. De Valera, by contrast, became a controversial figure amongst Irish nationalists
before he was 40 and, inevitably, living longer than any other major political figure, well into his 90s, continued to divide Irish politics thereafter.
This has made especially difficult an objective assessment of his achievements and defects within his own lifetime, or even within the generation
following his death in 1975.

The political system of the Irish state remains today largely based
upon a party system, the origins of which are to be found substantially
in a polarisation around de Valera. The issues that led to this polarisation
ceased to have any current relevance in domestic politics many decades
ago, and the two major political parties moved on to seek, and find, new
roles as they addressed the complex and difficult problems of Ireland in
the last third of the twentieth century. Nevertheless, the memory of the

circumstances that brought these two parties into existence lingers on and while virtually none of their members have any direct recollections of these events, even the youngest voters continue to associate these two parties vaguely with their historical origins. Because of this, many Irish people still have difficulty in seeing the two parties in question as they actually are today, with their current policies and different styles of leadership and organisation. To many Irish people, and especially to those who support other parties or none, they remain the two 'civil war parties'.

In a very real sense, therefore, de Valera's influence still pervades the Irish political system as it is perceived by those outside it, even though to the vast majority of those within the system, the active practical politicians, the divisions that led to their parties coming into existence are almost totally irrelevant and long forgotten.

Thus in twenty-seven years in active politics, I cannot recall a single disagreement or argument with an active politician of the Fianna Fáil party founded by de Valera that related to that distant past – the Anglo-Irish Treaty of 1921 or Civil War of 1922–23, or indeed to the other events of the 1920s and early 1930s that provided the original basis for the main divide in the party system that we know today. Consequently I – and I believe most other active Irish politicians of these two parties – are often frustrated, and indeed irritated, to hear people outside politics referring to 'the perpetuation of civil war politics' in our party system. Yet in so far as this is the external perception of so many outside politics it is, like all myths that are still believed, a reality we have to face.

I have made this point at the outset for several reasons. First, in so far as our existing political party system owes its origins to divisions eighty years ago in which de Valera played a crucial role, this represents a significant part of his influence on contemporary Ireland.

Second, because however anachronistic – in the eyes of active politicians at least – may be the common public perception that what divides the parties and their political representatives in parliament today is still 'civil war politics', this belief is a reality of modern Ireland that is equally a product of the controversial events eighty years ago.

And, third, because having made these two points I do not feel that it is necessary, or indeed, relevant to contemporary Ireland to discuss the controversial role of de Valera in those historical events, except where in very specific, but relatively limited, ways that role may impinge indirectly upon the contemporary scene.

What is, I think, more relevant is to consider how the actions and policies of de Valera in the period after the Civil War that ended in May 1923 have left their mark upon the institutions, and possibly in some respects upon the character, of contemporary Ireland. In attempting even a provisional assessment of this influence one must have regard, first, to the problems that faced the new Irish state in the aftermath of the Civil War, and, second, to the condition of Ireland today eighty years later. What has been achieved, what has been left undone, and what has been made worse over this period? And in relation to each of these questions, what was de Valera's role?

LEGITIMACY

The most fundamental problem facing the Irish state after the Civil War of 1922–23, in which those who wished to continue the struggle with Britain for an independent republic rejected dominion status within the British Commonwealth, was the stability of the state itself.

A substantial proportion of its people – at least one-third, on the evidence of the general election of summer 1923 called in the immediate aftermath of the Civil War – withheld their consent from the new state in its early years and by so doing challenged its legitimacy. The resolution of this fundamental problem of the legitimacy of the state required a development of its initial status. For, like the other dominions of the commonwealth at that time, that state when established was an autonomous, self-governing, political unit – but one with a question mark over its complete sovereignty vis-à-vis Britain.

Another different but related problem was that created by the partition of the island, that had been brought about by the decision of the provincial parliament in Northern Ireland to opt out of the new state on the day after its foundation as an internationally recognised political unit through the enactment of its constitution, vis., 6 December 1922. This right for Northern Ireland to opt out had been agreed as part of the Treaty terms and, contrary to popular mythology, had not been the subject of much discussion in the debate on the Treaty in Dáil Éireann which had preceded the outbreak of the Civil War. That debate had, of course, centred instead on the issue of the symbols of monarchy that the Treaty had imposed upon the independent Irish state. Would this division of the island, a division that had no historical precedent, endure – or could it be reversed, and the parts brought together again?

Next, there was a fundamental question as to what would be the political ethos of this new state. Would it be pluralist, giving full recognition to the cultural and religious tradition of many centuries of settlers, as well as the native cultural and religious tradition, or would it attempt to become mono-cultural, elevating to a position of primacy the native Gaelic and Catholic tradition of the great majority of its people – those who had sought and secured its independence – with all the problems that this might create for an eventual coming-together of the predominantly Protestant north with the overwhelmingly Roman Catholic state comprising the remainder of the island?

There was also the problem of the economics of a country that had suffered colonial exploitation in the eighteenth century and earlier, as well as considerable neglect at the hands of laissez-faire Britain during much of the nineteenth century. This unhappy economic history, together with the state's peripheral geographical location, had deprived Ireland of the possibility of industrial development. And this had left it a predominantly agricultural country with a high fertility and birth-rate.

In the absence of opportunities for employment in its weak agricultural sector, the state continued to suffer a massive erosion by way of emigration of a high proportion of those born within its territory during the first quarter-of-a-century of political independence. Of that generation one-third had emigrated by the age of 35, and one-sixth had died, principally due to infantile mortality or TB, thus reducing the size of each age cohort by one-half.

Finally, there was the question of the social organisation of the new state: would it develop into a property-owning democracy or into a socialist state; and, if the former, would it be a socially-conscious democracy, caring for the under-privileged in Irish society?

These were the five main challenges that faced the new state, although, of course, there were many others, including the immediate task of physical reconstruction in the immediate aftermath of a civil war that had involved much more damage to its infra-structure than the struggle against Britain that immediately preceded independence.

CONSENSUS AND LEGITIMACY

In the midst of the Civil War, in which the very foundations of the new state were challenged in arms, albeit unsuccessfully, the legitimacy of the new state was juridically established and internationally recognised. In 1923 it also became a member of the League of Nations. Moreover, by mid-1923 domestically the authority of the state was established with the defeat of those who opposed the Treaty.

But there remained the problem of securing free acceptance of this legitimacy and authority on the part of those who had rejected it at the outset. This posed a problem both for victor and vanquished in the Civil War.

The victors were, of course, the government led by W. T. Cosgrave, the supporters of which had during the latter stages of the Civil War formed themselves into a political party, Cumann na nGaedheal. Later, in the aftermath of their loss of power in 1932, and following a merger with several other groups, this party developed into the present Fine Gael party.

Cumann na nGaedheal's contribution to securing acceptance of the authority of the new state lay partly in a sustained external diplomatic campaign to transform the dominions of what was then commonly known as the British empire into sovereign independent states within a commonwealth in which Britain would no longer claim or exercise any authority over the countries enjoying dominion status. In this diplomatic battle Canada played a willing part, although the primary impetus in the crucial period from 1926 to 1931 has been attributed, with, I believe, some justice, to the Irish government. Indeed the extent of the Irish contribution has been well reflected in the title, as well as in the contents, of the authoritative work on the subject by David Harkness: *The Restless Dominion*.

By 1931, British resistance had been overcome and, through the Statute of Westminster, Ireland and Canada, as well as the other dominions, including a rather reluctant Australia and New Zealand, had secured their unfettered sovereignty.

But this achievement did not itself satisfy the aspirations of the many Irish people who remained hostile to the monarchical form of dominion status, under which the crown remained the nominal fount of authority in each of the several dominions. Given the importance of symbols, which in Ireland as in many other countries sometimes count for more than reality, this was an important qualification. In these early years of the new state there were in fact few indications that political independence and sovereignty achieved within a theoretical monarchical structure would induce those who had been defeated in the Civil War to go beyond a mere cessation of hostilities and enable them to accept and join in the political institutions that had been established.

Moreover, even if such a degree of popular acceptance of this status could have been achieved, there was the further potential problem of securing that, if and when the political representatives of the anti-Treaty tradition, having entered parliament, came to secure a popular mandate to govern, the resultant hand-over of power could be accomplished smoothly and without any attempt to inhibit it on the part of the army. For that army had established the authority of the state during the Civil War and might perhaps be expected not to relish serving within a few years under a government drawn from among those whom they had defeated in that struggle.

On the other hand, those who had been defeated in the Civil War faced the reverse side of this coin.

The de Valera of the post-Civil War era found himself the leader of a dispirited group, many of whom at that point did not hold him in high regard – a group which, after its military defeat, was overwhelmingly rejected by the Irish people politically in the post-Civil War general election of August 1923. In that election republicans – admittedly at the lowest ebb of their fortunes – received only about one-third of the votes cast.

And, in any event, those whom de Valera led had rejected the constitutional foundations of the new state, and were little disposed, as they emerged from internment in 1924, to sit down to work the system which they had fought to reject.

To many people in that situation the way ahead must have seemed hopeless – and many did indeed give up hope and emigrate to the United States. For what chance was there that, if a political U-turn were to be attempted involving the recognition and acceptance of that which they had just sought to reject in arms, the Irish people would accord respect or support to those who had undertaken this humiliating policy reversal? For such a U-turn was bound to leave those engaged in it open to a challenge: if you can accept the constitution now, why did you seek to reject it in arms several years ago and destroy much of the country in the process?

And even if de Valera were to attempt to lead the republicans of the post-Civil War era along such a constitutional path, how many would be willing to follow him? Would that number be sufficient to ensure stability and peace under the new dispensation, or would too many remain outside the system, continuing to challenge its legitimacy and to claim the right, if a suitable opportunity arose, of using arms against it?

It is for the historians to give their verdicts in due course on the manner in which de Valera tackled this problem. In particular it will be interesting to see to what extent historians eventually judge the events of the period 1926 to 1937 – from the decision to found a constitutional party, Fianna Fáil, in 1926 and to bring it into the Dáil in 1927, to the enactment of the new constitution of 1937 – to have been the result of a plan thought out from the outset, or to have been the product merely of a process of groping forward towards a goal perhaps only imperfectly defined, even in de Valera's own mind.

For the observer of contemporary Ireland it is sufficient to remark that the outcome of the process started in 1926 included a very substantial achievement, in the form of a largely successful conversion of the 1922 constitution (the verbal formulation of which – although not its real content – had necessarily been determined in a number of key respects by the outside force of the Anglo-Irish Treaty provisions), into a document expressed in the language of nationalism to a degree that rendered it acceptable to the vast majority of those who had rejected the Treaty.

Although the resultant reconciliation with extreme republicanism was incomplete – witness the amount of blood spilt in Ireland, north and south, in the following fifty years and especially in the past twenty-five years – it would be wrong to under-estimate the seminal importance of this process of establishing within the new state a national consensus – one that soon secured the acceptance by all but a tiny handful of irreconcilables of the legitimacy and authority of the institutions of the state.

It is to that achievement that we owe the preservation of peace within this state both during the last war, when the IRA lacked the support needed to create conditions of unrest that might have attracted German invasion, and again in the early 1970s when the cohesion of our political system was strong enough to resist the efforts of a handful of misguided politicians to embroil our state in the violence that engulfed Northern Ireland.

The fact that even today the extent of the potential dangers we faced on those two occasions remains largely unappreciated by public opinion is itself a tribute to the success of de Valera's stabilisation policy. His unexpected decision to oppose the Treaty had severely destabilised the state at the moment of its foundation, greatly increasing the difficulty of mastering the inevitable resistance by extremists to a compromise settlement with Britain. But he spent an important part of his life putting together again – successfully – the Humpty-Dumpty he had helped to push off the wall in December 1921.

The accession to power of Fianna Fáil under de Valera in 1932, only nine years after the defeat of the republicans in the Civil War, was a seismic event for all those who were politically active at the time. It involved what appeared to apparent contemporaries to be a sharp discontinuity in public policy, and especially in the state's relations with Britain – relations that immediately deteriorated into an Economic War centring on both constitutional and financial issues.

But in a historic perspective this discontinuity can be seen to be an illusion. The events between 1932 and 1937, when the new constitution was enacted, can now be seen to have been rather a continuation under a different leadership of the policy of seeking a separation of the new Irish state from Britain that Cumann na nGaedheal had been undertaking through successful diplomatic action. The difference lay in the fact that the new government was not committed to the terms of the 1921 Treaty and felt free to disregard some of its elements.

It was in this light, indeed, that the officials of the Department of External Affairs, as it was then, seem to have viewed the change of government, despite personal ties they had naturally formed with members of the Cumann na nGaedheal government that had appointed them and had built up the department.

Certainly within days of taking over the reins of government, de Valera's initial suspicion of that department (which he chose to head himself in addition to leadership of the government) had dissolved, encouraged by what today reads as a cloyingly sycophantic letter from its permanent head, Joe Walshe. This suspicion was replaced by a conviction that the External Affairs officials saw their role as helping him to pursue the achievement of the nationalist aim beyond the limits that had been imposed on the former government by their moral obligation to honour the Treaty.

The extent to which members of that first government had felt that this sense of moral obligation tied their hands in moving outside the Treaty obligations cannot be over-estimated; nor should the extent to which this sense of moral obligation was felt by them as a burden inhibiting the realisation of an aspiration which they largely shared with their anti-Treaty opponents. But, unhappily, having achieved sovereign independence within the commonwealth through the Statute of Westminster, their judgement of de Valera's effort to go further became seriously distorted. This reflected continuing bitterness at what they saw as his role in the initiation of the Civil War – a role, in their view, motivated by personal vanity and pique, rather than by principle.

The fact that complete continuity of public administration was provided after 1932 by the civil service, army and police that had served the Cumann na nGaedheal government during and since the Civil War was an achievement, the credit for which must be widely shared by: the public service itself, which thus established its political neutrality in the most difficult circumstances; the outgoing government which had consciously prepared the way for the change-over, including in particular W. T. Cosgrave and my own father whom he appointed as Minister of Defence with the task of taking tough steps to ensure that the army would be loyal to a future Fianna Fáil government; and, of course, by de Valera himself who effectively resisted great pressure to purge the army, the police, and the administration that he had inherited.

Apart from the removal of several police officers, he resisted this pressure – which paralleled very closely the pressures which the Cumann na nGaedheal government had faced from its supporters in 1923 (documented in minutes of party meetings), to purge its new administration of people who had served under the British government.

The constitution of 1937 came to provide the basis for a consensus on which the modern Irish state has been built. It represented an assertion of sovereignty in terms more acceptable to nationalists than those of the Statute of Westminster six years earlier. That statute had secured sovereign independence for the dominions, including the Irish state. In international law this independence clearly included the right to remain neutral in a conflict involving Great Britain. But many British politicians cherished the illusion that the member states of the commonwealth, while independent, must necessarily join with Britain in any major war in which she was engaged – relying in some cases upon the abstract concept of the indivisibility of the crown.

But for many Irish people, and particularly for de Valera himself, the right to remain neutral, and the assertion of that right, was the ultimate test of sovereignty and independence. A practical obstacle to the exercise of this right was the continued occupation and use of certain port facilities in the Irish state by British forces under the terms of the Treaty. In 1938, as part of the settlement that ended the Economic War, de Valera negotiated the return of these facilities and the departure of British forces, and despite discussion of a possible defence pact during these negotiations, eventually this was secured without any commitment to make these bases available again in time of war.

This obstacle to neutrality having been removed, de Valera, by that time disillusioned by the collapse of collective security under the League of Nations, first in the case of Manchuria and later in the case of Italy's invasion of Abyssinia, declared Irish neutrality, and maintained formal neutrality throughout the war – while at the same time secretly working closely with the British authorities.

This policy commanded the full support of the political opposition, with a single outstanding exception. James Dillon, who in 1942 retired from the position of deputy leader of the principal opposition party, Fine Gael, and became an independent member of the Dáil on an issue which he saw as one between good and evil – but significantly only after the USA had joined the war.

While the assertion of sovereignty was the primary motivation of neutrality it would be wrong to suggest that it was the sole consideration for de Valera, or indeed that it played any part in the ready acceptance of this policy by his political opponents. Amongst all political parties there was, I believe, the further, powerful, albeit for obvious reasons unspoken, consideration that to have entered voluntarily into the conflict on the allied side within sixteen years of the end of a civil war would have created the danger of a revival of that bitter conflict. This perceived danger had been increased by the IRA's immediate pre-war decision to 'declare war' on Britain and to set off bombs in British cities. As was very clear in Spain during the closing period of Franco's rule, a people who have experienced a civil war will go to immense lengths to avoid a recurrence of it.

The significance of this factor in securing all party support for neutrality, has, I believe, been under-estimated by historians because during the war it was never explicitly stated by any politician of any party – for obvious reasons. But it was, I believe, subsequently mentioned in retrospective interviews by two senior Fianna Fáil politicians, Seán Lemass and Seán McEntee, and I believe that explains my own father's support for neutrality despite his deep commitment to the allied cause.

Of course de Valera also used another argument for neutrality; vis., that so long as Ireland remained politically divided, with part of the island under British sovereignty, the Irish state should not engage in hostilities as an ally of Britain. The employment of this argument, largely perhaps for tactical reasons at the time, laid the ground for a decision of a later Irish government, led by de Valera's opponents, and in which Mr Seán McBride was Minister for External Affairs, not to join NATO in 1949 – a decision that subsequently hardened into a commitment to neutrality that has survived until the last decade of this century.

This commitment has since been strongly held by many who have forgotten the 'partition' factor that had been presented as the initial rationale of this policy, and who know nothing of the pragmatic basis for war-time neutrality – the fear of a renewal of civil war. There are indeed many today who would wish Irish neutrality to be maintained even if north and south were to be brought together politically.

What is more generally recognised by historians, however, is the extent to which the consensus on neutrality (as well as the entry to the army of many children of the leading members of both political parties) healed the divisions of the Civil War, uniting all in a common cause.

THE NORTHERN IRELAND QUESTION

But, to return to de Valera's concern to legitimise the Irish state in the eyes of republicans, there was a price to be paid for this, for it was inevitable that the single-mindedness with which de Valera felt it necessary to pursue this goal would impinge unfavourably on the attainment of certain other objectives.

First of all, by pressing ahead to remove the crown from the constitution – while avoiding at that stage declaring the state to be a Republic – and by the insertion in the new constitution of certain provisions designed to secure the assent of as many republicans as possible, and of other provisions designed to head off any potential opposition from the Roman Catholic Church, de Valera certainly made the resolution of the problem of Northern Ireland more difficult – to an extent greater than he himself perhaps recognised.

From the outset, the Northern Ireland entity had been based on shaky foundations. First of all, its boundaries were, of course, arbitrary – chosen to maximise the territory involved within the limits imposed by a concern to limit the Catholic, nationalist minority to one-third of the population.

And second, whatever may have been said publicly at that time there is, I believe, evidence that the most that many unionists then hoped to secure out of this arrangement, was a temporary postponement of the united Ireland that had been clearly envisaged as an outcome in the British act establishing a Northern Ireland parliament in 1920.

The survival of Northern Ireland for eighty years, and the determination of the majority of its unionist population today to resist unification, obscures the possibility that if the Irish state had evolved differently, the north-south relationship might also have turned out differently during this period. Even in 1937, when de Valera presented his new constitution to the people, the sense of the temporary character of the arrangement under which Northern Ireland remained part of the United Kingdom was still an underlying feature of northern unionist opinion – despite the rhetoric of 'no surrender'. This is, I believe, an under-researched element of the history of this island – partly, of course, because it is not documented, belonging as it does more to the minds rather than to the words and actions of those involved.

The constitution of 1937 helped to harden northern unionist attitudes in three respects.

First, the elimination of the crown from the constitution offended the monarchist sentiments of most northern unionists.

Second, they were upset at the inclusion in this constitution of provisions which had found no place in the 1922 constitution, which seemed to involve a claim to sovereignty over Northern Ireland on behalf of the government and parliament elected in the truncated Irish state – albeit a claim that was accompanied by an abrogation in practice of this claim to sovereignty.

And third, the inclusion of a provision recognising 'the special position of the Catholic, Apostolic and Holy Roman Church as the guardian of the faith of the great majority of the people' (a provision which, however, also recognised a list of named Protestant Churches and the Jewish community, and which was eliminated from the constitution in 1972 by an overwhelming majority in a popular referendum), served to confirm northern unionist prejudices about the predominantly Roman Catholic character of the Irish state.

This, incidentally, found further confirmation in their eyes in another new provision banning legislation for the dissolution of marriage, for, while most Protestants in Ireland at that time did not personally favour divorce for religious reasons, they saw this constitutional provision as evidence of influence by the Catholic Church on the government of the Irish state.

Finally, the policy of neutrality in the Second World War, designed both to proclaim Irish sovereignty and to maintain the consensus painfully brought about over the preceding years on the legitimacy of the Irish state, had the effect of further alienating unionist opinion in Northern Ireland, and of greatly increasing British sympathy with the unionist position. This was a further inevitable but unintended consequence of the policy to which de Valera had in practice given priority since the immediate post-Civil War period – vis., the achievement of a more complete separation of the Irish state from Britain.

Thus, in pursuing the unspoken objective of establishing the Irish state on a solid domestic foundation that would command the loyalty of all but a handful of its people, de Valera had found it necessary to pursue a course that divided this state more deeply from Northern Ireland and made re-unification more difficult, more distant and more problematic.

This was paradoxical, because he himself frequently publicly proclaimed the re-unification of Ireland as one of the two major national aims – the other, and prior, aim being the revival of the Irish language. His real order of priorities was, however, disclosed in a speech in reply to a debate in the Senate on 7 February 1939. There, in his customary rather tortured style, he said:

> Although freedom for a part of this island is not the freedom we want – the freedom we would like to have – this freedom for a portion of it, freedom to develop and to keep the kernel of the Irish nation, is something, and something that I would not sacrifice, if by sacrificing it we were to get a united Ireland and that united Ireland was not free to determine its own form of government, to determine its relations with other countries, and amongst other things, to determine for example, whether it would or would not be involved in war.

The relationship he saw between neutrality and sovereignty is there suggested, as well as the priority he always in practice accorded to the achievement and maintenance of sovereignty of the partitioned Irish state, as against political re-unification of the island.

In that same speech he even made it clear that re-unification came third and not even second in priority in his mind, for he emphasised that the object of restoring Irish as the spoken language of the majority of the people also took priority over re-unification:

> For instance, speaking for myself – I am not talking about government policy in the matter, which has been largely embodied in the constitution – I would not tomorrow, for the sake of a united Ireland, give up the policy of trying to make this a really Irish Ireland – not by any means. If I were told tomorrow: 'You can have a united Ireland if you give up your idea of restoring the national language to be the spoken language of the majority of the people', I would for myself, say no. I do not know how many would agree with me. I would say no, and I would say it for this reason: that I believe that as long as the language remains, you have a distinguishing characteristic of nationality which will enable the nation to persist. If you lose the language, the danger is that there would be absorption.

On the issue of partition itself, as distinct from the priority that he accorded to it, it is evident from the many oscillations in the position he took up in relation to Northern Ireland that de Valera himself shared to a high degree the ambivalence and confusion of thought about the nature of Irish nationhood which has been a feature of Irish nationalism throughout the present century.

Even in the brief period between 1917 and 1921 his ideas on this subject seem to have gone through several phases. As John Bowman has pointed out in *de Valera and the Ulster Question*, in 1917–1918 he advocated the expulsion or coercion of northern unionists. In 1919–1920, when in the United States, he modified this position to one of proposing that such unionists should be assimilated into the new Irish-Ireland. And in 1921, when the issue had to be faced in a practical way in preparing for the Treaty negotiations, he shifted his position to one of accommodating the unionists within a federal Ireland, externally associated with the British Commonwealth. Indeed at that time he even went so far as to propose that individual Ulster counties should have the right to opt out of the new Irish state.

There were further changes of approach later, through which it is not easy to detect any consistent pattern. However, it is possible that the view to which he ultimately came – and one which is in fact strikingly relevant to the problem as it is now seen by many people in both parts of Ireland after two decades of continuous violence – was expressed in a speech made towards the end of his first sixteen-year term of office as head of the Irish government. On 24 June 1947 he rejected as so often before the use of force as a solution:

> I believe that it [partition] cannot be solved, in any circumstances that we can now see, by force, and that if it were solved by force, it would leave a situation behind it which would mean that this state would be in an unstable position.

And he went on to observe that the problem was one primarily between north and south, and that Britain was not the ultimate obstacle to a solution – something now very generally understood in Ireland, although still not grasped by some Irish-Americans in the United States:

> In order to end this [partition] you will have to get concurrence of wills between three parties – we here who represent the people of this part of Ireland, those who represent the majority in the separated part of Ireland, and the will of those who are the majority for the time being in the British parliament. It is true, I think, that if there were agreement between the peoples of the two parts of Ireland, British consent to do the things that they would have to do could be secured.

At one period Britain's emotional and strategic commitment to Northern Ireland was, of course, a major additional obstacle to a united Ireland, but with the diminution in importance of this factor, the result has been to reveal in all its stark reality that, as de Valera implicitly recognised in that 1947 speech, the fundamental obstacle to the political unity of Ireland is the attitude of the unionist population. And this is a problem that the irredentist policies pursued by de Valera long after he made that speech in 1947 – policies that from 1949 until at least 1969 came to be pursued also by other parties in the Irish state in the period up to 1969 – served to intensify, rather than to moderate.

A PLURALIST OR A MONO-CULTURAL STATE?

From the outset, the new state had a clear choice between two approaches to the definition of its identity. The state could have founded itself on the tradition of the leaders of the Rebellion of 1798 and 1848 who, influenced by the French and American revolutions, had proclaimed that the national objective must be to unite Catholic, Protestant and Dissenter in the common name of Irishman. This would have entailed adopting an overtly pluralist approach, both in religious and in cultural matters, placing the different religions on a genuinely equal footing, and recognising the Irish and English languages as equally valid alternative means of expressing the Irish identity.

However, the path actually chosen by the new state in these matters was a very different one. In relation to the language, a clear policy had already begun to emerge during the period of office of Cumann na nGaedheal, at a time when de Valera was still in unconstitutional opposition. The language policy then adopted was determined by the sense of indebtedness felt by the leaders of the national political movement that had begun in the late nineteenth century, towards the language movement in which so many of them had found their inspiration – and had in many cases (including that of my own parents) found each other.

The pursuit of the objective of Irish language revival had led, even before the First World War, to the introduction of an Irish language requirement for entry to the colleges of the new National University of Ireland, to which the Catholic majority in the greater part of the island almost exclusively went, in search of university education until the 1960s. This had a profound influence on the teaching of the language at secondary level. But in the early days of the new state, W. T. Cosgrave's Cumann na nGaedheal government decided to make the Irish language a basic, required subject at primary level and to make it also a required subject in the national intermediate-level school certificate examinations taken at age 15-16.

De Valera, when he came to power, went on to make the Irish language an essential element in the school Leaving Certificate itself, taken at age 17-18, which was the qualification traditionally used by most employers as the educational test especially for clerical employment. Moreover, as mentioned earlier, in his speeches de Valera elevated the revival of the Irish language to the status of the first national aim, taking precedence even over national re-unification.

By thus making Irish an essential requirement for so many purposes, and by requiring a knowledge of Irish for entry to and promotion within the public service, in the hope of reviving a language which had been moving towards extinction for several centuries before the state was founded, successive governments were effectively making a choice against a culturally pluralist society. For this process involved a de facto – though unintended – discrimination against people of the Protestant tradition, north or south, whose culture had effectively always been exclusively English-speaking. And this was of course also true of other sub-cultures that had developed amongst those who maintained their adherence to Roman Catholicism but who in the cities and towns and throughout most of the province of Leinster and parts of other provinces had been English-speaking for several centuries.

By the 1950s the removal of this Irish language requirement for the purposes of school examination certificates and entry and promotion within the public service had started to become a political issue, provoking controversy, but during the long continuous period in office of the Fianna Fáil party from 1957 to 1973 no change was made. De Valera's successors as Taoiseach after his elevation to the constitutional presidency in 1959, Seán Lemass and Jack Lynch, were unwilling to tackle this problem, during his lifetime at least. It was left to the National Coalition government of 1973–1977, led by Liam Cosgrave, the son of W. T. Cosgrave, whose government had initiated this policy in all good faith in the 1920s, to make the changes that eliminated discrimination in examination and public employment against Irish people whose cultural tradition is not Gaelic, although the Irish language remains one of the three core subjects in all primary schools and is still taught throughout the second-level cycle to all pupils. It also remains a requirement for matriculation to the four NUI universities.

Religious pluralism is a somewhat different issue. Just as he intensified the divisive impact of the language policy formulated by his predecessors, so also did de Valera's religious policy drive a second wedge between north and south. The 1922 constitution had at least proclaimed a form of separation between Church and State, forbidding the endowment of religion by the state, although this did not, however, inhibit state support for an educational system that had always divided along religious lines – at all levels including the state's own primary school system. Nor did it prevent some of the state's leaders from addressing the Holy See in terms of what was described as 'filial piety'.

But de Valera had an additional concern over and above that of his predecessors. He had to dispel lingering suspicions amongst the Catholic Church authorities about his party – suspicions that derived from pronouncements by the Catholic hierarchy of the early 1920s against those who had opposed the Treaty in arms during the Civil War. And he also had reason to fear that triumphalist attitudes prevalent in the Catholic Church in the 1930s might lead the institutional Church to oppose his new constitution unless he gave some kind of formal recognition to that Church.

This led him to include in that constitution the provisions already referred to in relation to the specific position of the Catholic Church as the guardian of the faith of the great majority of the people, as well as a constitutional ban on legislation for divorce and other provisions in relation to education and private property, to all of which he then added non-judiciable provisions on social policy which derived directly from Catholic social teaching of that period.

All these must, of course, be seen in the context of a situation where he was under considerable pressure from Rome to declare Ireland a Catholic state (a constitutional proposal which de Valera firmly resisted) although oddly enough, in speeches he often, in referring to the state, used this phrase loosely himself.

It must be said that these constitutional provisions were not objected to by the Protestant Churches at the time they were enacted, and that de Valera, a fervent Catholic like his predecessor, W. T. Cosgrave, subsequently gained the respect of the leaders of the Protestant community in the Irish state and also at various stages in his career showed a measure of independence vis-à-vis the Catholic Church authorities.

Although he can be criticised in the light of hindsight for not having sustained religious pluralism in its fullest sense, like most of his supporters, and also his opponents, he was inevitably influenced in this by the climate of opinion of his time.

ECONOMIC DEVELOPMENT
De Valera's autarkic economic policies also proved divisive vis-à-vis Northern Ireland, for they involved imposing restrictions on imports from that part of the island.

In fairness, it must be said that almost none of those who emerged from the struggle for independence and survived the Civil War on either side had any deep interest in or understanding of economic or social questions – de Valera himself certainly did not have such an interest. Nevertheless, when he came to power in 1932, the cabinet that he led initiated significant economic changes that profoundly influenced the future economic development of the Irish state.

There are several ironies here. First, the policy of industrial protection which he implemented in the autarkic climate of the early 1930s had in fact been proclaimed as a nationalist dogma by Arthur Griffith, the leader of the pro-Treaty government who died during the Civil War. But Griffith's successors in the Cumann na nGaedheal government from 1922 to 1932 had not felt able to pursue a policy that would have been in such sharp conflict with the free trade spirit of the 1920s. Such a policy might, they feared, have provoked from other states retaliatory measures which could have been very damaging to a small, and export-dependent, economy.

In hesitating to initiate such a radical policy, so out of tune with the temper of the 1920s, that government had also been influenced by a more general consideration, vis. its concern with the establishment of the new state's credibility and credit vis-à-vis the outside world, a consideration to which it attached an over-riding importance.

Although de Valera almost certainly did not realise the impact a protectionist policy was going to have on Irish politics, the fact is that, by implementing in the quite different conditions of the 1930s the protectionist policy of Griffith, he laid the foundations of two new classes – protected industrialists and industrial workers – whose consequent support for Fianna Fáil across the class barrier supplemented the support of most small farmers which it had held from the outset. From this combination of sectoral groups that party thereafter derived its remarkable strength, both financial and electoral, which enabled it to secure between 44% and 51% of the popular vote at a score of general elections during the first sixty years of its existence.

De Valera envisaged protection as a means of making Ireland more self-sufficient and less dependent on trade and on exchanges with an outside world, which he regarded as ultimately dangerous to the Irish sense of identity. Yet ironically, the consequences of his protection policy were in fact to reduce Ireland's self-sufficiency sharply as materials for industrial processing flowed in and as the new class of industrial workers spent much of their wages on imported goods. By the time protection was firmly in place, around 1950, the share of external trade in Ireland's economy had consequently risen by almost a third, leaving the state much less self-sufficient than when de Valera had come to power!

However, the protection policy secured the establishment of many small and generally unspecialised industries. Their efficiency was relatively low because of the very high level of protection afforded to them, but they eventually provided an industrial base that was capable of being converted – albeit painfully and at great cost – to a structure over half of which survived the freeing of trade with Britain after 1965, and with other EC countries after 1973.

But, despite such moves as the establishment by the anti-Fianna Fáil Inter-Party Government in 1949 of the Industrial Development Authority (which then had a little-exercised tariff review function), this process of re-orientation of industry towards export markets was delayed long after the time it should have been undertaken in the early 1950s. This delay, for which de Valera's continued leadership of Fianna Fáil beyond the age of 70 was almost certainly largely responsible, contributed substantially to the economic stagnation of the Irish state during the 1950s, when in most other countries national output was expanding rapidly.

If de Valera had contested the constitutional presidency in 1952, his elevation to that position might have left the way clear for his eventual energetic successor, Seán Lemass, to tackle this problem when Fianna Fáil were in office at that time. In the event action was delayed until October 1956, when a subsequent coalition government started to challenge the traditional economic policies of protection and hostility to foreign investment, a policy reversal that was then vigorously expanded and developed by Seán Lemass, when he became Taoiseach following de Valera's eventual election as President at the age of almost seventy-seven.

SOCIAL OBJECTIVES

De Valera was a natural conservative; he venerated the past and wished to keep 'the old ways'. Frugal in his own way of life, like many of his generation who had entered politics through an idealistic national movement, he was unambiguously anti-materialist. In his conservatism he did not differ much from most of his political opponents. They had all become engaged before or during the First World War in a nationalist movement that, despite James Connolly's participation in the 1916 Rising, had for the most part little about it that was revolutionary.

De Valera's social philosophy was expressed in a St Patrick's Day broadcast during the Second World War, which has often been made the subject of humorous comment, and the language of which certainly resounds strangely in our ears, but which should be seen as the simple but sincere aspiration of a romantic conservative, talking in the kind of terms that may have been common enough during his childhood a century ago.

However, in the mid-twentieth century, and in the course of the most destructive war in history, these aspirations were so far removed from any reality that they served only to highlight the difficulty of posing any realistic alternative to the growth of materialism in an increasingly urbanised society.

In this respect, de Valera outlived his own era, and became irrelevant as an ideologue for the new generations that were growing up in the middle decades of this century. Ireland was moving on beyond him, to become an industrialised society with increasingly materialist values.

De Valera's most enduring achievement lies, I believe, in the manner in which he made the assertion of sovereignty not merely an end in itself but also the means of securing assent by the vast bulk of those who with him had challenged that legitimacy in arms in the Civil War to the legitimacy of the state established by his predecessor W. T. Cosgrave.

However, he does not seem himself to have articulated this objective clearly. Perhaps he recognised that he could not do so without endangering its achievement and that it could best be secured by subtleties and stealth. Nevertheless he dedicated an important part of his political career to it.

The dissonances of party politics have perhaps hidden from supporters of both of the political traditions of the Irish state the extent to which its first two governments, and their leaders, Cosgrave and de Valera, were successively responsible in different ways for establishing that state on a rock-like and enduring foundation.

The two aims to which de Valera himself gave priority in his utterance were, of course, quite different: the revival of the Irish language and the re-unification of Ireland. But he – and others – failed to stop the long-term decline of the Irish language as a natural means of communication, and he may even have contributed to some degree to the rate of this decline by endorsing and extending increasingly unpopular measures taken by his predecessors in office to make the language an essential element in the educational system and in public employment.

At the same time the methods he found it necessary to employ in order to secure his objectives of sovereignty and legitimisation of the state in the eyes of all but a dissident handful of its citizens helped to undermine seriously, perhaps fatally, the prospect of making progress with the second national aim, of political re-unification.

And his intensification of the language revival policy, together with the concessions he felt it necessary to make to the institutional Catholic Church when drafting his constitution, raised formidable additional obstacles to Irish re-unification – to which, on his own admission, he never gave a high priority.

The price we have had to pay for de Valera's successful post-Civil War stabilisation of our state has thus been substantial, and enduring.

In the economic sphere he sought self-sufficiency through industrialisation, but achieved industrialisation with a reduction in self-sufficiency. In the social sphere his influence was extremely limited because his conservatism – to which in the materialist society of Ireland today a small minority still look back with nostalgia – was too much a product of the nineteenth century to make an effective impact on the Ireland of the mid-twentieth century.

However, in the world outside Ireland, he added to his country's stature. A controversial figure at home, and for much of the time in his relations with Britain, he became known world-wide as an apostle of nationalism, but he was also an exponent in the 1930s of other values, such as the concept of collective security, which he sought, in vain, to have established through the League of Nations.

Many facets of his character and career will for long remain enigmas to historians, for he was an enigmatic man. Deeply concerned about the historical judgments that would be made on him, he sought to influence these consciously both through an 'authorised biography' and by calling together a group of historians to hear his answers to prepared questions on his career. Even today judgments on him are bound to be no more than provisional, both because we are too close to the man himself – barely two decades after his death – and because much research remains to be undertaken, and many veils remain to be removed, before the achievements and failures of this remarkable Irishman can be evaluated in a definitive way.

Appendix 1

Maternal mortality (Ireland) 1923–61. Rate and numbers. National, all-inclusive rate taken from *Statistical Abstracts*; breakdown and numbers taken from *Reports of Registrar-General*, 1923–49

Year	Total	Rate	Peurperal Sepsis		Other	
			Total	Rate	Total	Rate
1923	297	5.32	135	2.19	162	2.63
1924	303	5.21	123	1.94	180	2.84
1926	299	5.38	115	1.88	184	3.01
1927	271	4.80	77	1.28	194	3.23
1928	292	5.37	103	1.74	189	3.19
1929	239	4.85	80	1.37	159	2.73
1930	278	5.04	81	1.39	197	3.38
1931	246	4.76	66	1.16	180	3.15
1932	256	4.98	78	1.39	178	3.16
1933	255	5.16	80	1.39	175	3.05
1934	271	5.25	104	1.80	167	2.88
1935	272	5.10	89	1.53	183	3.14
1936	273	5.14	104	1.79	169	2.91
1937	203	4.19	51	0.90	153	2.71
1938	234	4.69	46	0.81	188	3.30
1939	190	3.89	38	0.68	152	2.71
1940	208	4.01	55	0.97	153	2.70
1941	182	3.68	43	0.76	139	2.45
1942	163	2.86	43	0.65	120	1.82
1943	144	2.51	36	0.56	108	1.69
1944	156	2.69	32	0.50	124	1.90
1945	159	2.63	35	0.50	124	1.90
1946	137	2.39	20	0.30	117	1.70
1947	130	2.15	31	0.40	99	1.40
1948	104	1.88	18	0.30	86	1.30
1949	116	2.01	18	0.30	98	1.50
1950	99					
1951	103					
1952	92					
1953	83					
1954	69					
1955	70					
1956	52					
1957	81					
1958	61					
1959	39					
1960	35					
1961	27					

Appendix 2

Major causes of maternal mortality in Ireland 1938–1950 for 1938–1950, from Table XXXI, *Annual Report of the Registrar-General 1950* (1953), xliii, and 1953, 1954 and 1958 (from tables in selected years, *Vital Statistics* 1953–58) as percentage of total deaths.

Year	Total Deaths	Toxaemia	Puerperal Sepsis	Haemorrhage	Other
1938	234	4.6%	39%	26%	11%
1939	190	4.6%	45%	23%	11%
1940	208	13%	34%	31%	10%
1941	182	17%	32%	23%	10%
1942	163	11.7%	31%	23%	17%
1943	145	11.6%	24%	33%	14%
1944	156	9.5%	34%	27%	17%
1945	159	16%	31%	28%	15%
1946	137	20%	11%	36%	16%
1947	130	24%	29%	23%	11%
1948	104	19%	20%	37%	13%
1949	116	16%	19%	32%	13%
1950	99	14%	20%	34%	25%
1953	83	19%	21%	19%	20%
1954	69	24%	26%	17%	11%
1958	61	26%	26%	14%	21%

Other minor causes of death included ectopic gestation, septic abortion, other or unspecified puerperal conditions, other diseases of pregnancy.

NOTES

The American identity of de Valera (pp. 11–28)
Owen Dudley Edwards

1. Lewis, C. S., *Prince Caspian*, Harper Collins, New York, 1951. Editions are so numerous that one can only indicate chapters: respectively 4 and 10. This book seems to me the one where Lewis most directly confronted problems of his Irish identity (pre-Catholic, Synge-Yeats style), although the sequel, *The Voyage of the Dawn Treader*, Harper Collins, New York, 1952, draws more on Celtic legend. The aged ape in *The Last Battle*, Harper Collins, New York, 1956, is evidently a relic of his Belfast Protestant youth, being an impression of Leo XIII. This is somewhat at variance with de Valera's 'nothing disgusts me so much as an analogy': I can only plead that my epigraphs mix symbols rather than pretending to exact parallels.

2. Schlesinger, Arthur, *A Thousand Days: John F. Kennedy in the White House*, Houghton Mifflin, Boston, 1965, says that 'the State Department drafts' of speeches for the European trip in June 1963 'were discarded' (London edition, p. 754). This is certainly not true of the speech to Dáil Éireann since it included much historical detail taken down from me by the Irish desk in the State Department, including one mistake reproduced by Kennedy and later corrected (the date of the battle of Fredericksburg, whose accurate citation was given by Basil Peterson in the *Irish Times* a few days after delivery). But Pierre Salinger in an interview the following day told me that 'you guys are going to be surprised by how much Irish history the President has read' and we were. Much of the humour in the Irish speeches was characteristic of Kennedy's off-the-cuff style at press conferences, rather than the rounded periods of Ted Sorenson's 'brilliant mind and pen' to which Schlesinger ascribes the speeches.

3. Earl of Longford, *Kennedy*, Weidenfeld & Nicolson, London, 1976, p. 151. Kenny O'Donnell opposed the visit on the grounds that he already had the Irish vote. McGeorge Bundy opposed it on grounds unknown, but in view of Bundy's character, that was not a bad compliment for Ireland.

4. Aedan O'Beirne, then counsel at the Irish Embassy in Washington, DC, conveyed this opinion to me in late 1959. Joseph P. Kennedy was remembered in August 1960 by Ambassador John Belton at Stockholm as having flown to Ireland in the autumn of 1939 to berate de Valera at a private but formal dinner in his honour, for his failure to enter the war in support of his friend Neville Chamberlain.

5. Brogan, Hugh, *Kennedy*, Longman, London, 1996, pp. 15–19 contains good perceptive comment on *Why England Slept* from a clever son of the shrewdest British commentator on mid-twentieth century USA. Joe Kennedy sent out many copies of the book long before he read it (if he ever did).

6. Reeves, Richard, *President Kennedy – Profile of Power*, Simon & Schuster, New York, 1993, p. 537: 'On the flight from Germany, Kennedy told Powers and O'Donnell about his only other trip to the land of his ancestors.' Admittedly Reeves then refers to Kathleen as 'Lady Hartigan' which would have been appreciated by the UCD History Department in the early 1960s. McTaggart, Lynne, *Kathleen Kennedy: Her Life and Times*, Doubleday, London, 1983, is interesting if gossipy on the family member who most successfully bridged the Atlantic (and made Kennedy Harold Macmillan's nephew-in-law's brother-in-law). Hamilton, Nigel, *J. F. K.: Reckless Youth*, Century, London, 1992, is the most useful if not faultless on Kennedy's early years.

7. Mitchell, Arthur, *J. F. K. and his Irish Heritage*, Moytura Press, Dublin, 1993, is an admirable rescue operation on crucial documents by a distinguished American historian of Irish politics, carrying the first Kennedy journalism (pp. 100–104) with the advertise-

ment 'WHY IRELAND CLINGS TO PEACE' on p. 89. See also Hennessy, Maurice N., *I'll Come Back in the Springtime – John F. Kennedy and the Irish*, Washburn, New York, 1966.

8. Fisk, Robert, *In Time of War*, Andre Deutsch, London, 1983.

9. Mitchell, Arthur, *J. F. K. and his Irish Heritage*, pp. 105–7. Kennedy ended his story with the magnificent tongue-in-cheek: 'At this weekend, the problem of partition seems very far from being solved'. The use of 'mist' for symbolic purposes in celebrating Ireland stayed with Kennedy to 1963.

10. Bromage, Mary C., *De Valera and the March of a Nation*, New English, London, 1956.

11. O'Connor, Edwin, *All in the Family*, Sphere edition, London, 1970, p. 83. A neglected classic.

12. Earl of Longford & O'Neill, T. P., *Eamon de Valera*, Hutchinson, London, 1970, p. 454. O'Neill insisted that Longford did not write a word of the book, his name being required on it by the London publishers, but the quotation from 'a guest at the large reception who watched the two presidents' seems to mean Longford, whose own book on Kennedy tells the same story with himself as the informant and de Valera now 'like a benignant uncle'; Earl of Longford, *Kennedy*, p. 4. It was of course Kennedy's extra-marital reputation which had become a little livelier in the interval, but Longford was tactful when he saw need of it. The Irish version of O'Neill's biography is fuller than the English but only goes up to 1937. O'Neill, Thomas P. & Ó Fiannachta, Pádraig, *De Valera*, 2 vols, Cló Morainn, Baile Átha Cliath, vol. 1, 1968, vol. 2, 1970.

13. I have gone into the implications of this in my *Eamon de Valera*, GPC, Cardiff, 1987. Subsequent to its appearance, Tim Pat Coogan, formerly as editor of the *Irish Press*, de Valera's hierophant-in-chief, now turned on his former employers to denigrate de Valera in every remotely plausible way in his biography. Pauric Travers in his *Eamon de Valera*, Historical Association of Ireland, Dundalgan Press, Dundalk, 1994, pp. 6, 52 comments that Coogan's 'intensive rootings' have not proven his allegation of de Valera's illegitimacy. Certainly Coogan has tried to go the whole hog throughout.

14. Moynihan, Maurice (ed.), *Speeches and Statements by Eamon de Valera, 1917–73*, Gill and Macmillan, Dublin, 1980, p. 93. In common with every other student, my debt to this work is endless, but in my case a personal debt of gratitude to a kind family friend from my childhood is even greater.

15. Travers, Pauric, *Eamon de Valera*, p. 3.

16. O'Connor, T. P. & McWade, Robert M., *Gladstone, Parnell and the Great Irish Struggle*, Hubbard, Boston, 1886, p. 506. For a good specimen of Sheehy's anti-clericalism in sermon see O'Brien, Conor Cruise, *States of Ireland*, Panther edition, London, 1974, pp. 22–3.

17. Farragher, Seán P., *Dev and his Alma Mater – Eamon de Valera's Lifelong Association with Blackrock College, 1898–1975*, Paraclete Press, Dublin, 1984, pp. 32, 51–4.

18. ibid., p. 58.

19. Earl of Longford & O'Neill, T. P., *Eamon de Valera*, pp. 7, 50; Travers, Pauric, *Eamon de Valera*, p. 13. Both works rather uniquely insist there is no 'evidence' or 'surviving records' supporting the thesis of American intervention. The US Consul was equally clear that there was, and his record survives. See Dudley Edwards, Owen, *De Valera*, GPC, Cardiff, 1987, p. 58 and 'American Aspects of the Rising' in Dudley Edwards, Owen & Pyle, Fergus (eds), *1916: The Easter Rising*, MacGibbon & Kee, London, 1968, p. 162.

20. Clarke was shot so quickly after the Rising that no diplomatic intervention was possible, especially as the consulate could not be reached by its staff until well over a week beyond it.

21. Dinneen, Revd Patrick S., SJ, *Foclóir Gaedhilge agus Béarla*, Irish Texts Society, Dublin, 1927, p. 145.

22. Yeats, W. B., 'Remorse for Intemperate Speech' in *The Winding Stair and Other Poems*, Macmillan, London, 1933. Yeats dated this poem 28 August 1931. It is written as though self-reflective but in spite – or perhaps because – of its confessional status it

could be read in allusion to de Valera, whose advent to power was clearly imminent. Brown, Thomas N., *Irish-American Nationalism 1870–90*, Lippincott, Philadelphia, 1966, applied it to Devoy (and his colleagues and rivals) appositely but in our context ironically.

23. Moynihan, Maurice (ed.), *Speeches and Statements by Eamon de Valera, 1917–73*, p. 93; Farragher, Seán P., *Dev and his Alma Mater*, pp. 23–4, 26. D'Alton reminisced that de Valera was 'good at mathematics but not outstanding otherwise' (ibid., p. 35). This might be modesty or judicious amnesia as to de Valera's defeating him successively in Christian Doctrine and Religious Instruction. De Valera is unlikely to have shared amnesia on the point: it was a useful recollection in Church-State debates of later years.

24. Ó Faoláin, Seán, *De Valera*, Penguin, London, 1939, p. 10.

25. Earl of Longford & O'Neill, T. P., *Eamon de Valera*, p. 52.

26. Dwyer, T. Ryle, *De Valera's Darkest Hour 1919–1932*, Mercier, Cork, 1982, title of Chapter One. This most important book with many invaluable quotations well merits re-issue, as does its successor *De Valera's Finest Hour 1932–1959*, Mercier, Cork, 1982.

27. Moynihan, Maurice (ed.), *Speeches and Statements by Eamon de Valera, 1917–73*, p. 6.

28. The Declaration of Independence was using the formula in part for the acquisition of a French alliance. De Valera's ambitions in that direction for Ireland at this juncture were certainly centred on the USA. Much later he would prove the most effective resistance to an American alliance in Irish political life, but that was in recognition of the dangers such an alliance must pose to the fulfilment of Wilsonian neutrality for Ireland.

29. Moynihan, Maurice (ed.), *Speeches and Statements by Eamon de Valera, 1917–73*, p. 6.

30. Earl of Longford & O'Neill, T. P., *Eamon de Valera*, p. 67.

31. Moynihan, Maurice (ed.), *Speeches and Statements by Eamon de Valera, 1917–73*, p. 8.

32. ibid., p. 14.

33. ibid., pp. 64, 74, 233–4, 465; Dwyer, Ryle T., *De Valera's Finest Hour 1932–1959*, pp. 79–80, 139, 152; Moynihan, Maurice (ed.), *Speeches and Statements by Eamon de Valera, 1917–73*, pp. 64, 74, 233–4, 465.

34. See Clemenceau, Georges, *American Reconstruction 1865–1870*, Dial Press, New York, 1928. This point is almost invariably overlooked.

35. John Mitchel's devotion to slavery and to the Confederacy is the extreme case. But William Smith O'Brien is another. A. M. Sullivan, editor of the *Nation*, no doubt acquired much such sentiment from his wife, late of New Orleans, and his popularisation of the term 'Home Rule' was connected to its post-war American use in 1870 and thereafter as an expression to cover ex-Confederate resumption of rule having ousted the republicans from political power.

36. Library of Congress, *The Impact of the American Revolution Abroad*, Library of Congress, Washington, 1976, my chapter on Ireland.

37. Moynihan, Maurice (ed.), *Speeches and Statements by Eamon de Valera, 1917–73*, pp. 14–5; Earl of Longford & O'Neill, T. P., *Eamon de Valera*, p. 80.

38. Ishmael, as commentators on Herman Melville's *Moby Dick* need to remember, survived against all odds, even when his mother turned aside from him in the desert.

39. Professor Cormac Ó Gráda misinterprets this in his preface to the recent reissue of the work in question, Dudley Edwards, R. & Williams, T. Desmond (eds), *The Great Famine: Studies in Irish History 1845–1852*, Browne and Nolan, Dublin, 1956; reprinted with new introduction and bibliography, Lilliput Press, Dublin, 1994.

40. De Valera's refusal to make the first move of reconciliation with Churchill for fear of a snub shows the same situation (Earl of Longford & O'Neill, T. P., *Eamon de Valera*, pp. 435–6, 441–3). Churchill made the move with congratulations on de Valera's seventieth birthday, to de Valera's delight.

41. Keogh, Dermot, *Twentieth Century Ireland: Nation and State*, Gill & Macmillan, Dublin, 1994, pp. 4–22. A textbook based on primary research is a beacon of freedom for historians.

42. Travers, *Eamon de Valera*, p. 31.

43. Keogh, Dermot & O'Driscoll, Finín, 'Ireland' in Buchanan, Tom & Conway, Martin (eds), *Political Catholicism in Europe 1918–1965*, Oxford University Press, Oxford, 1996. It wants an article on Austria.

44. Lee, Joseph, *Ireland 1912–1985: Politics and Society*, Cambridge University Press, Cambridge, 1989, p. 203.

45. Keogh, Dermot & O'Driscoll, Finín, 'Ireland', p. 290, but see also Tierney, M., 'Ireland and the Corporate State', *United Ireland*, 16 December 1933 in Deane, Seamus, et al (eds), *Field Day Anthology of Irish Writing*, Field Day, Derry, 1991, vol. iii, pp. 760–62. In an analysis of Irish writers in favour of the corporate state and/or Catholic Action, on the pro-Treaty side my student Thomas Villis found only one whose thought could be termed fascist, but there was no doubt about him: Tierney.

46. Briscoe's invaluable autobiography (with Alden Hatch but unmistakably Briscoe in tone), *For the Life of Me*, Little, Brown & Co., Boston, 1958, is a rich and beautiful celebration of de Valera's Jewish sympathies. But for all of its excellent humour it does not disguise the intolerance of the physical force men for Jews. The notable advocate of physical force in Irish nationalist thought who identified with the causes of non-whites was Patrick Ford, owner-editor of the *Irish World*, flourishing in New York 1870–90.

Eamon de Valera and the Civil War in Ireland, 1922–1923 (pp. 45–73)
Dermot Keogh

1. See Dwane, David T., *Early Life of Eamon de Valera*, Talbot Press, Dublin, 1927, for an example of a very reverential and pious work. One highly interesting study is Ó Faoláin, Seán, *The Life Story of Eamon de Valera*, Talbot Press, Dublin and Cork, 1933. Subsequently disowned by its author, this book proved to be an embarrassment given the very positive evaluation of its subject contained therein. McCartan, Patrick, *With de Valera in America*, Brentano, New York, 1932 is a useful but uncritical account of the author's time in the United States in the company of de Valera. MacManus, M. J., *Eamon de Valera*, Talbot Press, Dublin and Cork, 1944 was very severely reviewed by Ó Faoláin in *The Bell*; see Ó Faoláin, Seán, 'Eamon De Valera', *The Bell*, vol. 10, no. 1, April 1945. A central text is Macardle, Dorothy [with a preface by de Valera], *The Irish Republic: a Documented Chronicle of the Anglo-Irish Conflict and the Partitioning of Ireland, with a Detailed Account of the Period 1916–1923*, Irish Press edition, Dublin, 1951. This is as close to an official account of the early life of de Valera as came to be written before the publication of the Longford/O'Neill biography. It is a very useful work as it provides access to a wide range of documentary sources. Bromage, Mary C., *De Valera and the March of a Nation*, New English, London, 1956 was written with a little assistance from de Valera who tended to be shy in helping his many biographers; it is, however, an interesting account of his life. Browne, Kevin J., *Eamon de Valera and the Banner County*, Glendale, Dublin, 1982 provides some useful information on de Valera's local career in Clare politics.

2. Ó Faoláin, Seán, *The Life Story of Eamon de Valera*, pp. 94–5.

3. Ó Faoláin, Seán, *De Valera*, Penguin, London, 1939, pp. 105–6.

4. MacManus, *Eamon de Valera*, p. 229.

5. ibid, pp. 228–9.

6. The critical works abound and contemporary accounts tend to be increasingly more critical of de Valera. See Gwynn, Denis, *De Valera*, Jarrolds, London, 1933. This is a relatively gentle but critical account of de Valera's life. Ryan, Desmond, *Unique Dictator – a study of Eamon de Valera*, Arthur Barker, London, 1936, is the work of a left-wing journalist and political activist who reveals his disappointment with de Valera in power.

Ó Faoláin, Séan, *De Valera*, provides a radically revised view of de Valera – written after experiencing Fianna Fáil in power since 1932. See also O'Faoláin, 'Eamon De Valera', *The Bell*, op. cit., for a very severe review of the MacManus biography. The title of Ireland, Denis, *Eamon de Valera Doesn't See it Through: a Study of Irish Politics in the Machine Age*, Forum Press, Cork, 1941 speaks for itself. Younger, Calton, *A State of Disunion: Arthur Griffith, Michael Collins, James Craig, Eamon de Valera*, Fontana, London, 1972, provides a useful comparative sketch of de Valera. Regarding McInearney, Michael (ed.), *Eamon de Valera 1882–1975*, Irish Times, Dublin, 1976, like Desmond Ryan, the writer provides a critique of de Valera from the perspective of the republican left. It is a book of some insight. Coogan, Tim Pat, *De Valera: Long Fellow, Long Shadow*, Arrow Books, London, 1995. This book is the most critical to date. It is unrelentingly hostile to de Valera. But it is based on considerable research in archives in Ireland and abroad. Dwyer, T. Ryle, *Eamon de Valera*, Gill and Macmillan, Dublin, 1980; Dwyer, T. Ryle, *De Valera: the Man and the Myths*, Poolbeg, Dublin, 1992; Dwyer, T. Ryle, *Big Fellow, Long Fellow: a Joint Biography of Collins and De Valera*, Gill and Macmillan, Dublin, 1999. This author has provided a range of studies based on work in Irish archives and abroad, in particular the United States.

7. Coogan, Tim Pat, *De Valera: Long Fellow, Long Shadow*, p. 300.
8. ibid.
9. ibid., p. 305.
10. ibid., p. 315.
11. ibid., p. 311.
12. ibid., p. 314.
13. ibid.
14. ibid., pp. 312, 313 and 316.
15. A number of studies of de Valera, or of an aspect of his life, do not fit in either of the two extreme categories. See in particular, Dudley Edwards, Owen, *Eamon de Valera*, GPC, Cardiff, 1987. This work provides a very strong analysis of de Valera's career and seeks to set in wider historical context the role played by him in the struggle for Irish independence and the development of the Irish state. Also McCartney, Donal, *The National University of Ireland and Eamon de Valera*, University Press of Ireland, Dublin, 1983; this work treats of a very important aspect but usually neglected part of de Valera life. Farragher, Seán P., *Dev and his Alma Mater –Eamon de Valera's Lifelong Association with Blackrock College, 1898–1975*, Paraclete Press, Dublin 1984; his work is of major historical significance. It has opened up many avenues of research yet to be undertaken by other historians. McMahon, Deirdre, *Eamon de Valera and the Irish Americans*, Woodrow Wilson Center, Washington, 1986; this work ought to be read together with her excellent monograph, *Republicans and Imperialists – Anglo Irish Relations in the 1930s*, Yale University Press, New Haven, 1984. Bowman, John, *De Valera and the Ulster Question, 1917–1973*, Oxford University Press, Oxford, 1989; this work is a critical but fair analysis of the partition policies of de Valera; O'Carroll, J. P. & Murphy, John A. (eds), *De Valera and his Times*, Cork University Press, Cork, 1984; this edited volume provides a good review of different aspects of de Valera's life; Brennan, Paul, et al, *Eamon De Valera*, Université de la Sorbonne Nouvelle Paris III, Paris, 1986; a satisfactory collection of essays. Travers, Pauric, *Eamon de Valera, Historical Association of Ireland*, Dundalgan Press, Dundalk, 1994, offers a good short summary of de Valera's life. Lee, J. J., *Ireland 1912–1985: Politics and Society*, Cambridge University Press, Cambridge, 1989; this volume is among the most detailed accounts of the life and times of de Valera, containing a portrait that is the distilled analysis of years of work in archives.
16. Anon., *Correspondence of Mr Eamon de Valera and Others*, Alex. Thom, Dublin, 1922.
17. Anon., *The Hundred Best Sayings of Eamon de Valera*, Dublin and Cork, 1924, National Library of Ireland P2027. See footnote reference to this pamphlet in Murphy, John A., 'The Achievement of Eamon de Valera' in O'Carroll, J. P. & Murphy, John A. (eds), *De

Valera and his Times, p. 16. The editor of this pamphlet may have been Frank Gallagher, a veteran of the period 1916–1923, an author, a future editor of the *Irish Press* and a member of the Irish Government Information Service. Robert Brennan, another veteran of those years and a future Irish ambassador to the United States, may also have been involved in its production.

18. Anon., *Peace and War: Speeches by Mr de Valera on International Affairs*, Gill & Son, Dublin, 1944.

19. Anon., *Ireland's Stand: Being a Selection of the Speeches of Eamon De Valera During the War (1939–1945)*, M. H. Gill, Dublin, 1946.

20. Moynihan, Maurice (ed.), *Speeches and Statements by Eamon de Valera, 1917–73*, Gill and Macmillan, Dublin, 1980.

21. Mac Aonghusa, Proinsias, *Eamon de Valera: na Blianta Réabhlóideacha*, Clóchomhar, Baile Átha Cliath, 1982; Mac Aonghusa, Proinsias, *Quotations from Eamon de Valera*, Mercier Press, Cork, 1983.

22. Earl of Longford & O'Neill, T. P., *Eamon de Valera*, Hutchinson, London, 1970, Acknowledgements, xv–xvi.

23. See Bowman, John, 'Eamon de Valera: Seven Lives' in O'Carroll, J. P. & Murphy, John A. (eds.), *De Valera and his Times*, p. 191.

24. O'Neill, Thomas P. & Ó Fiannachta, Pádraig, *De Valera*, 2 vols, Cló Morainn, Baile Átha Cliath, 1970.

25. Earl of Longford & O'Neill, T. P., *Eamon de Valera*, p. 185.

26. ibid., pp. 187–8.

27. ibid., p. 211.

28. Hopkinson, Michael, *Green against Green: The Irish Civil War*, Gill and Macmillan, Dublin, 1988; Garvin, Tom, *1922: the Birth of Irish Democracy*, Gill and Macmillan, Dublin, 1996; Regan, John, *The Irish Counter-Revolution 1921–1936*, Gill and Macmillan, Dublin, 1999. The paucity of scholarship on the period is further reflected in the absence of studies on almost every major figure on the government and anti-Treatyite side, the exceptions being Richard Mulcahy, Kevin O'Higgins, Mary MacSwiney, Erskine Childers, Liam Mellowes and Liam Lynch. Frank Aiken, whose papers became available to researchers in 2001, is a very good example where no full-length biography has yet been published.

29. The opening of the de Valera papers was a most important event for the historical profession with a specialist interest in the twentieth century, in the development of Irish nationalism and in the establishment of the Irish state. The Franciscan community, in whose possession the papers resided for many years, worked heroically to open up the collection to bona fide scholars. Without any warning to the Irish scholarly community, the de Valera papers were transferred to University College Dublin. Most of the collection had been closed indefinitely while the entire archive was being catalogued again. Scholars should congratulate the Franciscans, and Fr Ignatius Fennessy in particular, for the manner in which such an extensive collection was opened for research while under their jurisdiction. UCD are to be congratulated for the manner in which the archives have now been catalogued and opened.

30. Dáil Éireann (private sessions), 14 December 1921, cols 110–111.

31. De Valera to John Hagan, 13 January 1922, Hagan papers, Irish College, Rome.

32. Moynihan, Maurice (ed.), *Speeches and Statements by Eamon de Valera*, pp. 94–117.

33. ibid., p. 98.

34. ibid., pp. 99–101.

35. Coogan, Tim Pat, *De Valera: Long Fellow, Long Shadow*, p. 313.

36. Williams, T. Desmond, 'From the Treaty to the Civil War' in Williams, T. Desmond (ed.), *The Irish Struggle 1916–1926*, Routledge and Kegan Paul, London, 1966, pp. 127–8.

37. O'Faoláin, Seán, *The Life Story of Eamon de Valera*, pp. 93–4.

38. Brennan, Robert, *Allegiance*, Browne and Nolan, Dublin, 1950, p. 343.

39. Moynihan, Maurice (ed.), *Speeches and Statements by Eamon de Valera*, p. 107.

40. Bromage, Mary C., *De Valera and the March of a Nation*, p. 179.

41. De Valera papers, 205/3 (see also note 29).

42. T. P. O'Neill minute, de Valera papers, 205/3.

43. Bromage, Mary C., *De Valera and the March of a Nation*, p. 183.

44. De Valera diary, 11 August 1922, de Valera papers, 2122.

45. Bromage, Mary C., *De Valera and the March of a Nation*, pp. 182–3.

46. De Valera diary, 12 August 1922, de Valera papers, 2122.

47. Bromage, Mary C., *De Valera and the March of a Nation*, p. 183.

48. De Valera diary, 13 August 1922, de Valera papers, 2122.

49. ibid. 14 August 1922, de Valera papers, 2122.

50. T. P. O'Neill minute, de Valera papers, 205/3.

51. MacArdle, Dorothy, *The Irish Republic: a Documented Chronicle of the Anglo-Irish Conflict and the Partitioning of Ireland, with a Detailed Account of the Period 1916–1923*, pp. 711–2.

52. ibid. p. 712.

53. O'Kelly to Hagan, 26 August 1922, Hagan papers, Irish College, Rome.

54. ibid.

55. Mulcahy to Hagan, 11 September 1922, Hagan papers, Irish College, Rome.

56. De Valera to Ms Ryan, 21 September 1922, Hagan papers, Irish College, Rome.

57. Earnan Ó Maille to de Valera, 3 September 1922, de Valera papers, 215.

58. Keogh, Dermot, *The Vatican, the Bishops and Irish Politics*, Cambridge University Press, Cambridge, 1986, p. 96.

59. Moynihan, Maurice, *Speeches and Statements by Eamon de Valera*, p. 108; see also de Valera papers, 1452.

60. Thomas O'Doherty to Hagan, 11 November 1922, Hagan papers, Irish College, Rome.

61. He had been caught in possession of a pistol which had been given to him as a gift by Michael Collins. On the morning Childers stood trial at Portobello Barracks, 17 November, four men who had been caught in Dublin in possession of weapons were executed.

62. The first death sentences under the new legislation had been handed down in Kerry but they had not been carried out.

63. Dáil Éireann Debates, 28 November 1922, cols 2356–74; 29 November, cols 2387–431, 2445–60.

64. Patrick O'Donnell to Hagan, 25 November 1922, Hagan papers, Irish College, Rome.

65. Keogh, Dermot, *The Vatican, the Bishops and Irish Politics*, p. 97.

66. Keogh, Dermot, *Twentieth Century Ireland*, Gill and Macmillan, Dublin, 1994, p. 14.

67. Davitt, Cahir, Memoir (unpublished), p. 51.

68. ibid., pp. 50–54.

69. Keogh, Dermot, *The Vatican, the Bishops and Irish Politics*, p. 98.

70. ibid., p. 97.

71. Madge Hales to Donal Hales, 9 June 1923, Hales papers, Cork Archives Institute.

72. *Cork Examiner*, 11 December 1924, clipping kept in Hales papers, Cork Archives Institute.

73. Davitt, Cahir, Memoir, pp. 75–6.

74. Cronin, Seán, *The McGarrity Papers*, Anvil Books, Tralee, 1972, pp. 132–5.

75. Interview with John Moher, former Fianna Fáil TD for North Cork and close friend of Seán Moylan.

76. Diary of Lieutenant Patrick Quinlan, 13 December 1922, copy in author's possession.

77. Davitt, Cahir, Memoir, pp. 58–9.

78. Andrews, C. S., *Dublin Made Me: An Autobiography*, vol. 1, Mercier Press, Cork, 1979, pp. 243–4.

79. Cronin, Seán, *The McGarrity Papers*, p. 133.

80. This was said by Cosgrave in the course of an interview to representatives of neutral IRA men on 27 February 1923, NAI, DT S8139.

81. The last executions took place on 30 May 1923 when two men, Michael Murphy and Joseph O'Rourke, were shot dead for the armed robbery on 24 May of the Munster and Leinster Bank in Athenry.

82. *Donegal Vindicator*, 17 March 1923; reference kindly supplied by Tom Cannon, Drumcondra, Dublin.

83. Daly to Fr Brennan, PP of Castlemaine, 7 February 1923. Daly papers, in possession of Tony and Aine Meade, Cork.

84. Daly to his father, 14 March 1923, Daly papers.

85. McMullen to Fr Brennan, 21 March 1923, Daly papers. In the same letter, Fr McMullen wrote that 'Charlie did not ask me to write to the Bishop [O'Sullivan of Kerry]. I fancy he considered himself more or less in disfavour with his Lordship.' In fact, Charlie Daly's father's grandmother and the father of Dr O'Sullivan were brother and sister. His father had gone to see 'his big Cousin' in mid-February about his son's predicament. He had not found the bishop 'in very good humour' but he was 'prepared for him' and they talked about old times; 'so we had a long shanachee so I got him into the humour I wanted him.' He found he had enough 'of the Old Nature' in him and concluded that 'he is a good Old Fellow after all – Oh by the way he asked a good deal about you'; Letter from Daly's father, 19 February 1932, Daly papers. Daly replied to his father on 25 February stating that he had been told about his visit to 'your old school chum, big cousin as you call him'. The purpose 'I can only guess but I don't for a moment imagine that it was for the sake of "influence" in the vulgar sense of that word. Even in a case like this you, no more than I, would dream of seeking such "influence". Nobody can object to intervention though where neither principle or honour are involved.' He also pointed out that he had heard that his father had been surrounded by 'Job's comfortors' who said that his teaching had been responsible for the situation in which his sons had found themselves. (His two brothers were also jailed anti-Treatyites.)

86. Keogh, Dermot, *The Vatican, the Bishops and Irish Politics*, p. 258.

87. See *Donegal Vindicator*, 24 March 1923. The house at Kilraine belonged at that time to the bishop's brother. Bonnyglen House, Inver, was also burned down by armed men who were not even disguised. They told the caretaker that they were burning the place as a reprisal for the executions at Drumboe. The house was owned by the British Consul General in Philadelphia, W. H. M. Sinclair. The house of the father of Commandant Joseph Cunningham near Carrick was also burned down. He was OC Killybegs barracks. The house of Captain O'Boyle, Adjt. 46th Batt. Mallinmore, Killybegs was also destroyed by fire around the same time. The *Donegal Vindicator*, 24 March 1923 recorded the events which followed in the wake of the Drumboe executions and commented in an editorial: 'Dead Irishmen are Ireland's loss.' I am very grateful to Dr James M. McCloskey, and to many other people in Glenties who helped me to research this incident. The family and relatives of Cardinal O'Donnell kindly showed me the home and papers in their possession. Mary Campbell of Glenties gave me a valuable taped interview of a number of elderly people from the area which I used as background. I am also grateful to Tom Cannon who gave me research notes.

88. *Donegal Vindicator*, 24 March 1923.

89. Keogh, Dermot, *The Vatican the Bishops and Irish Politics*, chapter iv, pp. 101–23.

90. Macardle, Dorothy, *The Irish Republic*, pp. 769–70.

91. ibid., pp. 774–5

92. Letter from Hagan to Mrs Ryan, 26 December 1923, Hagan papers, Irish College, Rome.

93. Earl of Longford & O'Neill, T. P., *Eamon de Valera*, p. 229.

94. Mansergh, Nicholas, *The Irish Free State: its Government and Politics*, Allen and Unwin, London, 1934, p. 228.

95. Dudley Edwards, Owen, *Eamon de Valera*, p. 110.

The aftermath of the Irish Civil War (pp. 74–83)
Tom Garvin

1. Garvin, Tom, *1922: the Birth of Irish Democracy*, Gill and Macmillan, Dublin, 1996, pp. 27–62.
2. Garvin, Tom, *Nationalist Revolutionaries in Ireland*, Clarendon Press, Oxford, 1987, pp. 139–66.
3. Pyne, Peter, 'The Third Sinn Féin Party, 1923–26,' *Economic and Social Review*, vol. 1, 1969–70, pp. 29–50, 229–57.
4. Garvin, Tom, *Nationalist Revolutionaries in Ireland*, pp. 139–66.
5. The standard works are Hopkinson, Michael, *Green against Green*, Gill and Macmillan, Dublin, 1988; Litton, Helen, *The Irish Civil War*, Wolfhound, Dublin, 1995.
6. Garvin, Tom, *1922: the Birth of Irish Democracy*, pp. 119–20.
7. ibid., p. 183 and passim.
8. Mansergh, Nicholas, *The Unresolved Question*, Yale University Press, New Haven and London, 1991.
9. Litton, Helen, *The Irish Civil War*, p. 132.
10. ibid.
11. Pyne, Peter, passim.
12. Garvin, Tom, *1922: the Birth of Irish Democracy*, pp. 135–6.

De Valera imagined and observed (pp. 84–103)
Ged Martin

1. Quoted in Lee, Joseph and Ó Tuathaigh, Gearóid, *The Age of de Valera*, Ward River Press, Dublin, 1982, p. 206. I have taken the spelling of MacLennan's surname from his entry in *Who's Who*.
2. Coogan, Tim Pat, *De Valera: Long Fellow, Long Shadow*, Hutchinson, London, 1993, pp. 246–8; Macardle, Dorothy, *The Irish Republic*, with preface by de Valera, Corgi, London, 1968 edition, first published 1937.
3. Lord Garner, former British diplomat, quoted in Lee, Joseph and Ó Tuathaigh, Gearóid, *The Age of de Valera*, p. 203.
4. Article in the *Sunday Express* (London), 21 August 1921, quoted in Callanan, Frank, *T. M. Healy*, Cork University Press, Cork, 1996, p. 562.
5. MacDonald, Malcolm, *Titans and Others*, Collins, London, 1972, p. 55.
6. Lee, J. J., *Ireland 1912–1985: Politics and Society*, Cambridge University Press, Cambridge, 1989, p. 75.
7. Callanan, Frank, *T. M. Healy*, p. 563.
8. ibid., pp. 538, 563. In private letters, Healy usually wrote of 'Valera'.
9. Quoted in Lyons, F. S. L., *John Dillon: a Biography*, Routledge and Keegan Paul, London, 1968, p. 423.
10. Quoted in Wilson, Trevor (ed.), *The Political Diaries of C. P. Scott, 1911–1918*, Collins, London, 1970, p. 349.
11. Quoted in Callanan, Frank, *T. M. Healy*, p. 538.
12. The veteran MP braced himself for a defeat first by a thousand votes, then by 'about two thousand' and was finally swept away by a majority of well over four thousand, in a two-to-one landslide. Dillon attributed his defeat in large measure to organised intimidation, overlooking the inconvenient point that de Valera had been equally heavily defeated challenging Joseph Devlin in West Belfast. Wilson, Trevor (ed.), *The Political Diaries of C. P. Scott*, pp. 362–3; Lyons, F.S.L., *John Dillon: a Biography*, pp. 451–3.
13. Lyons, F. S. L., *John Dillon: a Biography*, p. 467.
14. Responsible for the welfare of British prisoners of war in 1917, Newton had found himself in the odd position of indirectly negotiating with the Germans. His visit to Ireland in April 1919 did not persuade him to extend the same approach to Sinn Féin. He was

also puzzled by the fact that 'I do not remember seeing a single pig'. Lord Newton, *Retrospection*, John Murray, London, 1941, p. 269.

15. Quoted in Sommer, Dudley, *Haldane of Cloan: His Life and Times 1856–1928*, Allen & Unwin, London, 1960, p. 363.
16. Quoted in Lord Riddell's *Intimate Diary of the Peace Conference and After 1918–1923*, John Murray, London, 1933, p. 260.
17. ibid., p. 288.
18. Quoted in Churchill, Randolph S., *Lord Derby 'King of Lancashire'*, Heinemann, London, 1959, p. 405.
19. ibid., p. 420.
20. Quoted in Self, Robert (ed.), *The Austen Chamberlain Diary Letters*, Cambridge University Press, Cambridge, 1995, Camden Fifth series, p. 161.
21. Earl of Midleton, *Records and Reactions 1856–1939*, Oahspe, Herts., 1939, pp. 258–62.
22. Quoted in Hancock, W. K., *Smuts: II The Fields of Force 1919–1950*, Cambridge University Press, Cambridge, 1968, p. 51. For his early career see Hancock, W. K., *Smuts: I The Sanguine Years 1870–1919*, Cambridge University Press, Cambridge, 1962.
23. Hancock, W. K., *Smuts: II The Fields of Force 1919–1950*, chap. 9.
24. One of the 1914 rebels, Jopie Fourie, had been shot by firing squad, refusing a blindfold as he met his death. Smuts was widely blamed for the sentence. Davenport, T. R. H., *South Africa: a Modern History*, Palgrave, London, 1977, pp. 184–6; Hancock, W. K., *Smuts: I The Sanguine Years 1870–1919*, pp. 392, 406.
25. Taylor, A. J. P., *English History 1914–1945*, Oxford University Press, Oxford, 1965, p. 82.
26. For the mythic version see ibid., p. 156; Hancock, W. K., *Smuts: II The Fields of Force 1919–1950*, pp. 51–5; Murphy, John A., *Ireland in the Twentieth Century*, Gill and Macmillan, Dublin, 1975, p. 25–6. The government's control over the speech is made clear in Self, Robert (ed.), *The Austen Chamberlain Diary Letters*, p. 161 and Rose, Kenneth, *King George V*, Phoenix, London, 1984, p. 238. According to Chamberlain, the positive response to the speech persuaded the king that the initiative had been his own idea.
27. Quoted in Hancock, W. K., *Smuts: II The Fields of Force 1919–1950*, pp. 55–6.
28. ibid., pp. 50–56.
29. For the letter of 4 August 1921, Van Der Poel, J. (ed.), *Selections from the Smuts Papers: V September 1919–November 1934*, Cambridge University Press, Cambridge, 1973, pp. 100–105, and p. 106 for his unease at the use Lloyd George might make of it. De Valera protested at its publication, Macardle, Dorothy, *The Irish Republic*, pp. 446–7.
30. Hancock, W. K., *Smuts: II The Fields of Force 1919–1950*, p. 56.
31. Gogarty, Oliver St John, *As I Was Going Down Sackville Street*, Rich & Cowan, London, 1937, chapter 21.
32. Quoted in Van Der Poel, J. (ed.), *Selections from the Smuts Papers: V September 1919–November 1934*, p. 96 (from a Buckingham palace memorandum of Smuts' report to the king, 7 July 1921).
33. ibid., p. 102 (letter of 4 August 1921).
34. ibid., p. 97.
35. ibid., p. 96. Griffith had organised perhaps the most unlikely event in the pantheon of Irish historical commemoration, the 1798 centenary celebrations in Johannesburg.
36. Dangerfield, George, *The Damnable Question: a Study in Anglo-Irish Relations*, Quartet, London, 1977, p. 209. The whole strategy was best summed up by Healy: 'To enlist the great Boer statesman to string the government proposals into nursery rhymes set to African lullabies for Irish ears was crudely inartistic.' Callanan, Frank, *T. M. Healy*, p. 562.
37. Quoted in Van Der Poel, J. (ed.), *Selections from the Smuts Papers: V September 1919–November 1934*, p. 94.
38. Macardle, Dorothy, *The Irish Republic*, p. 434. Afrikaners formed the majority of the white population of the Cape Colony, and so sympathised with the former Boer Republics.

Natal settlers were intensely pro-British, but in 1910 they numbered fewer than 100,000, barely larger than the Protestant population of Tyrone and Fermanagh. Natal whites were outnumbered ten-to-one by an African majority over which they had come close to losing control in 1906. Durban, Natal's principal port, depended upon the Transvaal for much of its trade. Northern Ireland had been delineated to ensure that there would never be a nationalist majority. Unionists needed nobody's support to maintain internal control, and Belfast looked outwards for its prosperity.

39. Quoted in Van Der Poel, J. (ed.), *Selections from the Smuts Papers: V September 1919–November 1934*, p. 113 (letter of 23 February 1923).

40. Quoted in Wilson, Trevor (ed.), *The Political Diaries of C. P. Scott*, p. 391. In fairness, it should be added that Scott received precisely the same report from A. D. Lindsay, the Oxford don who also tried to contact the Sinn Féin leadership. 'He shared Smuts' view of de Valera as a man without much sense of reality and obsessed by a sort of poetic vision of an ideal Ireland.' ibid., p. 392.

41. Taylor, A. J. P. (ed.), *Lloyd George: a Diary by Frances Stevenson*, Hutchinson, London, 1971, pp. 227–8 (17 July 1921). The Welsh word for 'people' is 'pobl'.

42. Wilson, Trevor (ed.), *The Political Diaries of C. P. Scott*, p. 395.

43. From Lloyd George's letter of 24 June 1921. In a speech on 14 July, he called de Valera 'the Chieftain of the vast majority of the Irish race'. Macardle, Dorothy, *The Irish Republic*, pp. 431, 439.

44. Meeting of 17 July 1921, reported in Taylor, A. J. P. (ed.), *Lloyd George: a Diary by Frances Stevenson*, p. 229.

45. Calton Younger describes this as 'the error of an honest man who believes other men are as honest as he'. Younger, Calton, *Arthur Griffith*, Gill & Macmillan, Dublin, 1981, p. 109.

46. Quoted in Wilson, Trevor (ed.), *The Political Diaries of C. P. Scott*, pp. 392, 394. De Valera had taken a similar line to Smuts, Van Der Poel, J. (ed.), *Selections from the Smuts Papers: V September 1919–November 1934*, pp. 97–8.

47. Quoted in Nicolson, Harold, *King George V: His Life and Reign*, Constable, London, 1952, p. 358. Austen Chamberlain similarly dismissed de Valera as 'a dreamer', adding that Griffith was 'a poet', Barton 'a small solicitor' and Stack 'a crooked-faced solicitor's clerk and gunman'. Self, Robert (ed.), *The Austen Chamberlain Diary Letters*, p. 163.

48. Churchill, Winston S., *The Aftermath: Being a Sequel to the World Crisis*, Macmillan, London, 1941, p. 309. Poyning's Law dated from 1494. Tales of de Valera's historical disquisitions soon passed into popular legend (e.g., Gunther, John, *Inside Europe*, Harper, New York, 1938, p. 310). Malcolm MacDonald thought it promising evidence of de Valera's 'present practical mood' at a meeting during the 1936 British-Irish negotiations that 'he never mentioned Oliver Cromwell' or any other episode prior to 1921. When a draft communiqué describing talks in 1938 referred to an opening statement of the Irish position, de Valera 'beamed a smile' and suggested that the press would report 'that by the end of a long harangue I was still describing the wrongs done to Ireland by Oliver Cromwell'. The draft was amended. Quoted in Harkness, David, 'Mr de Valera's Dominion: Irish relations with Britain and the Commonwealth 1932–38', *Journal of Commonwealth Political Studies*, vol. 8, 1970, p. 217; MacDonald, Malcolm, *Titans and Others*, pp. 75–6.

49. Callanan, Frank, *T. M. Healy*, pp. 558, 584–5.

50. ibid., pp. 586, 588.

51. ibid., pp. 607–10.

52. Healy was using the term 'half-breed Spaniard' by February 1923, Callanan, Frank, *T. M. Healy*, p. 606, and see p. 625 for the 1928 newspaper interview and p. 736 for Devoy. De Valera denied Jewish ancestry: Dwyer, T. Ryle, *Eamon de Valera*, Gill and Macmillan, Dublin, 1980, p. 90. Coogan, Tim Pat, *De Valera: Long Fellow, Long Shadow*, pp. 4–10 suggests that de Valera may have been illegitimate, but sees no reason to doubt his

parentage. Lady Lavery spread the story that the decision not to renew Healy's appointment as governor-general in 1928 was taken 'with an idea to make things easier if de Valera should come in'. Barnes, J. and Nicholson, D. (eds), *The Leo Amery Diaries I: 1896–1921*, Hutchinson, London, 1980, p. 538. Callanan, Frank, *T. M. Healy*, pp. 622–4 does not mention the story but supplies practical reasons for getting Tim out of the Viceregal Lodge. Nor was there any cause for Cosgrave to make life easier for his opponents.

53. Ethnic abuse of de Valera is scattered through Gogarty, Oliver St John, *As I was Going Down Sackville Street*. These examples are taken from chapter 4, where Gogarty commented that de Valera 'is more Irish perhaps than any of us, seeing that he looks like something uncoiled from the Book of Kells'.

54. MacDonald, Malcolm, *Titans and Others*, p. 55.

55. Gunther, John, *Inside Europe*, p. 302. Other European leaders born outside the countries they ruled were Pilsudski of Poland, Turkey's Kemal Ataturk and von Schuschnigg of Austria. Neville Chamberlain, who had dealt with both, also drew a parallel between de Valera and Hitler. McMahon, Deirdre, *Republicans and Imperialists Anglo-Irish Relations in the 1930s*, Yale University Press, New Haven, 1984, p. 243.

56. O'Leary, Grattan, *Recollections of People, Press and Politics*, Macmillan, Toronto, 1977, p. 94.

57. Van Der Poel, J. (ed.), *Selections from the Smuts Papers: V September 1919–November 1934*, p. 520.

58. The prominence of Ireland in the world picture of the British elite can be over-estimated: Gladstone grew up in Liverpool and enjoyed a country estate in north Wales, but managed only one visit despite devoting part of his career to the Irish Question. Gladstone visited great houses and their destruction destroyed a network of hospitality. On a visit to Dublin in 1948, Harold Nicolson lunched at the Kildare Street Club, 'a strange Victorian relic' full of 'broken-down peers'. Nor was cross-channel travel much easier than in Victorian times. On a previous visit, Nicolson had flown to Ireland, noting that the aircraft 'smelled of sick'. The Dublin universities, which invited Keynes in 1933 and figured in both of Nicolson's visits, were hardly able to finance extensive intellectual exchanges. Commonwealth links before 1932 were still tentative. The British Dominions Secretary, L. S. Amery, wrote generously of the impact that O'Higgins made in London, but privately seems to have been more concerned by the degree to which the organisation might influence him. McGilligan seems to have been respected in British government circles, and was the target of a charm offensive by the Prince of Wales at the Imperial Conference of 1930, but it is doubtful if he established close friendships. Nicolson seems to have been embarrassed by McGilligan's pro-British sentiments at a UCD debate in 1942. Morley, John, *The Life of William Ewart Gladstone*, Lloyd, London, 1903, vol. 2, p. 571; Nicolson, Nigel (ed.), *Harold Nicolson: Diaries and Letters 1945–1962*, Collins, London, 1971, p. 143; Nicolson, Nigel (ed), *Harold Nicolson: Diaries and Letters 1939–1945*, Collins, London, 1970, pp. 214–6; de Vere White, Terence, *Kevin O'Higgins*, Anvil, Dublin, 1986, p. 247; Barnes, J. and Nicholson, D. (eds), *The Leo Amery Diaries I, 1896–1929*, pp. 483, 485, 512–3; Harkness, D. W., *The Restless Dominion: the Irish Free State and the British Commonwealth of Nations, 1921–1931*, Macmillan, London, 1969, pp. 225–8; Harkness, David, 'Patrick McGilligan: Man of Commonwealth', *Journal of Imperial and Commonwealth History*, vol. 8, 1979, pp. 117–35.

59. Skidelsky, R., *John Maynard Keynes II: The Economist as Saviour 1920–1937*, Macmillan, London, 1992, pp. 479–80. For the policy of encouraging wheat see Lee, J. J., *Ireland 1912–1985*, p. 185.

60. MacDonald, Malcolm, *Titans and Others*, p. 67. For Ireland and the Abdication see Hancock, W. K., *Survey of British Commonwealth Affairs I: Problems of Nationality 1918–1936*, Oxford University Press, London, 1937, pp. 387–90, 625–30; McMahon, Deirdre, *Republicans and Imperialists: Anglo-Irish Relations in the 1930s*, pp. 198–209.

61. Roskill, S. W., *Hankey: Man of Secrets, III: 1931–1963*, Naval Institute Press, London, 1974, p. 254.

62. Garner, Joe, *The Commonwealth Office 1925–1968*, Heinemann, London, 1978, p. 70. On one occasion, Batterbee telephoned his opposite number, Joe Walsh of External Affairs, over an open line to discuss 'the cook giving notice and engaging someone to take his place.'

63. Gunther, John, *Inside Europe*, p. 304.

64. Garner, Joe, *The Commonwealth Office*, p. 118.

65. MacDonald, Malcolm, *Titans and Others*, pp. 55–8.

66. Lee, J. J., *Ireland 1912–1985*, p. 213. For British-Irish negotiations generally see Canning, Paul, *British Policy Towards Ireland 1921–1941*, Oxford University Press, Oxford, 1985, pp. 121–238.

67. MacDonald, Malcolm, *Titans and Others*, pp. 64–5, 73–4.

68. Quoted in Feiling, Keith, *The Life of Neville Chamberlain*, Macmillan, London, 1946, p. 310.

69. Simon (Viscount), *Retrospect: the Memoirs of Viscount Simon*, Hutchinson, London, 1952, p. 230. There is an irresistible similarity between this staged incident and the restoration, in Wilde's *The Importance of Being Earnest*, of Miss Prism's long-lost handbag. ('The bag is undoubtedly mine. I am delighted to have it so unexpectedly restored to me. It has been a great inconvenience being without it all these years.') Malcolm Mac-Donald was keen to cement relations with the austere de Valera with a gift. After joking about the parsimony of the Scots, de Valera finally mentioned a mathematics text that he had seen in a London bookshop. On purchasing it, MacDonald found that de Valera had tactfully chosen a volume costing just five shillings. In a more curious gesture of co-operation, de Valera contributed a memorandum to a British government discussion of penal reform, based on his experience of British prisons. MacDonald, Malcolm, *Titan and Others*, pp. 77–9.

70. Lee, J. J., *Ireland 1912–1985*, p. 212.

71. Duff Cooper, Alfred (Viscount Norwich), *Old Men Forget: the Autobiography of Duff Cooper*, Rupert Hart-Davis, London, 1953, p. 229. De Valera's warm message of support to Chamberlain ('one person at least is completely satisfied that you are doing the right thing') is in Feiling, Keith, *The Life of Neville Chamberlain*, p. 364. But a week earlier, de Valera had equated Hitler's claims in the Sudetenland with the nationalist areas of Northern Ireland, angrily telling a British politician that he sometimes thought of 'going over the boundary and pegging out the territory, just as Hitler was doing'. Quoted in Dwyer, T. Ryle, *Eamon de Valera*, p. 109.

72. Quoted in Gilbert, Martin, *Winston S. Churchill V: 1922–1939*, Heinemann, London, 1976, p. 1049.

73. Feiling, Keith, *The Life of Neville Chamberlain*, p. 311.

74. Quoted in Harkness, David, 'Mr de Valera's Dominion', p. 227. Had he remained in office, it seems likely that Chamberlain would have attempted to trade the return of the bases for a British declaration in favour of a united Ireland in 1940. Gilbert, Martin, *Finest Hour: Winston S. Churchill VI: 1939–1941*, Heinemann, London, 1983, p. 577; Canning, Paul, *British Policy Towards Ireland 1921–1941*, pp. 272–5.

75. Gunther, John, *Inside Europe*, pp. 305–6, 303.

76. ibid., pp. 306, 309, 310.

77. ibid., pp. 303, 305. Gunther's belief that Irish people 'are not particularly prone to give nicknames' (p. 302) casts some doubt on his powers of observation.

78. Menzies, R. G., *Afternoon Light*, Penguin, London, 1967, p. 40.

79. MacDonald, Malcolm, *Titans and Others*, pp. 58–9.

80. Gunther, John, *Inside Europe*, p. 309.

81. Nicolson, Nigel (ed.), *Harold Nicolson: Diaries and Letters 1939–1945*, p. 217. J. P. Walshe alarmed British ministers by discussing the forthcoming abdication with de Valera in Irish over an open telephone line while visiting the Dominions Office. Walshe reassured them by explaining that nobody in the Dublin telephone exchange under-

stood Irish. McMahon, Deirdre, *Republicans and Imperialists: Anglo-Irish Relations in the 1930s*, p. 199.

82. Foot, Michael, *Aneurin Bevan II*, Paladin, London, 1975, p. 587. Bevan promptly claimed that it had been 'written by a Welshman', a romantic interpretation of the origins of Thomas Jefferson, and not a sentiment to appeal to an Irish leader who had dealt with Lloyd George. See also Nicolson, Nigel, *Harold Nicolson: Diaries and letters 1939–1945*, p. 217.

83. Gilbert, Martin, *Finest Hour*, p. 67. *See* also Canning, *British Policy Towards Ireland*, pp. 241–309.

84. Menzies, R. G., *Afternoon Light*, p. 41. For the British use of an arms embargo as a means of putting pressure on Ireland, see Canning, Paul, *British Policy Towards Ireland*, pp. 289–91, 305–6.

85. Nicolson, Nigel, *Harold Nicolson: Diaries and Letters 1939–1945*, p. 140.

86. O'Leary, Grattan, *Recollections*, p. 94.

87. Menzies, R. G., *Afternoon Light*, p. 37.

88. Nicolson, Nigel, *Harold Nicolson: Diaries and Letters 1939–1945*, p. 298.

89. O'Leary, Grattan, *Recollections*, pp. 93–4. De Valera's reply was that it was 'a British Army recruiting speech'. According to the *Dictionary of National Biography 1941–1950*, pp. 394–5, Cardinal Hinsley devoted 'all his energies ... to the spiritual service of the Allies'. In 1942, Oxford University hailed him as 'a great Englishman'.

90. Nicolson, Nigel, *Harold Nicolson: Diaries and Letters 1939–1945*, p. 214.

91. The provocative verb chosen by Churchill in his 1945 victory speech. Earl of Longford and O'Neill, T. P., *Eamon de Valera*, Houghton Mifflin, Boston, 1971, pp. 413–4 for the speech and de Valera's response.

92. Quoted in Gilbert, Martin, *Finest Hour*, p. 43.

93. MacDonald, Malcolm, *Titans and Others*, p. 85.

94. Nicolson, Nigel, *Harold Nicolson: Diaries and Letters 1939–1945*, p. 215.

95. Menzies, R. G., *Afternoon Light*, p. 41.

96. ibid., pp. 36–43. Day, David, *Menzies and Churchill at War*, Angus & Robertson, North Ryde, 1986 argues that Menzies hoped to emulate the role of Smuts in the First World War and even to oust Churchill from the premiership. The Dublin visit is seen as part of that strategy, pp. 111–3. The episode is played down by Cameron Hazelhurst in *Menzies Observed*, Allen & Unwin, Sydney, 1979, p. 215.

97. Menzies, R. G., *Afternoon Light*, pp. 38–40.

98. MacDonald, Malcolm, *Titans and Others*, pp. 82–5; Canning, Paul, *British Policy Towards Ireland*, pp. 274–87. Lee suggests that de Valera was more concerned to maintain the unity of Fianna Fáil than to secure the unity of Ireland, but Dermot Keogh sees a 'missed opportunity'. Lee, J. J., *Ireland 1912–1985*, p. 249. Keogh, Dermot, *Twentieth Century Ireland: Nation and State*, Gill and Macmillan, Dublin, 1994, p. 114. De Valera demanded immediate reunification, but could not promise a declaration of war. Mac-Donald was convinced that he expected a German victory. In any case, a 'profoundly shocked and disgusted' Craigavon interposed a veto. Bardon, J., *A History of Ulster*, Blackstaff, Belfast, 1992, p. 559.

99. Garner, Joe, *The Commonwealth Office*, pp. 246–7.

100. Nicolson, Nigel, *Harold Nicolson: Diaries and Letters 1939–1945*, pp. 217–8. Gunther was less impressed by de Valera's Irish accent: 'He speaks with a perceptible brogue; words like "that" and "this" come out with the "th's" thickened.' Gunther, John, *Inside Europe*, p. 309.

101. Morgan, K. O., *Labour in Power 1945–1951*, Oxford University Press, Oxford, 1984, pp. 199–200. Herbert Morrisson met de Valera in 1946 after a holiday in west Cork, but of all Attlee's ministers, he was perhaps the most identified with Ulster. Donoghue, B. and Jones, G. W., *Herbert Morrison: Portrait of a Politician*, Weidenfield and Nicolson, London, 1973, pp. 308, 385–6.

102. For Nicolson's comment *see* Nicolson, Nigel, *Harold Nicolson: Diaries and Letters 1939–1945*, p. 464.

103. Earl of Longford and O'Neill, T. P., *Eamon de Valera*, pp. 435–6.

104. ibid., pp. 442–3.

105. Lord Moran, *Winston Churchill: the Struggle for Survival 1940–1965*, Houghton Mifflin, London, 1967, p. 473.

106. See note 42.

107. Cf. Murphy, *Ireland in the Twentieth Century*, p. 140.

108. Dwyer, T. Ryle, *De Valera*, p. 148 and see Bowman, J., *De Valera and the Ulster Question*, Oxford University Press, Oxford, 1982.

109. Menzies, R. G., *Afternoon Light*, p. 38. Buckland, P., *The Factory of Grievances: Devolved Government in Northern Ireland 1921–1939*, Gill and Macmillan, Dublin, 1979.

110. Thus a note addressed to the British government, for domestic political reasons in 1951, complaining about the conditions faced by Irish migrant workers in the Birmingham area, went unanswered. An attempt by de Valera to draw Churchill into further correspondence about the return of Casement's remains also met with silence. Coogan, Tim Pat, *De Valera: Long Fellow, Long Shadow*, pp. 662–3; Earl of Longford and O'Neill, T. P., *Eamon de Valera*, p. 443.

111. O'Leary, Grattan, *Recollections*, p. 134.

112. Coogan, Tim Pat, *De Valera: Long Fellow, Long Shadow*, p. 520, and *see* MacDonald, Malcolm, *Titans and Others*, pp. 76–7.

113. MacDonald, Malcolm, *Titans and Others*, p. 86.

Women in de Valera's Ireland 1932–42: a reappraisal (pp. 104–114)
Catriona Clear

1. Journalistic examples are numerous, in the journalism of, e.g., Emily O'Reilly, Fintan O'Toole, Kathryn Holmquist, Nuala O'Faolain (to name but four) in the *Irish Times*, *Sunday Business Post*, *Irish Press*, *Sunday Press*, 1990–1997. Lichfield, John, 'Ireland's comely maidens are doing it for themselves' in *Independent on Sunday* 15 September 1996, is one example of the genre. There are several other examples of this doom-laden scenario in the fields of sociology and political science, and women's studies; see, for example, Rose, Catherine, *The Female Experience: the Story of the Woman Movement in Ireland*, Arlen House, Galway, 1975; Mahon, Evelyn, 'Women's Rights and Catholicism in Ireland' *New Left Review*, no. 166 (November–December 1978), pp. 53–78, and 'From Democracy to Femocracy: the Women's Movement in the Republic of Ireland' in Clancy, P., et al (eds), *Irish Society: Sociological Perspectives*, IPA, Dublin 1995, pp. 675–708; Beale, Jenny, *Women in Ireland: Voices of Change*, Gill and Macmillan, Dublin, 1986; Gardiner, Frances, 'The Unfinished Revolution', *Canadian Journal of Irish Studies*, vol. 18, no. 1, 1992, pp. 15–39. Rose's and Beale's books are very thoroughly researched and each was ground-breaking when it first appeared. It is impossible to disagree with Beale's summary of the first fifty years after independence as 'fifty years of inequality', however much one might disagree with some of her other conclusions. Professor Joseph Lee in his *Ireland 1912–85: Politics and Society*, Cambridge University Press, Cambridge, 1989, p. 335 uses the William Trevor short story 'The Ballroom of Romance', published in 1972 and actually set in 1971, to underline women's particularly hard lives in rural Ireland in the 1940s and 1950s.

2. See, for example, Wieners, Amy, 'Rural Irishwomen, their Changing Role, Status and Condition' *Eire–Ireland*, Earrach–Spring 1994, pp. 76–91. It is Maryann Valiulis however who proposes most vigorously that Ireland in the 1920s and 30s was a protofascist state as far as women were concerned; see Valiulis, M., 'Defining their Role in the New State: Irishwomen's Protest Against the Juries Act', *Canadian Journal of Irish*

Studies, vol. 18, no. 1, 1992, pp. 43–60; 'Power, Gender and Identity in the Irish Free State' *Journal of Women's History*, vols 6/7, nos 4/5, Winter/Spring 1994–5, pp. 117–136; 'Neither Feminist Nor Flapper: the Ecclesiastical Construction of the Ideal Irish Woman' in O'Dowd, M. and Wichert, S. (eds), *Chattel, Servant or Citizen? Studies in Women's History*, Institute of Irish Studies, Belfast, 1995, pp. 168–78.

3. Scannell, Yvonne, 'The Constitution and the Role of Women' in Farrell, B. (ed.), *De Valera's Constitution and Ours*, Gill and Macmillan, Dublin, 1988, pp. 123–36; Clancy, Mary, 'Aspects of Women's Contribution to Oireachtas Debate in Ireland 1922–37' in Luddy, M. and Murphy, C. (eds), *Women Surviving: Studies in Irish Women's History in the Nineteenth and Twentieth Centuries*, Poolbeg, Dublin, 1990, pp. 206–32.

4. The argument set out in this paper is developed more fully in Clear, C., *Women of the House: Women's Household Work in Ireland 1921–1961*, PhD, NUI (UCD), 1997, chapters 1–7 inclusive. See also Clear, C., 'The Women Cannot be Blamed: the Commission on Vocational Organisation, Feminism and "Home-Makers" in Independent Ireland in the 1930s and 1940s' in O'Dowd, M. and Wichert, S. (eds), *Chattel, Servant or Citizen?*, pp. 179–86.

5. Macardle, Dorothy, 'Irish Women in Industry' *Irish Press*, 5 September 1931.

6. *Woman's Life: the Irish Home Weekly*, 1936–1954 (National Library of Ireland).

7. Laverty, Maura, *Never No More: the Story of a Lost Village*, Longmans, London, 1942; *Kind Cooking*, ESB, Dublin, 1946; *Lift Up Your Gates*, Longmans, London, 1946.

8. Curtayne, Alice, 'The New Woman': text of a lecture given in the Theatre Royal, Dublin, 22 October 1933, under the title, *The Renaissance of Woman*, np, Dublin, 1933, with an imprimatur by the Bishop of Ferns. I am grateful to Alan Hayes for this reference.

9. 'Clarion Call of Lenten Pastoral – Clonfert', *Connacht Tribune*, 17 February 1934.

10. L'Observateur, 'Causes and Consequences of Depopulation: Notes from France', *Catholic Bulletin* vol. 15, January–December 1925, pp. 911–8, and 'Paternal Authority in the French Family', *Catholic Bulletin*, vol. 28, January–June 1938, pp. 299–303.

11. See, for example, MacDonagh, W. F., SJ, 'The Position of Woman in Modern Life', *Irish Monthly*, vol. 67, June 1939, pp. 389–99; Hayden, Mary, 'Woman's Role in the Modern World', *Irish Monthly*, vol. 68, August 1940, pp. 392–402; Guthrie, Hunter, SJ, 'Woman's Role in the Modern World', *Irish Monthly*, vol. 69, August 1941, pp. 246–52.

12. Stafford, Brigid, 'Equal Pay for Women', *Irish Monthly*, vol. 79, July 1951, pp. 308–14; Shannon, Rev. G. J., 'Woman: Wife and Mother' *Christus Rex*, vol. 5, 1952, pp. 155–74.

13. ibid.; for stories and articles disapproving of fashion, clothes and work in cities and towns, see *Irish Messenger of the Sacred Heart*, 1924–1940, *passim*, e.g., Bauer, Maria, 'Dress and Fashion', ibid., vol. xlix, August 1936, p. 87; Dease, A., 'Those Nuns!', ibid., vol. xl, October 1927; O'Connor, E., SJ, 'The Pope Speaks to Women Workers', ibid., vol. lxiv, February 1951, pp. 109–10, see also editorial comment p. 1.

14. The personal testimony which I solicited for this research brought me into contact with many women who were running houses in Ireland in this period, and who have only been made aware of the constitution in recent years, see Clear, C., *Women of the House*, 1997. It is interesting that while women's organisations (see below) protested strongly against the constitution for the limits they feared it would place on women's work, a sweep through the two largest selling daily newspapers, the *Independent* and the *Press* for 1937, did not reveal any letters from individual women objecting to this. And it is not that women did not write to newspapers; see the long-running controversy on 'Can Irish Girls Cook?' in the *Irish Independent* (March–May 1938) for a sample of the articulacy of women of the house from a variety of social backgrounds.

15. Valiulis, 'Power, Gender and Identity', p. 120.

16. Clancy, Mary, 'Aspects' *loc. cit.*; Clear, C., *Women of the House*, 1997, chapter 4; Beaumont, Caitriona, 'Women and the Politics of Equality: the Irish Women's Movement 1930–43' in O'Dowd, M. and Valiulis, M. (eds), *Women and Irish history: Essays for Margaret MacCurtain*, Wolfhound, Dublin, 1997, pp. 173–88.

17. The Irish Countrywomen's Association, the Joint Committee of Women's Societies and Social Workers (a 28,000-strong organisation in 1940), the Catholic Federation of Secondary School Unions (past-pupil) and the National Council of Women in Ireland, all gave evidence to the Commission on Vocational Organisation in 1940, the ICA in a session on its own, the other three together. For ICA see Minutes of evidence, 12 November 1940, NLI 930, vol. 9. The evidence given by the other three organisations is also in NLI 930, vol. 9.

18. Tweedy, Hilda, *A Link in the Chain: the Story of the Irish Housewives Association 1942–1992*, Attic, Dublin, 1992, and *The Irish Housewife* (annual publication of the IHA, vol. 1, 1946).

19. Lucy Franks, Maire MacGeehin (Or Máire F. Nic Aodháin, as she also signed herself) and Louie Bennett were the three female members of the twenty-five-strong Commission on Vocational Organisation, which delivered its report in 1943 (*Report of the Commission on Vocational Organisation*, K76/1); Louie Bennett and Agnes Ryan (later replaced by Brigid Stafford) were members of the Commission on Youth Unemployment (R/82) which reported in 1951 (18 members in all); Mrs Agnes McGuire and Mrs Frances Wrenne were members of the Commission on Emigration and Other Population Problems (1956), R/84 (24 members in all).

20. Correspondence between Department of Education and INTO, 1932–54, National Archives S7985, A, B, C, D. See also O' Leary, Eoin, 'The INTO and the Marriage Bar for Women National Teachers 1933–58', *Saothar: Journal of the Irish Labour History Society*, vol. 12, 1987, pp. 47–52.

21. Daly, Mary E., *Industrial Development and Irish National Identity 1922–39*, Syracuse University Press, New York, 1992, and 'Women in the Irish Free State 1922–39: the Interaction between Economics and Ideology', *Journal of Women's History*, vol. 6/7, no. 4/5, Winter–Spring 1994–5, pp. 99–116.

22. Kessler-Harris, Alice, 'Gender Ideology in Historical Reconstruction: a Case from the 1930s', *Gender and History*, vol. 1, no. 1, 1989, pp. 31–49.

23. Jones, Mary, *Those Obstreperous Lassies: a History of the Irish Women Workers Union*, Gill and Macmillan, Dublin, 1988, chapters 7–9.

24. See Clancy, Mary, op. cit., and Daly, Mary E., *Industrial Development and Irish National Identity*, pp. 122–7.

25. ibid.; Scannell, Yvonne, op. cit.; also McGinty, Mary, *A Study of the Campaign for and against the Enactment of the 1937 Constitution*, MA, NUI (UCG), 1987. Article 41.2 reads 'In particular the state recognises that by her life within the home, woman gives to the State a support without which the common good cannot be achieved. The State shall, therefore, endeavour to ensure that mothers shall not be obliged by economic necessity to engage in labour to the neglect of their duties in the home.'

26. For an invaluable breakdown, country by country, of the climate of opinion on women's working rights and citizenship, see all the articles in, and the editorial introduction to, Bock, Gisela and Thane, Pat (eds), *Maternity and Gender Policies: Women and the Rise of European Welfare States*, Routledge, London, 1991; Koven, Seth and Michel, Sonya (eds), *Mothers of a New World: Maternalist Politics and the Rise of Welfare States*, Routledge, London, 1993 is also useful. On Irish women and emigration, see Travers, Pauric, 'Emigration and Gender: the Case of Ireland 1922–1960' in O'Dowd and Wichert (eds) *Chattel, Servant or Citizen*, pp. 187–99.

27. See note 20.

28. *Dublin Opinion*, June 1941, p. 3. This cartoon, like so many others on this theme, was by the editor Charles E. Kelly. Kelly's daughter, Pauline Bracken, in her autobiographical *Light of Other Days*, Mercier, Cork, 1994 tells us that the Kellys always had maids.

29. *Census of Ireland* 1926, 1936, 1946, 1951, 1961: occupational tables for the country as a whole; 'No Wives For Farmers', *Irish Times*, 18 December 1936. I am grateful to Anne Byrne, agricultural journalist, Co. Wicklow, for bringing this news item to my attention.

30. 'Help Wanted' advertisements, *Irish Independent*, 27 September 1950.

31. Anon, 'I am a Model Mistress but where are the Model Maids?' *Irish Independent*, 12 May 1947.

32. Bennett, Louie, 'The Domestic Problem', *The Irish Housewife*, vol. 1, 1946, pp. 29–30; 'Joan', 'The Homefront', *The Irish Housewife*, vol. 4, 1950, pp. 103–5; 'Statement by Miss Louie Bennett Regarding her Refusal to Sign the Report', *Youth Unemployment Commission Report*, 1951, pp. 51–2.

33. *Emigration Commission Report*, pp. 171–3, and Roberts, Ruaidhri, *Reservation*, no. 11, pp. 247–56. In most of the personal testimony which I collected for the thesis, and in my own family (lower middle-class/skilled working-class) I never heard a whisper of the shortage of servants being a problem, there had never been any servants to begin with. Clear, C., *Women of the House*, chapter 1 and passim.

34. Boyle, Elizabeth, 'A Plan for the Northern Houseworkers', *The Irish Housewife*, vol. 1, 1946, pp. 31–3, is typical of the tone of such well-meaning recommendations.

35. *Census of Ireland*, 1926–1961, occupational tables; Bourke, Joanna, *Husbandry to Housewifery: Women, Economic Change and Housework in Ireland 1890–1914*, Oxford University Press, Oxford, 1993.

36. *Census of Ireland*, 1926–61, occupational tables; see also Hannan, Damian, 'Patterns of Spousal Accommodation and Conflict in Traditional Farm Families', *Economic and Social Review*, vol. 10, no. 1, 1978, pp. 61–84, and 'Changes in Family Relationship Patterns', *Social Studies: an Irish Journal of Sociology*, vol. 2, no. 6, December 1973, pp. 550–63.

37. Clear, C., *Women of the House*, chapters 8, 9 & 10; McNabb, Patrick, 'Social Structure' in Newman, J. (ed.), *The Limerick Rural Survey 1958–64*, Muintir na Tíre, Tipperary, 1964, pp. 226–7; see also, for example, the short story 'Fine China' by Elizabeth Brennan in *The Irish Countrywoman*, vol. 9, 1963–4, pp. 23–7. The Emigration Commission also noted the problem of multigenerational families. Eamon de Valera had been worried about this for some time, and had set up the Interdepartmental Committee on the Question of Making Available a Second Dwelling House on Farms, which reported in 1943 (NA S13413/1) that such a provision might encourage subdivision, and advised against it. However many of the Land Commission inspectors who responded to the questionnaire sent out by the Committee (the only research which they carried out) noted the problem of the extended rural farm family. Useful and readable surveys of the Irish family in the twentieth century are to be found in Curtin, C. and Gibbon, P., 'The Stem Family in Ireland', *Comparative Studies in Society and History*, vol. 20, no. 3, July 1978, pp. 429–53, and Fahey, Tony, 'Family and Household in Ireland' in Clancy, Patrick (ed.), *Irish Society: Sociological Perspectives*, IPA, Dublin, 1995, pp. 206–33.

38. See tables in Appendices, compiled from the Office of the Registrar General, *Annual Report 1923–52*, up to 1949, Table 10, 15 or 17 (variously), Marriage, Birth and Death Rates by Provinces, Counties and County Boroughs. After 1952 there was no longer a regional breakdown of maternal mortality. From 1953, Central Statistics Office, *Vital Statistics 1953* (1955) T3/33, table XXVII, xxxv; ibid., *1954* (1957), T3/34, xxxiii; ibid., *1955* (1958), T3/35, xxx; and so on.

39. Loudon, Irivine, *Death in Childbirth*, Oxford University Press, Oxford, 1992. This is the most comprehensive and readable survey of death in childbirth over the past several hundred years, up to the present day.

40. Barrington, Ruth, *Health, Medicine and Politics in Ireland 1900–1970*, IPA, Dublin, 1987, passim; *Revised Midwives Bill 1931*, NA S942.

41. See Appendix 2. Apart from the distinction between deaths from puerperal sepsis/fever and other causes of maternal mortality, which were set out in the annual statistics cited in note 39, all information on the breakdown of causes of maternal mortality 1938–1950 is to be found in *Annual Report of Registrar-General 1950*, table XXXI, xliii, and for selected years in the 1950s, from the Vital Statistics for those years.

42. Dockeray, G. C. and Fearon, W. R., 'Ante-Natal Nutrition in Dublin: a Preliminary Survey', *Irish Journal of Medical Science*, no. 175, 1939, pp. 80–84.

43. In 1936, 98 out of the 273 maternal deaths, or 35%, took place 'elsewhere', i.e., some-where other than a hospital or nursing home, effectively, at home; in 1950, 36 of the 99 maternal deaths, or 36%, took place at home. Abstract V: 'Causes of Deaths in Saor-stát Éireann by Sexes, Ages and Places of Occurrence', *Report of the Registrar-General for 1936*; Table 20, 'Deaths in 1950 Classified by Cause Showing Place of Occurrence', *Report of the Registrar-General for 1950*.

44. Spain, Alex, 'Maternity Services in Éire', and Quinn, James, 'A Suggested Maternity Ser-vice for Éire', in *Irish Journal of Medical Science*, no. 229, January 1945, pp. 1–23. A num-ber of similar opinions were expressed in letters to medical journals, see for example, letter from P. J. Greene, GP, Loughrea, to the *Journal of the Medical Association of Éire*, vol. 14, no. 3, 1944, pp. 57–8.

45. Healy, Mary, *For the Poor and For the Gentry: Mary Healy Remembers Her Life*, Geography Publications, Dublin, 1989, pp. 84–7; Humphreys, Alexander, *New Dubliners: Urbani-sation and the Irish Family*, Routledge and Keegan Paul, London, 1966, p. 120.

46. A comparison of the maternal mortality rates and services in counties Mayo and Kil-dare up to 1953 (one of the worst and one of the best serviced areas respectively) is made in Clear, C., *Women of the House*, chapter 6, and it is suggested that a higher pro-portion of midwives and services in a largely rural area did not significantly reduce maternal mortality.

47. Barrington, *Health, Medicine and Politics*, p. 131. My own research also indicated that 'handywomen' or female relatives were very common as birth attendants in rural areas up to the 1950s.

48. The information on women attending ante-natal clinics is taken from the annual reports of the Department of Local Government and Public Health up to 1946. The hostility of trained midwives to handywomen is evident in the appendices to these reports and in numerous articles in nurses' newspapers, see, for example, 'Editorial', *Irish Nurses Union Gazette*, no. 13, May 1925.

49. Connolly, G., 'Extract from the Annual Report' (Discussion of the Dublin Maternity Re-ports), *Irish Journal of Medical Science*, no. 371, November 1956, p. 528.

50. Barrington, *Health, Medicine and Politics*, chapters 6 & 7.

51. Children's Allowances were introduced in 1944, conceived of as subsidies to low bread-winner incomes, payable to the fathers of families. Lee, *Ireland 1912–1985*, pp. 277–85. See also correspondence on family allowances, 13/11/39–16/3/43, and *Report of Inter-departmental Committee on Family Allowances* NA S12117, A, B.

52. My own evidence for this is the personal testimony which I solicited, in which women – and men – from this period thought of these allowances as women's money, and had to be reminded by me that they were in fact payable initially to fathers. It is strik-ing that even in families where the male head was mean with money and otherwise domineering, the woman still collected this. Because of the manner in which I solici-ted testimony (by letters in newspapers), there was a higher probability that the infor-mants (because of their very survival) would have had a positive experience of 'family life'. Yet it was striking that these allowances were seen as payable to women by a variety of informants, urban and rural, farming (on good land and on bad) and non-farming, lower-middle-class and working-class, male-dominated or female-domi-nated families.

53. Healy, John, *No One Shouted Stop*, formerly *Death of an Irish Town*, Mercier, Cork, 1968, chapters 1–4; McCourt, Frank, *Angela's Ashes*, Flamingo, London, 1996.

54. Department of Health, *National Nutrition Survey Parts I–VII (1948–52)*, K53/1–6; *Gene-ral Survey*, Table 22, p. 23.

55. Loudon, *Death in Childbirth*, op. cit.

56. Recent revelations about Sweden's eugenic policies up to the 1970s in the work of Scan-dinavian historian Gunnar Myrdal.

57. There was a strong eugenic strand in the 'voluntary motherhood' movement and the

feminism of the first half of this century was often associated with eugenicism, see Greer, Germaine, *Sex and Destiny: the Politics of Human Fertility*, Secker and Warburg, London, 1984, passim, but especially chapter 6; Bock, Gisela and Thane, Pat, *Maternity and Gender Policies: Women and the Rise of the European Welfare States 1880–1950s*, Routledge, New York, 1992; Koven, Seth and Michel, Sonya, *Mothers of a New World, Maternalist Politics and the Origins of Welfare States*, Routledge, New York, 1993. Lucy Kingston, Irish feminist and pacifist highly active in the defence of women's citizenship. and working women's rights in the 1920s, 1930s and 1940s, revealed eugenic beliefs in her diaries, see Lawrenson Swanton, Daisy, *Emerging from the Shadow: the Lives of Sarah Anne Lawrenson and Lucy Olive Kingston*, Attic, Dublin, 1994. For a eugenically-minded health manual of the period, see Stone, Abraham & Stone, Hannah, *A Marriage Manual: a Practical Guidebook to Sex and Marriage*, Simon & Schuster, New York, 1940.

58. *Emigration Commission Report*, Reservation no. 8 by Mr Arnold Marsh, pp. 234–7; for a non-eugenic advocacy of birth control and smaller families, see Reservation no. 1 by W. R. F. Collis and Arnold Marsh, pp. 220–21 and Reservation no. 6 by Rev. A. A. Luce, pp. 230–1.

59. ibid., pp. 98–101, and in Dr Lucey's *Minority Report*, p. 341. These were not universal, but common enough, and exacerbated by poor nutrition and exhaustion; piles, varicose veins, neuralgia, fallen arches; then the dangers for subsequent pregnancies of a prolapsed womb, slack uterine muscles which might not contract efficiently in labour, placenta praevia, anaemia, high blood pressure, and of course, any condition the mother had, like heart disease or weakness in the lungs, could be worsened by continual pregnancy. See, for example Feeney, J. K., Master, Coombe Hospital, Dublin, 'Complications Associated with High Multiparity: a Clinical Survey of 518 cases', *Journal of the Irish Medical Association*, vol. 32, 1953, pp. 36–55; Solomons, Michael, *Pro-Life? The Irish Question*, Lilliput, Dublin, 1992, pp. 5–6 on his own experience and that of his father, both Dublin obstetricians in this century; O'Connell, John, *Doctor John: Crusading Doctor and Politician*, Poolbeg, Dublin, 1989, p. 30.

60. Ó Gráda, Cormac, *Ireland: a New Economic History*, Oxford University Press, Oxford, 1994, pp. 218–25.

61. Healy, *For the Poor and For the Gentry*, p. 87. It is however likely that such a sense of grievance might not have been expressed to me, for a number of reasons.

62. Lee, *Ireland 1912–1985*, p. 193.

63. See note 52, above, and Clear, C., *Women of the House*, passim.

64. See correspondence on children's allowances, reference given note 51.

Better sureshot than scattergun:
Eamon de Valera, Seán Ó Faoláin and arts policy (pp. 115–131)
Brian P. Kennedy

1. Author's interview with Seán Ó Faoláin, 7 February 1987.

2. Paddy Woodworth, interview with Charles J. Haughey, *Irish Times*, 31 December 1990.

3. ibid.

4. *The Echo* (Wexford), 7 February 1953.

5. Anon, 'Art Treasures in Limerick Exhibition', *Irish Times*, 27 May 1952.

6. Anon, 'Four Pillars of Wisdom', *Kavanagh's Weekly*, 19 April 1952.

7. Examples include: 'The Intentions of the Arts Council', *Cork Examiner*, 10 March 1952; 'Save Historic Sites Call: Arts Council Chief Opens Drama Week' (Scariff, Co. Clare) *Irish Press*, 24 March 1952; 'Architects Told of Council's Progress', *Irish Independent*, 4 December 1952; 'Public Bodies Urged to Foster Art', *Irish Times*, 13 March 1953; 'Art and Education', *Irish Catholic*, 19 March 1953.

8. Interview with Dr O'Sullivan, 31 January 1987.

9. An Chomhairle Ealaíon (CE), file 3, Dr O'Sullivan to Secretary, Department of Posts and Telegraphs, 5 August 1953.

10. CE 19, 'Agreed memorandum of meeting between the Taoiseach and representatives of the Arts Council', 15 January 1953.

11. MacLysaght, Edward, *Changing Times*, Gerrard's Cross, Buckinghamshire, 1978, p. 167.

12. Henderson, Gordon, 'An Interview with Mervyn Wall', *The Journal of Irish Literature*, vol. xi, no. 1 & 2, January–May 1982, p. 72.

13. Moynihan, Maurice, *Speeches and Statements of Eamon de Valera 1917–73*, Gill and Macmillan, Dublin, 1980, pp. 154–5.

14. ibid., p. 205

15. Interview with Dr George Furlong, 29 May 1984.

16. Moynihan, Maurice, *Speeches and Statements by Eamon de Valera*, pp. 220–23.

17. Dail Debates, vol. 125, 24 April 1951, cols 1337–8.

18. Trinity College, Dublin (TCD), MS 7003/2719, Bodkin to Costello, 28 November 1956.

19. TCD, MS 7003/273a, Bodkin to Archbishop McQuaid, 20 December 1956.

20. Author's interview with Seán Ó Faoláin, 7 February 1987.

21. TCD, MS 7003/273a, Bodkin to Archbishop McQuaid, 20 December 1956.

22. Private source.

23. ibid.

24. TCD MS 7006/665, 24 December 1956.

25. CE 551.

26. Editorial headed 'The Arts Council', *Irish Times*, 22 December 1956.

27. ibid., 29 December 1956.

28. CE 384, memorandum on Council policy by Dr O'Sullivan in response to queries by Professor Bodkin, undated.

29. CE 553, 29 December 1956.

30. CE 574, Earl of Rosse to Seán Ó Faoláin, 4 March 1957.

31. CE 574, minutes of Council meeting, 6 March 1957.

32. CE 29/3.

33. CE 637, minutes of Council meeting, 14 January 1958.

34. CE 637, minutes of Council meeting, 14 January 1958.

35. S. Ó Faoláin to the editor, *Irish Times*, 5 June 1959.

36. CE 656, Dr Nolan to S. Ó Faoláin, 24 July 1957.

37. CE 615, S. Ó Faoláin to C. de Baróid, 30 April 1959, and minute 8 of Council meeting, 14 July 1959.

38. CE 628 and National Archives, Department of Taoiseach S14996B, 10 December 1957.

39. CE 628.

40. See Ó hAodha, Michael, 'Ireland's Amateur Drama', *Ireland of the Welcomes*, vol. 6, no. 3, September–October 1957, pp. 12–4.

41. *Irish Independent*, 20 February 1959.

42. CE 560, 22 May 1957.

43. CE 598, Dr Nolan to Dr O'Sullivan, 15 June 1957.

44. CE 598, Seán Ó Faoláin to Mervyn Wall, telegram, 15 June 1957.

45. ibid., Dr O'Sullivan to Dr Nolan, 28 June 1957. Wall (born 1908) was a prominent member of the literary scene in Dublin and was friendly with Ó Faoláin. He was educated at University College Dublin, and worked for Radio Éireann. His novels, which are satirical, humorous and poignant, include *The Unfortunate Fursey*, Pilot, London, 1946; *The Return of Fursey*, Pilot, London, 1948; *Leaves for the Burning*, Methuen, London, 1952; and *No Trophies Raise*, Methuen, London, 1956. See Kilroy, Thomas, 'Mervyn Wall: The Demands of Satire', *Studies*, Spring 1958; and Hogan, Robert, *Mervyn Wall*, Bucknall University Press, Lewisburg, 1972.

46. CE 587, Maurice Moynihan to Mervyn Wall, 19 July 1957.

47. CE 14, Ó Faoláin to Secretary, Department of the Taoiseach, 13 September 1956.

48. ibid., 16 September 1958.
49. ibid., 20 September 1958.
50. ibid., Dr Nolan to Ó Faoláin, 1 October 1958.
51. CE 350, Council decision, 4 January 1957.
52. CE 555, circular letter, 14 March 1957.
53. See 'Many Rural Advertising Signs to Go', *Irish Press*, 27 August 1957; 'Subtopia Limited', *Irish Times*, 27 August 1957.
54. CE 555, Moran & Ryan, Solrs, to Ó Faoláin, 31 August 1958.
55. ibid., Ó Faoláin to Moran & Ryan, Solrs, 23 September 1958.
56. 'Advertising Hoardings Still Deface Countryside', *Irish Times*, 7 October 1959.
57. 'No Reprieve for Georgian Houses', *Irish Times*, 3 July 1957.
58. CE 578, Dr O'Sullivan to each Council member, 29 June 1957.
59. '22 Nations Show Books in Dublin', *Irish Press*, 8 November 1957.
60. CE 618, Council meeting, 12 November 1957.
61. CE 747, Mervyn Wall to Mrg de Brun, 21 October 1959.
62. CE 551, 29 April 1958.
63. TCD, MS 6966/170, 17 November 1958.
64. ibid., MS 6966/171, 22 November 1958.
65. 'Seán Ó Faoláin for US post', *Irish Press*, 2 July 1959.
66. See Walsh, Caroline, 'Joseph Sheridan Le Fanu and Dublin', *Irish Times*, 24 May 1977.
67. 'New Home for the Arts', *Evening Press*, 28 October 1959.

Public holidays, commemoration and identity in Ireland,
north and south, 1920–60 (pp. 138–154)
Brian Walker

1. *Northern Ireland Parliament*, vol. ii, 15 July 1922; vol. vi, 19 May 1925.
2. Public Record Office of Northern Ireland, CAB/4/125, no. 8, 20 October 1924; CAB/4/147, no. 2, 10 August 1925.
3. *Northern Whig*, 13 July 1922.
4. ibid., 13 July 1923.
5. ibid., 14 July 1925.
6. ibid., 13 July 1926.
7. ibid., 13 July 1927.
8. McDonnell, A. D., *The Life of Sir Denis Henry, Catholic Unionist*, Ulster Historical Foundation, Belfast, 2000.
9. Bardon, Jonathan, *A History of Ulster*, Blackstaff, Belfast, 1992, p. 511.
10. Jeffery, Keith, 'Parades, Police and Government in Northern Ireland, 1922–69' in Fraser, T. G. (ed.), *The Irish Parading Tradition: Following the Drum*, Macmillan, London, 2000, pp. 84–6.
11. *Northern Whig*, 13 July 1933.
12. ibid., 13 July 1932.
13. ibid., 13 July 1939.
14. *Portadown News*, 13 July 1940, 12 July 1941, 4 and 18 July 1942, 17 July 1943.
15. *Northern Whig*, 13 July 1955, 14 July 1958.
16. ibid., 12 July 1960.
17. ibid., 13 July 1960 and 13 July 1961.
18. ibid., 13 July 1960.
19. *Irish Times*, 12 November 1919.
20. Leonard, Jane, *The Culture of Commemoration: the Culture of War Commemoration*, np, Dublin, 1996, p. 20.
21. *Irish News*, 12 November 1924.

22. Jeffery, Keith, 'The Great War in Modern Irish Memory' in Fraser, T. G. and Jeffery, Keith (eds), *Men, Women and War: Historical Studies XVIII*, Lilliput Press, Dublin, 1993, p. 151.
23. Leonard, Jane, *Culture of Commemoration*, p. 20.
24. Jeffery, Keith, *Ireland and the Great War*, Cambridge University Press, Cambridge, 2000, p. 133.
25. Jeffery, Keith, 'The Great War in Modern Irish Memory', p. 150.
26. ibid., pp. 150–1.
27. *Belfast Telegraph*, 11 November 1930.
28. *Belfast Newsletter*, 11 November 1937; *Londonderry Sentinel*, 13 November 1934.
29. *Belfast Newsletter*, 11 November 1946, 13 November 1950
30. ibid., 11, 12 November 1955; 11, 12 November 1956; *Northern Whig*, 11, 12 November 1955, 11, 12 November 1956; *Irish News*, 11, 12 November 1955, 11, 12 November 1956.
31. *Northern Whig*, 18 March 1930.
32. Cathcart, Rex, *The Most Contrary Region: the BBC in Northern Ireland, 1924–84*, Blackstaff, Belfast, 1984, p. 32.
33. *Irish News*, 18 March 1932; *Belfast Newsletter*, 17 March 1932.
34. *Northern Whig*, 18 March 1930.
35. *Belfast Newsletter*, 18 March 1946, 18 March 1950, 17 March 1952.
36. Document is quoted in *Belfast Newsletter*, 1 January 1996.
37. *Irish Independent*, 18 March 1954; for complaints about schools not closing see *Belfast Newsletter*, 16 March 1961.
38. ibid., 17 March 1961.
39. *Belfast Telegraph*, 17 March 1956.
40. *Belfast Newsletter*, 17 March 1961.
41. *Irish Independent*, 19 March 1956; *Belfast Telegraph*, 10 March 1964.
42. *Northern Ireland Parliament*, vol. ix, 15 May 1928.
43. ibid., vol. xiv, 22 March 1932.
44. See Jarman, Neil and Bryan, Dominic, 'Green Parades in an Orange State' in Fraser, T. G. (ed.), *The Irish Parading Tradition*, pp. 95–110.
45. *Irish News*, 22 April 1935.
46. ibid., 17 April 1933.
47. ibid., 6 April 1942.
48. ibid., 10 April 1950.
49. Jarman, Neil and Bryan, Dominic, 'Green Parades in an Orange State', pp. 103–5 op cit.
50. *Irish Independent*, 18 March 1926.
51. ibid., 16 March 1930.
52. ibid., 18 March 1931.
53. ibid., 18 March 1932, 19 March 1934.
54. See speech by Eamon de Valera in Moynihan, Maurice (ed.), *Speeches and Statements by Eamon de Valera*, Gill and Macmillan, Dublin, 1980, pp. 217–9.
55. *Irish Independent*, 18 March 1935.
56. *Northern Whig*, 18 March 1939.
57. *Irish Independent*, 18 March 1939.
58. Moynihan, Maurice, *Speeches and Statements by Eamon de Valera*, p. 46.
59. *Irish Independent*, 18 March 1950.
60. ibid., 18 March 1953.
61. ibid., 18 March 1955.
62. *Capuchin Annual*, 1962, p. 218.
63. See Ryan, Rosemary, et al, 'Commemorating 1916', *Retrospect*, 1984, pp. 59–62.
64. Fitzpatrick, David 'Commemorating in the Irish Free State: a Chronicle of Embarrassment' in McBride, Ian (ed.), *History and Memory in Modern Ireland*, Cambridge University Press, Cambridge, 2001, p. 196
65. *Irish Independent*, 2 April 1934.

66. Fitzpatrick, David, 'Commemorating in the Irish Free State', p. 197
67. *Irish Independent*, 5 April 1935.
68. Hill, Judith, *Irish Public Sculpture*, Four Courts Press, Dublin, 1998, pp. 188–9.
69. *Irish Independent*, 14 April 1941.
70. ibid., 19 April 1954.
71. Ryan, Rosemary, 'Commemorating 1916', p. 61.
72. Leonard, Jane 'The Twinge of Memory: Armistice Day and Remembrance Sunday in Dublin since 1919' in English, Richard and Walker, Graham (eds), *Unionism in Modern Ireland*, St Martin's Press, New York, 1996, p. 101.
73. ibid.
74. Hill, Judith, *Irish Public Sculpture*, pp. 189–90.
75. See Jeffery, Keith, *Ireland and the Great War*, pp. 107–23.
76. *Irish News*, 12 November 1924.
77. Leonard, Jane, 'The Twinge of Memory: Armistice Day and Remembrance Sunday in Dublin since 1919', p. 105.
78. Hanley, Brian, 'Poppy Day in Dublin in the '20s and '30s', *History Ireland*, vol. 7, no. 1, Spring 1999, pp. 5–6.
79. Leonard, Jane, 'The Twinge of Memory: Armistice Day and Remembrance Sunday in Dublin since 1919', p. 106.
80. Fitzpatrick, David, 'Commemorating in the Irish Free State', p. 195
81. ibid., pp. 194-5
82. Girvin, Brian and Roberts, Geoffrey, 'The Forgotten Volunteers of World War II', *History Ireland*, vol. 6, no. 1, Spring 1998, pp. 46–51.
83. *Belfast Newsletter*, 13 November 1950.
84. Leonard, Jane 'Facing the "Finger of Scorn": Veterans' Memories of Ireland after the Great War' in Evans, Martin and Lunn, Kenneth (eds), *War and Memory in the Twentieth Century*, Oxford University Press, Oxford, 1997, pp. 59–72.
85. *Northern Whig*, 13 July 1923.
86. ibid., 14 July 1925.
87. ibid., 14 July 1930.
88. *Londonderry Sentinel*, 15 July 1930.
89. *Northern Whig*, 14 July 1931.
90. ibid.; *Irish Independent*, 13 August 1931.
91. McClelland, Aiken 'Orangeism in County Monaghan', *Clogher Record*, 1978, pp. 401–2.
92. Special meeting of the County Monaghan Grand Orange Lodge, 28 June 1932, recorded in minutes of the County Monaghan Grand Orange Lodge, May 1932–May 1943 (in private possession).
93. Recorded in above minutes.
94. *Belfast Newsletter*, 11 July 1936.
95. Jeffery, Keith, *Ireland and the Great War*, p.107. This comment about 11 November was made by General Sir William Hickie.
96. See Craig's comments in 1934 and 1938, Kennedy, Dennis, *The Widening Gulf: Northern Attitudes to the Independent Irish State, 1919–49*, Blackstaff, Belfast, 1988, pp. 166, 173–4.
97. Arthur, Paul, *Government and Politics of Northern Ireland*, Longman, London, 1980, p. 92; Bloomfield, Kenneth, *Stormont in Crisis: a Memoir*, Blackstaff, Belfast, 1994.

De Valera's other Ireland (pp. 155–165)
Gearóid Ó Crualaoich

1. Moynihan, Maurice (ed.), *Speeches and Statements by Eamon de Valera, 1917–1993*, Gill and Macmillan, Dublin, 1980, p. 454.
2. Ó Faoláin, Seán, 'This is Your Magazine', *The Bell*, vol. 1, no. 1, 1940, p. 8.

3. Almqvist, Bo, 'The Irish Folklore Commission: Achievement and Legacy', *Béaloideas*, vol. 45–7, 1979, p. 26.

4. Foster, Roy, *W. B. Yeats: A Life. 1: The Apprentice Mage. 1865–1914*, Oxford University Press, Oxford, 1997, p. 126.

5. ibid., p. 136.

6. Lee, J. J., *Ireland 1912–1985: Politics and Society*, Cambridge University Press, Cambridge, 1989, p. 211.

7. Linke, Uli, 'Power and Culture Theory: Problematising the Focus of Research in German Folklore Scholarship' in Bendix, R. and Zumwolt, R. L. (eds), *Folklore Interpreted: Essays in Honour of Alan Dundes*, Garland, New York, 1995, pp. 417–8.

8. Quoted in Foster, Roy, *W. B. Yeats: A Life*, p. 126.

9. Rechnenbach, H., untitled article in *Volk und Rasse*, vol. 10, 1935, p. 376.

10. Ziegler, M., 'Volkskunde auf rassischer Grundlage: Voranssetzungen und Aufgaben', *Nationalsozialistische Monatshefte*, vol. 4, 1936, pp. 711–7.

11. Moynihan, Maurice (ed.), *Speeches and Statements by Eamon de Valera*, p. 354.

12. Connolly, S., 'Approaches to the History of Irish Popular Culture', *Bullán*, vol. 2, no. 2, 1996, pp. 83–100.

13. Ó Crualaoich, G., 'The Vision of Liberation in Cúirt an Mhéan Oíche', in de Brún, P., Ó Coileáin, S., Ó Riain, P. (eds), *Folia Gaedlica*, Cork University Press, Cork, 1983, pp. 95–104.

14. Hyde, D., 'The Necessity of De-Anglicising Ireland' in Ó Conaire, Breandán (ed.), *Language, Lore and Lyrics: Essays and Lectures – Douglas Hyde*, Irish Academic Press, Dublin, 1986, p. 154.

15. Moynihan, Maurice (ed.), *Speeches and Statements by Eamon de Valera*, p. 131.

16. Hannerz, Ulf, *Cultural Complexity: Studies in the Social Organisation of Meaning*, Colombia University Press, New York, 1992.

17. Ó Crualaoich, G., Ó Giolláin, D., Huttunen, H., 'Irish-Finnish Research Collaboration: The Cork Northside Project', *NIF Newsletter*, vol. 21, 1993, pp. 17–8.

18. A seminal statement of these issues is Clifford, J. and Marcus, G. (eds), *Writing Culture: The Poetics and Politics of Ethnography*, University of California Press, Berkeley, 1985. Their importance in relation to folklore is reflected in Jackson, B. and Ives, E. (eds), *The World Observed: Reflections on the Fieldwork Process*, University of Illinois Press, Urbana, 1996.

Cultural visions and the new state: embedding and embalming (pp. 166–184)
Gearóid Ó Tuathaigh

1. Barry, Kevin, et al (eds), *The Irish Review*, no. 12, 1992; Deane, Seamus (ed.), *The Field Day Anthology of Irish Literature*, 3 vols, Faber/Field Day, London/Derry, 1991; Eagleton, Terry, *Heathcliffe and the Great Hunger, Studies in Irish Culture*, Verso, London, 1995; Foster, John Wilson, *Colonial Consequences*, Lilliput, Dublin, 1991; Gibbons, Luke, *Transformations in Irish Culture*, Cork University Press, Cork, 1991; Howe, Stephen, *Ireland and Empire: Colonial Legacies in Irish History and Culture*, Oxford University Press, Oxford, 2000; Longley, Edna, *Poetry in the Wars*, Blackstaff, Belfast, 1986; Lloyd, David, *Anomalous States: Irish Writing and the Post-Colonial Moment*, Lilliput, Dublin, 1993; Lloyd, David, *Ireland After History*, Cork University Press, Cork, 1999; Kiberd, Declan, *Inventing Ireland: The Literature of the Modern Nation*, Jonathan Cape, London, 1995; Brady, Ciarán (ed.), *Interpreting Irish History: The Debate on Historical Revisionism*, Irish Academic Press, Dublin, 1994.

2. In this essay, discussion of the Irish experience is situated in the wider context of the debate on colonialism and post-colonialism addressed in the following works amongst others: Anderson, Benedict, *Imagined Communities: Reflections on the Origins and Spread*

of *Nationalism*, Verso, London, 1983; Ashcroft, Bill, et al (eds), *The Empire Writes Back: Theory and Practice in Post-Colonial Literatures*, Methuen, London, 1989; Bhabha, Homi K. (ed.), *Nation and Narration*, Routledge, London, 1990; Fishman, Joshua, *Language and Nationalism*, Newbury House Inc., Rowley, Mass, 1972; Said, Edward, *Yeats and Decolonisation* (Field Day Pamphlet no 15), Lawrence Hill/Field Day, London, 1988; Said, Edward W., *Culture and Imperialism*, Vintage, London, 1994; Said, Edward W., *Representations of the Intellectual*, Vintage, London, 1994; Smith, Anthony D., *The Ethnic Origins of Nations*, Blackwell, Oxford, 1986; Williams, Patrick & Chrisman, Laura (eds), *Colonial Discourse and Post-Colonial Theory*, Columbia University Press, New York, 1994; Woolf, Stuart (ed.), *Nationalism in Europe: 1815 to the present: a Reader*, Routledge, London and New York, 1996.

3. Some of the issues explored in this essay were identified in an earlier essay of mine on decolonisation and identity in González, Rosa (ed.), *Culture and Power: Institutions*, Promociones y Publicaciones Universitarias, Barcelona, 1996, pp. 27–44.

4. Ó Cuív, Brian (ed.), *A View of the Irish Language*, Rialtas na hÉireann, Dublin, 1969.

5. Leerssen, Joep, *Remembrance and Imagination*, Cork University Press, Cork, 1996; Murray, Damien, *Romanticism, Nationalism and Irish Antiquarian Societies, 1840–80*, NUI Maynooth, Maynooth, 2000.

6. Ó Tuathaigh, M. A. G. (ed.), *Community, Culture, and Conflict*, Officina Typographica/ Galway University Press, Galway, 1986; Ní Dhonnchadha, Máirín (ed.), *Nua-Léamha: Gnéithe de Chultúr, Stair agus Polaitíocht na hÉireann c.1600–c.1900*, An Clóchomhar, Baile Átha Cliath, 1996.

7. Hutchinson, John, *The Dynamics of Cultural Nationalism*, Allen and Unwin, London, 1987; Ó Tuama, Seán (ed.), *The Gaelic League Idea*, Mercier Press, Cork, 1972; Ó Cuiv, Brian, *A View of the Irish Language*; Ó Tuathaigh, M. A. G., 'The Irish Ireland Idea: Rationale and Relevance' in Longley, Edna (ed.), *Culture in Ireland: Division or Diversity?*, Institute of Irish Studies, Belfast, 1991.

8. Ó Cuiv, Brian, *A View of the Irish Language*.

9. Maume, Patrick, *The Long Gestation: Irish Nationalist Life 1891–1918*, Gill and Macmillan, Dublin, 1999; Garvin, Tom, *Nationalist Revolutionaries in Ireland 1858–1928*, Clarendon Press, Oxford, 1987.

10. Daly, Dominic, *The Young Douglas Hyde*, Irish University Press, Dublin, 1974; Dunleavy, Janet Egleson & Dunleavy, Gareth W., *Douglas Hyde: A Maker of Modern Ireland*, University of California Press, Berkeley, 1991; Ó Conaire, Breandán (ed.), *Language, Lore and Lyrics: Essays and Lectures – Douglas Hyde*, Irish Academic Press, Dublin, 1986.

11. All quotations from Hyde, unless otherwise indicated, are from the edited collection of his essays, Ó Conaire, Breandán (ed.), *Language, Lore and Lyrics: Essays and Lectures – Douglas Hyde*.

12. Ó Cuiv, Brian, *A View of the Irish Language*; Mac Aonghusa, Proinsias, *Ar Son na Gaeilge: Conradh na Gaeilge 1893–1993*, Conradh na Gaeilge, Baile Átha Cliath, 1993.

13. Blanning, T. C. W. (ed.), *The Oxford Illustrated History of Modern Europe*, Oxford University Press, Oxford, 1996, p. 140.

14. Leerssen, Joep, *Mere Irish and Fíor-Ghael*, Second edition, Cork University Press, Cork, 1996.

15. Maume, Patrick, *The Long Gestation: Irish Nationalist Life 1891–1918*.

16. Bartlett, Thomas, *The Fall and Rise of the Irish Nation: The Catholic Question 1690–1830*, Gill and Macmillan, Dublin, 1992; Corish, Patrick, *The Irish Catholic Experience: a Historical Survey*, Gill and Macmillan, Dublin, 1985; Ó Tuathaigh, M. A. G. (ed.), *Community, Culture, and Conflict*.

17. Curtis, L. P. Jr, *Anglo-Saxons and Celts*, Conference on British Studies, Bridgeport, 1968.

18. Martin, F. X. and Byrne, F. J. (eds), *The Scholar Revolutionary*, Irish University Press, Shannon, 1973; Tierney, Michael, *Eoin Mac Néill: Scholar and Man of Action 1867–1945*, Oxford University Press, Oxford, 1980; Hutchinson, John, *The Dynamics of Cultural Nationalism*.

19. Maume, Patrick, *D. P. Moran*, Historical Association of Ireland, Dundalk, 1995.
20. Garvin, Tom, *Nationalist Revolutionaries in Ireland 1858–1928*, p. 78.
21. McBride, Lawrence, *The Greening of Dublin Castle*, Catholic University of America, Washington, 1991; Paseta, Senia, *Before the Revolution: Nationalism, Social Change and Ireland's Catholic Elite 1879–1922*, Cork University Press, Cork, 1999.
22. O'Donoghue, Thomas A., *Bilingual Education in Ireland, 1904–1922*, Murdoch University, Perth, 2000.
23. Farrell, Brian (ed.), *De Valera's Constitution and Ours*, Gill and Macmillan, Dublin, 1988; Ó Máille, Tomás, *The Status of the Irish Language: A Legal Perspective*, Bord na Gaeilge, Dublin, 1990.
24. Ó Cuiv, Brian, *A View of the Irish Language*; Kelly, A., *Compulsory Irish: Language and Education in Ireland 1870s–1970s*, Irish Academic Press, Dublin, 2002.
25. Ó Cuiv, Brian, *A View of the Irish Language*; Ó Tuathaigh, M. A. G., *The Development of the Gaeltacht as a Bilingual Entity*, Institiúid Teangéolaíochta Éireann, Dublin, 1990; Ó Tuathaigh, Gearóid, et al (eds), *Pobal na Gaeltachta: A Scéal agus a Dhán*, Cló Iar Chonnachta, Indreabhán, 2000; Hindley, Reg, *The Death of the Irish Language*, Routledge, London, 1990; Walsh, John, 'Díchoimisiúnú Tenaga: Comisiún na Gaelteachta 1926', *Cois Lífe*, Baile Átha Cliath, 2002.
26. Lee, J. J., *Ireland 1912–1985: Politics and Society*, Cambridge University Press, Cambridge, 1989; Girvin, Brian, *Between Two Worlds: Politics and Economy in Independent Ireland*, Gill and Macmillan, Dublin, 1989; Regan, John M., *The Irish Counter-Revolution 1921–1936*, Gill and Macmillan, Dublin, 1999.
27. Whyte, John, *Church and State in Modern Ireland 1923–1970*, Gill and Macmillan, Dublin, 1971; Keogh, Dermot, *Twentieth Century Ireland: Nation and State*, Gill and Macmillan, Dublin, 1994.
28. Manning, Maurice, *James Dillon: A Biography*, Wolfhound, Dublin, 1999; Corish, Patrick, *The Irish Catholic Experience: a Historical Survey*.
29. Brown, Terence, *Ireland: A Social and Cultural History 1922–1979*, Fontana, London, 1981; Fallon, Brian, *An Age of Innocence: Irish Culture 1930–1960*, Gill and Macmillan, Dublin, 1988; Ó Faoláin, Seán, *Vive Moi!*, Ruper Hart-Davis, London, 1965.
30. Moynihan, Maurice (ed.), *Speeches and Statements by Eamon De Valera 1917–1973*, Gill and Macmillan, Dublin, 1980.
31. Ó Tuathaigh, M. A. G., 'De Valera and Sovereignty: a note on the pedigree of a political idea', in O'Carroll, J. P. and Murphy, John A. (eds), *De Valera and his Times*, Cork University Press, Cork, 1983.
32. Williams, Raymond, *The Country and the City*, Oxford University Press, Oxford, 1973.
33. Whyte, John, *Church and State in Modern Ireland 1923–1970*.
34. Hickey, D. J. & Doherty, J. E., *A Dictionary of Irish History since 1800*, Gill and Macmillan/ Barnes and Noble, Dublin and New Jersey, 1980.
35. Kennedy, Kieran A., Giblin, Thomas and McHugh, Deirdre (eds), *The Economic Development of Ireland in the Twentieth Century*, Routledge, London, 1988; Ó Tuathaigh, M. A. G., 'The Land Question, Politics and Irish Society, 1922–1960' in Drudy, P. J. (ed.), *Ireland: Land, Politics and People*, Cambridge University Press, Cambridge, 1982.
36. Lee, J. J., 'Aspects of Corporatist Thought in Ireland: The Commission on Vocational Organisation, 1939–43' in Cosgrove, Art and McCartney, Donal (eds), *Studies in Irish History: Presented to R. Dudley Edwards*, University College Dublin, Dublin, 1979.
37. Miley, Jim (ed.), *A Voice for the Country: 50 Years of Macra na Feirme*, Macra na Feirme, Dublin, 1994.
38. Ó Tuama, Seán, *The Gaelic League Idea*; Ó Cíosáin, Éamon, *An tÉireannach; 1934–1937*, An Clóchomhar, Baile Átha Cliath, 1993; Kelly, A., *Compulsory Irish: Language and Education in Ireland 1870s–1970s*.
39. Ó hAnluain, Eoghan (ed.), *Léachtaí Uí Chadhain*, An Clóchomhar, Baile Átha Cliath, 1989; Ó Cíosáin, Éamon, *An tÉireannach; 1934–1937*.

40. Ó Riagáin, Pádraig (ed.), *International Journal of the Sociology of Language: Language Planning in Ireland*, Mouton de Gruyter, Amsterdam, 1985; Ó Riagáin, Pádraig, *Language Policy and Social Reproduction. Ireland 1893–1993*, Oxford University Press, Oxford, 1997; Ó Riain, Seán, *Pleanáil Teanga in Éirinn 1919–85*, Carbad/Bord na Gaeilge, Baile Átha Cliath, 1994.

41. Ó hAnnracháin, Stiofán (ed.), *An Comhchaidreamh: Crann a Chraobhaigh*, An Clóchomhar, Baile Átha Cliath, 1985.

42. Ó Súilleabháin, Donncha, *Scéal an Oireachtais 1897–1924*, An Clóchomhar, Baile Átha Cliath, 1984; Mac Aonghusa, Proinsias, *Ar Son na Gaeilge: Conradh na Gaeilge 1893–1993: Stair Sheanchais*, Conradh na Gaeilge, Baile Átha Cliath, 1993; Ó Cearúil, Mícheál, *Gníomhartha na mBráithre*, Coiscéim, Baile Átha Cliath, 1996.

43. Ó Buachalla, Séamas, *Education Policy in Twentieth-Century Ireland*, Wolfhound Press, Dublin, 1988.

44. Lee, J. J. & Ó Tuathaigh, M. A. G., *The Age of De Valera*, Ward River Press, Dublin, 1982; Lee, J. J., *Ireland 1912–1985: Politics and Society*; Keogh, Dermot, *Twentieth-Century Ireland: Nation and State*.

45. Ó Conaire, Breandán, *Myles na Gaeilge*, An Clochomhar Tta, Baile Átha Cliath, 1986.

46. Ó hAnluain, Eoghan (ed.), *Léachtaí Uí Chadhain*; Ó Cadhain, Máirtín, *An Ghaeltacht Bheo: Destined to Pass*, Coiscéim, Baile Átha Cliath, 2002.

47. Ó Tuama, Seán, *The Gaelic League Idea*; Maume, Patrick, *'Life that is Exile': Daniel Corkery and the Search for Irish Ireland*, Institute of Irish Studies, Belfast, 1993.

48. An Coimisiún um Athbheochan na Gaeilge, *An Tuarascáil Dheiridh*, Oifig an tSoláthair, Baile Átha Cliath, 1994, pp. xiv–xv.

49. Crotty, Raymond, *Ireland in Crisis: a Study in Capitalist Colonial Underdevelopment*, Brandon, Dingle, 1986; Tobin, Fergal, *The Best of Decades: Ireland in the 1960s*, Gill and Macmillan, Dublin, 1984; Lee, J. J., *Ireland 1912–1985: Politics and Society*; Kennedy, Kieran A., *Ireland in Transition*, Mercier Press, Cork, 1986; Litton, Frank (ed.), *Unequal Achievement: The Irish Experience 1957–1982*, Institute of Public Administration, Dublin, 1982; Ó Caollaí, Maolsheachlainn, *Tiarnas Cultúir: Craolachán in Éirinn*, Conradh na Gaeilge, Baile Átha Cliath, 1980.

50. Ó Tuama, Seán, *The Gaelic League Idea*, p. 30.

INDEX

Also available from
Mercier Press

MICHAEL COLLINS AND THE MAKING OF THE IRISH STATE
EDITED BY GABRIEL DOHERTY AND DERMOT KEOGH

Collins has generally been portrayed in writing and film as a revolutionary guerrilla leader, a military tactician and a figure of great personal charm, courage and ingenuity. This collection of essays challenges that over-simplified view. It is a professional evaluation of Michael Collins and his contribution to the making of the Irish state, which brings to light his multifaceted and complex character. With contributions from many leading historians working in the field, and written in an accessible style, the essays make full use of archival material and provide new findings and insights into the life and times of Michael Collins.

THE STONES & OTHER STORIES
Daniel Corkery
selected & edited by Paul Delaney

Daniel Corkery's short stories rank amongst the finest in the history of Irish literature. His stories have been acclaimed and anthologised, and have exerted a profound influence on generations of Irish writers including Frank O'Connor, Seán O'Faoláin and Michael McLaverty. This new volume provides a comprehensive selection of these stories, and restores to print the work of one of Ireland's greatest storytellers.

THE COURSE OF IRISH HISTORY
Edited by T. W. Moody and F. X. Martin

A revised and enlarged version of this classic book provides a rapid short survey, with geographical introduction, of the whole course of Ireland's history. Based on a series of television programmes, it is designed to be both popular and authoritative, concise but comprehensive, highly selective but balanced and fair-minded, critical but constructive and sympathetic. A distinctive feature is its wealth of illustrations.

The Legacy of History
Martin Mansergh

The value of looking back is to understand where we are and why; to honour that which was noble; to acknowledge and try to correct what went wrong. Ireland's history has had a profound influence on the Irish as a people and it has certainly shaped the character of the State. *The Legacy of History* helps to flesh out and put into perspective the background to the problems with which we have had to deal, as well as highlighting what remains to be done.

Sarsfield & the Jacobites
Kevin Haddick-Flynn

Patrick Sarsfield's career as the leading Irish soldier of the Williamite War (1688–91) is the stuff of legend. In this military biography – the first written on Sarsfield by an Irishman in over 100 years – all the known facts of this great soldier's career are probed. Special attention is given to the great battles and sieges of the war: the Boyne, Aughrim, Athlone, Derry, Cork and more. Sarsfield's heroic defence of Limerick and his part in negotiating the famous Treaty of Limerick are considered and weighed. His celebrated raid on the Williamite siege train at Ballyneety is fully covered, as are his final days with the 'Wild Geese' in Flanders. *Sarsfield & the Jacobites* is a compelling narrative and an illuminating critique of the seventeenth-century military and political mindset. It is a perfect reference for both the student and the general reader.

Police Casualties in Ireland, 1919–22
Richard Abbott

The year 1919 saw the beginning of a serious challenge to the Royal Irish Constabulary, a force whose members had peaceably served the community for many years. Within three years, policing had changed out of all recognition throughout Ireland. This book tells the story of those turbulent years and charts the history of both the RIC and the nationalist groups that rose to oppose them, leading to the establishment of the Irish Free State and the eventual disbandment of the force in 1922.